Special-Needs Adoption

SPECIAL-NEEDS ADOPTION

A STUDY OF INTACT FAMILIES

James A. Rosenthal

Victor K. Groze

*Foreword by Drenda S. Lakin
and Kathryn S. Donley*

New York
Westport, Connecticut
London

Library of Congress Cataloging-in-Publication Data

Rosenthal, James Aaron.
    Special-needs adoption : a study of intact families / James A.
Rosenthal, Victor K. Groze ; foreword by Drenda S. Lakin and
Kathryn S. Donley.
      p. cm.
    Includes bibliographical references and index.
    ISBN 0-275-93790-9 (alk. paper)
    1. Adoption—United States. 2. Older child adoption—United
States. 3. Handicapped children—United States. 4. Children of
minorities—United States. I. Groze, Victor K. II. Title.
HV875.55.R68 1992
362.7'34'0973—dc20   91-30278

British Library Cataloguing in Publication Data is available.

Library of Congress Catalog Card Number: 91-30278
ISBN: 0-275-93790-9

First published in 1992

Praeger Publishers, One Madison Avenue, New York, NY 10010
An imprint of Greenwood Publishing Group, Inc.

Printed in the United States of America

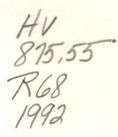

The paper used in this book complies with the
Permanent Paper Standard issued by the National
Information Standards Organization (Z39.48-1984).

10 9 8 7 6 5 4 3 2 1

Copyright Acknowledgments

Grateful acknowledgment is given for permission to adapt excerpts from the following articles:

Groze, V. (1991). Adoption and single parents: A review. *Child Welfare, 70* (3), 321–322. By permission of the Child Welfare League of America (CWLA).

Groze, V. & Gruenewald, A. (1991). Partners: A model program for special needs adoptive families in stress. *Child Welfare, 70,* 581–589. By permission of CWLA.

Groze, V. & Rosenthal, J. A. (1991). Single parents and their adopted children: A psychological analysis. *Families in Society: The Journal of Contemporary Human Services, 72* (2), 67–77.

Groze, V. & Rosenthal, J. A. (1991). A structural analysis of families adopting a special-needs child. *Families in Society: The Journal of Contemporary Human Services, 72* (8), 469–481. By permission of the publisher.

Rosenthal, J. A. & Groze, V. (1991). Behavior problems of special needs adopted children. *Children and Youth Services Review, 13* (5&6), 343–361. By permission of Pergamon Press plc.

Rosenthal, J. A. & Groze, V. (1990). Special needs adoption: A study of intact families. *Social Service Review, 64,* 475–505. By permission of the University of Chicago Press.

Rosenthal, J. A., Groze, V., & Aguilar, G. (1991). Adoptive outcomes for children with handicaps. *Child Welfare, 70* (6), 623–636. By permission of CWLA.

Rosenthal, J. A., Groze, V., & Curiel, H. (1990). Race, social class, and special needs adoption. Reprinted with permission from *Social Work, 35* (6), 532–539. Copyright October 1990, National Association of Social Workers, Inc.

Rosenthal, J. A., Groze, V., Curiel, H., & Westcott, P. A. (1991). Transracial and inracial adoption of special needs children. *Journal of Multicultural Social Work, 1* (3), 331–332. By permission of Haworth Press.

To families and kids, to moms and dads, to brothers and sisters, and to all those who help make adoption work. —jar and vkg

To Mom, Dad, my sister, Ethel, and my brothers, George and Owen, for their love and support. —vkg

To Mom and Dad, to Cindy, who leads the way, and to my favorite friends, Catie and Aaron. —jar

Contents

Tables and Figures

FIGURES

Foreword

"No child is unadoptable" has long been a basic tenet of the special-needs adoption field. This study by James Rosenthal and Victor Groze supports another basic tenet: most committed families, if given information, preparation, and on-going support, can successfully adopt. A child's special needs or parents' age, income, type of housing, marital status, education, race, or culture have little to do with success in adoption. Special-needs adoptions work!

Those of us who have been working in the field for some time tend to forget that the special-needs adoption field is a fairly new one—only about 20-years-old. It is rewarding work where we have seen "miracles" happen: the child whose physical and cognitive development catches up to his or her chronological age; the child who has been in numerous placements and is able to stabilize. But we are also now seeing things we did not see in the past, either because we did not recognize them or because they are more prevalent: the effects of sexual abuse, alcohol, and drug abuse. This study reflects the real world experiences of children with traumatic histories joining families with optimistic expectations. What they find is a mixture of pleasure and pain. As the field matures, it becomes increasingly clear that love is not necessarily enough, that permanency does not always heal old wounds, and that being a healing resource for a traumatized child can be very painful.

This study of 800 intact adoptive families by Rosenthal and Groze reveals a substantial majority of families who have adopted children with special needs feel that they have gained satisfaction and rewards from their adoptions. The five stories of adoption by young adults who have experienced it and the words of real people tucked among the results of samples, tables, findings, and interpretations highlight the strengths and difficulties in these adoptions.

In addition, the authors identify and summarize earlier research, adding to the book's usefulness as a resource for policymakers and practitioners. They have integrated their extensive research findings with recommendations for practice which also have implications for policy. Many of their findings and recommendations support current practice and will challenge those for whom it is not current practice, both in child welfare and mental health. And their careful analysis of family functioning normalizes adoptive family functioning, which too often has been characterized as dysfunctional.

This research supports outreach to and placement with families of color, families with modest incomes, older parents, and other "non-traditional" families. The result is a confirmation of the practice wisdom that special-needs adoption works well for youngsters and their families but is not problem-free. There are hard-nosed observations here and suggestions for improvements in policies and practices, but, most of all, the book provides the foundation for renewed efforts to ensure that every child has a permanent family and a framework of respect and attentive analysis of the heroic efforts of children and families who have beat the odds.

Drenda S. Lakin, ACSW
Director

Kathryn S. Donley, MSW
Trainer/Consultant

National Resource Center for
Special Needs Adoption
Southfield, Michigan

Preface

This preface is the last "chapter" of this book to be written. While it provides the reader with a place to begin, it provides us with an opportunity to look back.

This survey of 800 families provides empirical justification for what many adoption professionals already know, that adoption of older children and children with handicaps is rewarding and satisfying for a substantial majority of families. It shows that the outreach in special-needs adoptive practice to what would once have been termed "nontraditional" families—minority families, lower-income and less-educated families, single parents, relatives of the child, the child's foster parents—has been wise and effective policy. These nontraditional families, on balance, experience excellent adoptive outcomes. Clearly, special-needs adoption works, and it works for children and families from all walks of life.

The study seeks to integrate research findings, both quantitative and qualitative, with practical recommendations for special-needs adoptive practice. While the study's strongest contribution is the development of a solid data base to guide practice and policy, we have tried to keep most statistics simple and to make the book readable for practitioners and academics alike. While many recent studies have focused on disruption, or the termination of an adoption, we have shifted the perspective and instead focused on the everyday (and not so everyday) experiences of intact special-needs families.

Looking back, we are impressed by the dedication of parents. Their care, concern, dedication, and commitment come through in the good response rate and in the lengthy, thoughtful comments that many wrote. While the study findings support special-needs adoption, we have avoided the temptation to create a rosy picture. As the chapter that is focused on parent comments shows, the great rewards of special-needs adoption for most families are counterbalanced by difficult and painful experiences for some others.

The book begins with an overview of issues and research in special-needs adoption and presents the study design and methodology. Next, findings are overviewed, using traditional quantitative methods. Important areas studied include perceptions of social work and other services, parent-child relationships, school, and the impact of adoption on the families. Qualitative methods are used to study two topics. First, parent perceptions of the rewards and difficulties of special-needs adoption are assessed via content analysis methods. Second, case vignettes developed from in-depth interviews capture the adoptee's perspective of events. Subsequent chapters focus on special topics, including family dynamics, single-parent adoptions, minority children and families, children with disabilities and handicaps, and behavior problems. The concluding chapter summarizes findings, presents practice recommendations, and looks towards the year 2000.

We hope that this book is enjoyable and that it helps in developing effective services for children and families.

Acknowledgments

Many organizations contributed to this study. The University of Oklahoma and the University of Iowa provided funding and in-kind support. The Oklahoma Department of Human Services (ODHS), the Kansas Department of Social and Rehabilitation Services (KDSRS), the Illinois Department of Children and Family Services (IDCFS), and Project Adopt of Oklahoma City contributed in-kind support for copying, postage, and the like. Also, considerable staff time at these agencies was directed to the tasks of sample selection and locating missing addresses.

Many helped the study go forward. They include: at the Oklahoma DHS, Jane Conner and Elaine McGuire; at the Kansas DSRS, Barbara Stodgell, Dorothy Tenney and Joyce Resnick; at the Illinois DCFS, Judy Pence, Sadari Bhasin, Joe Coffey, and Dixie Smedley; and at Project Adopt, Carole Patten and Ina Javellas.

Many graduate social work students carried out various study tasks. At the University of Oklahoma, Patricia Westcott assisted with sampling, locating missing addresses, key punch, and literature review. Louanna Law, Sheryl Glover, and Linda Evans-Cummings helped in all facets of the content analysis of parent comments. Susan Barker-Buchert, Betsy O'Hara, and Lauren Smith helped in the classification of children with handicaps. Amy Morris, Heather Curless, Robert Canon, and Sandy Quintano also helped with various study tasks. At the University of Iowa, Mary Brown, Cynthia Keeley, Sandra Eshelman, and David Strabla assisted with everything from locating obscure references to trekking across campus for computer printouts. In addition, Hwi Ja Canda assisted in the content analysis. Jo Conroy and Mary Ann Wright assisted with typing and tables throughout the project.

Three faculty at the University of Oklahoma School of Social Work contributed to the study. Herman Curiel contributed to the chapter on minority children and families, in particular generating key ideas for the chapter section entitled "Minority Family Systems." Gloria Aguilar contributed to the chapter on children with handicaps, in particular to the analysis of parent comments. Man Keung Ho read several chapters and generated ideas that guided analysis and writing.

Cindy Simon Rosenthal took the writing of two academics, one with a dense, choppy style (JAR) and one inclined towards theoretical formulation (VKG) and blended them together to form a friendlier and more readable book. We thank her greatly for her thorough, careful work in organizing and editing the manuscript, all the while with two kids making mischief nearby. Thank you!

Special-Needs
Adoption

Chapter 1

Change and Challenge in Adoption

A HISTORICAL PERSPECTIVE

Adoption changed dramatically in the 1970s and 1980s due to trends in the society at large and in child welfare practice. A healthy infant placed with an infertile, middle-class, usually white couple no longer typifies the traditional adoption (Hartman, 1979). Children of various races, ages, and backgrounds and often with significant emotional, physical, or mental impairments comprise an increased proportion of the population of adopted children. Similarly, what was once described as the "model adoptive couple" (Hartman, p. 21) has been supplemented by other family forms including single parents, minority parents, parents of modest financial means, and foster parents who adopt.

In the larger society, the legalization of abortion, availability of more sophisticated means of contraception, and increased acceptance of single parenthood have combined to reduce the number of babies available for adoption. At the same time, the demand for babies has increased as couples have delayed parenthood and subsequently experienced fertility problems.

In child welfare, the Adoption Assistance and Child Welfare Act of 1980 (P.L. 96-272) reversed the dramatic increase in the foster care population seen during the 1970s and codified the concept of permanency planning. The legislative intent was to provide permanent homes for children through goal-directed and time-limited social work and legal services. Towards this end, it provides incentives to develop programs to prevent foster care placement and, where placement can not be prevented, to shorten the time children spend in foster care. In particular, the legislation seeks to reduce "foster care drift"—the succession of multiple and often unplanned placements experienced by many children in substitute care. While continued residence in the family of origin is the preferred permanency goal, adoption is preferred over long-term foster care when the child cannot live in the birth home.

At least in the early 1980s, the act accomplished its purpose of reducing the size of the foster care population. Between 1970 and 1977, the number of children in foster care nationwide had climbed to 502,000, a 54 percent jump stemming, in part, from the parallel increase in reported child abuse and neglect (Gershenson, 1984b). At the same time, the proportion of foster care children from poverty and minority families increased (Gershenson). Yet by 1982, in part due to the increased practice of special-needs adoption, the foster care population had declined to less than one-half of the 1977 level (Gershenson). Significant numbers of children, about 18,000 in Fiscal Year (FY) 1985, are adopted under the auspices of public child welfare agencies (Tatara, 1988). At the conclusion of FY 1985, about 19,000 children residing in substitute care were legally free for adoption and awaiting adoptive placement (Tatara).

With the impetus of permanency planning, special-needs children—older children and adolescents, handicapped children, sibling groups, and children with emotional and behavioral problems—began to be adopted. Previously, many of these children would have grown up in foster care. The term special needs has also been extended to minority and biracial children because of the greater difficulty encountered in implementing these adoptive placements. Minority children (even those who are not older or handicapped) must often wait long periods of time before adoptions can be arranged and are at higher risk for not being adopted. In FY 1985, for instance, Blacks represented 38 percent of the total of children who were awaiting adoption but only 23 percent of the total of children who were adopted (Tatara, 1988).

Unfortunately, the trend towards a reduction of children in foster care in the late 1970s and early 1980s appears to have reversed across the balance of the 1980s; some estimates are that the foster care population in 1990 had returned to its peak level of about 500,000 (*Roundtable*, 1990, p. 18). This increase, traceable in part to the increased poverty rate for children, suggests that even greater numbers of children with special needs will become eligible for adoption in the 1990s.

Clearly, the concomitant trends in the society at large, that is, more couples experiencing problems with fertility and fewer infants available for adoption, and in child welfare, namely, more children with special needs in foster care placement and an increased emphasis on adoptive placement, led many couples who previously would have adopted infants to consider the adoption of children with special needs.

Increased flexibility in adoption agency policies and procedures have opened adoption to prospective parents who might not previously have qualified. This follows Joyce Ladner's (1977) recommendation that adoption agencies should screen in rather than screen out applicants. Among the most important changes, agencies have reached out more actively to minority families, developed financial subsidies for adopting families, and recruited foster parents for adoption. Selection criteria have been broadened so that low-income or single-parent status are less likely to disqualify the applicant.

The 1988 Standards for Adoption Service of the Child Welfare League of America (CWLA), the major professional accrediting body in the adoption field, state that "applicants should be accepted on the basis of their capacity to understand and meet the needs of a particular available child at the point of the adoption and beyond into the future. . . . The ability to protect, nurture and care for a child makes up the primary qualifications of applicants" (pp. 49–50). These standards specifically state that marital status, sexual preference, age, and social or economic position should not be used narrowly to rule applicants in or out.

The more flexible selection criteria are in accord with an ecological approach to decision making in adoption (Hartman, 1979). Within an ecological framework, families are assessed in relationship to their ability to meet each child's specific needs. The focus shifts from one of worker as expert and judge to one of participation and learning for both family and worker (Hartman, 1979).

The shift towards the adoption of special-needs children has required changes in the delivery of adoption services and has not always been without problems. As special-needs adoption increased in the 1970s, so also did the percentage of adoption disruptions, terminations of the adoption prior to legal finalization, and dissolutions, terminations following legalization. A 1985 study estimated the disruption rate at 13 percent (Urban Systems). In addition to the increase in adoption disruption, research studies have documented deviant, sometimes dangerous behavior on the part of children whose adoptions disrupted (Sack & Dale, 1982; Schmidt, Rosenthal, & Bombeck, 1988). Further, some adoptive parents have reported that adoption agencies have not provided adequate background information regarding the child or have misrepresented the severity of the child's problems or handicaps (Schmidt et al., 1988; Valentine, Conway, & Randolph, 1988; Nelson, 1985).

Changes in selection and screening practices have been paralleled by a recognition that many adoptive families require postplacement services

(Hartman, 1984). Increasingly, such services include support groups and counseling for parents, children, and families and specialized medical and educational services. Services for adult adoptees may also be offered. Although such services may be available when an infant is adopted, postplacement support often ends with the adoption's finalization.

Finally, there is some evidence of a disturbing trend towards a two-tiered system for adoption. On the one hand, many couples with high socioeconomic status—those who fit the earlier description of the typical adoptive couples—often adopt healthy babies independently or through private agencies. On the other hand, many (but not all) of the couples adopting special-needs children through the public agencies are of more modest means. Some experts in adoption have also questioned whether agencies tend to place the "best-qualified" children (i.e., "blue-ribbon" babies), with the best-qualified applicants (often the typical couple). While the development of flexible selection criteria increases the pool of adoptive families, the practice may inadvertently contribute to the two-tier phenomenon.

OBJECTIVES OF STUDY

The increase in disruption triggered numerous studies of its causes (see the next section). The current study, in contrast, focuses on intact families. Just as the term *disruption* should not always be interpreted as failure, this study questions whether intact adoptions should always be viewed as successful. The study seeks to determine whether the majority of parents in intact families experience their adoption of special-needs children as rewarding and fulfilling. The primary objective is to provide empirically based data to guide policy, practice, and theory.

The study examines support and approval from relatives and friends, social work and other services delivered to the child and family, perceptions of the helpfulness of services, child behavior, school performance, the parent-child relationship, family functioning, and the impact of the adoption on the family. With 799 special-needs adoptive parents responding to a mailed survey, the large sample size allows analysis of different types of adoptions. For instance, adoptions by those who were previously foster parents are contrasted with those for "new" adopters. Similarly, the age of the child at adoption and at the time of the survey are examined in relationship to adoptive outcome. Separate chapters focus in depth on adoptions by single parents, adoptions of children with disabilities and handicaps, and adoptions of minority children, both transracial and inracial. Based on data collected using standardized instruments, child behavior and adoptive family functioning are also explored in depth. While most of the findings are quantitative in nature, the study also examines comments of parents about the rewards and difficulties of the adoptive experience. A series of vignettes captures the experiences and perspective of several young adults who were adopted as older children. Another chapter explores selected topics, including visits between children and members of their birth families, adoptions of sibling groups, the children's self-esteem, and adoptive placement patterns (who tends to adopt whom). The closing chapter offers recommendations for practice and policy and identifies the challenges that the 1990s present for the adoption field.

The balance of this chapter reviews studies of the outcomes of adoption including infant adoption, adoption disruption, and intact special-needs families. Greater depth is provided in the reviews of minority and transracial adoptions, single-parent adoptions, adoptive family functioning, behavior problems, and children with handicaps than are found in the separate chapters focused on these issues.

RESEARCH ON ADOPTION OUTCOMES

Special-needs adoption must be understood within the broader context of adoption generally and the successes and difficulties encountered by traditional adopting families and their children. Alfred Kadushin and Judith Martin's review of 24 studies suggests that 66 percent of infant adoptions can be characterized as "unequivocally successful," and only 16 percent as "unsuccessful" (1988, p. 618). Other research suggests that adopted children are more likely to experience emotional adjustment difficulties. Brinich and Brinich (1982) cite 13 authors who contend that adopted children are overrepresented in mental health clinics and eight who disagree. McRoy, Grotevant, and Zurcher (1988), summarizing data from 15 studies, conclude that adopted children may be two to five times more likely to require psychological treatment. The overrepresentation of adoptees in psychological treatment may reflect an increased propensity on the part of adoptive parents to seek treatment services. However, increased emotional problems have also been observed in nonclinical samples of adopted children (Bohman & Sigvardsson, 1980; Hoopes, 1986; Lindholm & Touliatos, 1980; Brodzinsky, Schechter, Braff, & Singer, 1984). Brodzinsky (1987), for instance, states that "although most adopted children are within normal limits for psychological development, as a group, they show a higher incidence of behavioral, emotional, and academic problems than their non-adopted peers" (p. 43).

Kadushin's (1970) study of abused and neglected children who were adopted at age 5 or older was a landmark for the yet-to-emerge special-needs adoptive field. The study showed favorable outcomes, comparable with those observed in his review of traditional adoption. Most adoptive parents

were well satisfied with their decisions to adopt. Important sources of
parental satisfaction included "the child himself: personality, temperament,
disposition" (p.80), the child's relationship to extended family, and companionship with and for the parent. The study demonstrated the "reversibility of trauma" and paved the way for the development of special-needs
adoption in the 1970s (Kadushin, 1967).

As mentioned earlier, as special-needs placements increased, so too did
the percentages of disruptions and dissolutions. For instance, the statewide
disruption rate for California public agencies increased from 2.7 percent
in 1970 to 7.6 percent in 1973 (Festinger, 1986). In Ontario province, the
disruption rate increased from 4 percent in 1971 to 7 percent in 1978
(Festinger). In contrast to its increase in the 1970s, the disruption rate
appears to have stabilized in the 1980s (Barth & Berry, 1988). In 1981 in
13 California counties, 14.9 percent of placements of children aged 3 and
older ended in disruption (Barth & Berry). The disruption rate in a 1985
five-state study was 13 percent (Urban Systems). In Oklahoma, about 12
percent of placements made from 1982 to 1985 resulted in disruption.

Predictors of Adoption Disruption

With the increase in disruption, research attention has focused on
identification of associated factors. Figuring prominently in the disruption
research are a complex of demographic characteristics, social and family
criteria, and agency practices.

Age and gender of child. Older age at adoptive placement has been linked
with increased risk of disruption in numerous studies (Rosen, 1977;
Kadushin & Seidl, 1971; Cohen, 1984; Festinger, 1986; Barth & Berry,
1988; Urban Systems, 1985; Nelson, 1985; Rosenthal, Schmidt, & Conner,
1988; Partridge, Hornby, & McDonald, 1986; Boneh, 1979; Boyne, Denby,
Kettenring, & Wheeler, 1984; Groze, 1986). For instance, at Spaulding for
Children in New Jersey, disruption rates were 7 percent for children aged
birth to 5 years at placement, 15 percent for those 6 to 8, 25 percent for
those 9 to 11, and 47 percent for those 12 to 17 (Boyne et al., 1984). Barth
and Berry's (1988) study of more than 900 children placed in 13 California
counties showed lower disruption rates on the whole than the Spaulding
study, but the same increasing risk of disruption with older children
emerges: age 3 to 5, 5 percent disruption rate; age 6 to 8, 10 percent; age
9 to 11, 17 percent; age 12 to 14, 22 percent, and age 15 to 18, 26 percent.

Boys are overrepresented in disruptions and dissolutions in six studies
(Rosenthal et al., 1988; Rosen, 1977; Boneh, 1979; Nelson, 1985; Barth
& Berry, 1988; Sack & Dale, 1982). No statistically significant gender-as-
sociated differences are evident in five others (Boyne et al., 1984; Festinger,

1986; Kadushin & Seidl, 1971; Urban Systems, 1985; Zwimpfer, 1983). A study of adoptive placements made by the Oklahoma Department of Human Services between 1982 and 1985 found that among children age 8 and younger, disruption was more likely for boys; among children age 9 and above, the disruption rate was modestly higher for girls (Rosenthal et al., 1988).

*Child handicaps and behavior problems.*The combined results from six studies suggest that developmental disability (orthopedic or physical handicap, retardation, reduced cognitive functioning, or serious developmental delays) may predict disruption, but only to a limited degree (Partridge et al., 1986; Boneh, 1979; Boyne et al., 1984; Nelson, 1985; Rosenthal et al., 1988; Urban Systems, 1985). Coyne and Brown (1985) found a disruption rate of 8.7 percent in a sample of 693 developmentally disabled children, a rate that was lower than had been anticipated.

In contrast to developmental disability, emotional and behavioral problems strongly predict disruption (Sack & Dale, 1982; Reid, Kagan, Kaminsky, & Helmer, 1987; Boneh, 1979; Barth & Berry, 1988; Boyne et al., 1984; Rosenthal et al., 1988). Aggressive, acting-out behavior as contrasted with inhibited, withdrawn behavior is most centrally linked to disruption (Partridge et al., 1986; Barth & Berry; Reid et al.; Sack & Dale). For example, Partridge and colleagues (1986) identified six behaviors that predicted disruption: sexual promiscuity, physically injuring others, stealing, vandalizing, threatening or attempting suicide, and wetting or soiling bed or clothes.

Ethnicity, family structure, and sociodemographics. In general, the associations of ethnicity, family structure, and income and education levels to risk for disruption are weak in strength.

Several disruption studies show modestly reduced risk in minority families (Rosenthal et al., 1988; Urban Systems, 1985), others demonstrate no relationship to race (Festinger, 1986; Boyne et al., 1984; Barth & Berry, 1988), while others demonstrate higher risks for minority families (Partridge et al., 1986). Groze (1986) found increased risk for disruption in transracial placements but two other studies found no such linkage (Partridge et al.; Barth & Berry, 1988).

Two studies demonstrate an association between adoptions by single-parent adoptions and increased risk of disruption (Boneh, 1979; Partridge et al., 1986), but four others show no such association (Reid et al., 1987; Barth & Berry, 1988; Boyne et al., 1984; Festinger, 1986; Urban Systems, 1985). Festinger found that six of seven placements with single fathers resulted in disruption.

Recent studies suggest that lower socioeconomic status may be associated with reduced risk. Boneh (1979) observed a higher disruption rate when fathers were in professional occupations. Barth and Berry (1988) and Festinger (1986) found that higher education of the mother predicted disruption. (Festinger concluded that less educated parents were over-represented in foster parent adoptions, which seldom disrupted.) Rosenthal and colleagues (1988) and Urban Systems (1985) also found that higher educational level predicted disruption. Two additional studies show educational level and disruption to be unrelated (Partridge et al., 1986; Boneh, 1979). Four studies demonstrate modest associations between higher income level and increased risk (Rosenthal et al., 1988; Groze, 1986; Barth & Berry; Urban Systems). Income level and disruption risk were unassociated in the Partridge (1986) study. Two studies suggest that middle-class families may have more difficulty coping with and tolerating behavior problems that run counter to community norms (Schmidt, Rosenthal, & Bombeck, 1988; Unger, Dwarshuis, & Johnson, 1981).

Some disruption studies evidence different patterns. Zwimpfer (1983) found that lower social class status increased risk in her New Zealand study. Boyne and colleagues (1984) found that increased education of the mother was weakly associated with reduced risk, particularly for younger children.

Family functioning. Flexibility as contrasted with rigidity in family decision-making patterns may reduce the risk of disruption (Kagan & Reid, 1986; Rosenthal et al., 1988; Sack & Dale, 1982). Findings from many studies concur that unrealistic or unmet expectations of the child portend instability (Gill, 1978; Schmidt et al., 1988; Barth & Berry, 1988; Festinger, 1986; Kadushin & Seidl, 1971; Nelson, 1985; Unger et al., 1981). In one study, families who adopted older, emotionally disturbed children reported three major areas of disappointment, those involving their "expectations concerning the child's personality, expectations of improvement in the child, and expectations of reciprocal caring for the child" (Kagan & Reid, p. 147). Even when the adoption social worker emphasizes the problems that may be encountered, the prospective adoptive parents may maintain idealized, unrealistic expectations. As one parent who had experienced a disruption stated, "We were told [about his problems], but we really thought we could handle this and anyway, our child would never act that way" (Schmidt et al., p. 125). The husband's noninvolvement in decision making and child care was the pivotal variable in Cohen's (1984) disruption study. Similarly, research by Westhues and Cohen (1990) found that if the father is "actively involved in parenting, and able to nurture and support the mother in her role, placements are more likely to be sustained" (p. 141).

Type of adoption. Adoptions by foster parents have consistently been associated with stability (Rosenthal et al., 1988; Festinger, 1986; Barth & Berry, 1988; Nelson, 1985). Rosenthal and colleagues found that 41 percent (11 of 27) of adoptive placements in a sample of intact families were foster adoptive placements. In contrast only 21 percent (13 of 62) of placements in a sample of disruptions were foster family placements. The increased stability may be due to the fact that foster children who are adjusting well are more likely to be adopted than those who are not. Barth and Berry (1988) found that adoption of children age 12 and younger by foster parents was more likely to result in stability. Adoption by foster parents was not an important factor affecting stability for older adoptees.

Research on placement of siblings offers mixed findings as to the likelihood of disruption. Some research suggests that the placement of siblings in the same home is associated with increased risk (Davis & Bouck, 1955; Boneh, 1979; Kadushin & Seidl, 1971; Urban Systems, 1985; Boyne et al., 1984). For instance, data compiled from three states showed that sibling placements represented 20 percent of all placements, but 43 percent of disrupted placements (Urban Systems). Yet several studies show no association of sibling placement with risk (Barth & Berry, 1988; Groze, 1986; Rosenthal et al., 1988, Oklahoma sample), while others show reduced risk for sibling placements (Rosenthal et al., Colorado sample). For instance, Kagan and Reid's (1986) study of emotionally disturbed children who were adopted when older showed better outcomes for those adopted with siblings. Festinger (1986) also observed a lower disruption rate among sibling placements but posited that siblings with more problematic backgrounds are more likely to be separated.

Some studies suggest that sibling placements may be problematic only when there are other children in the home. Boneh (1979), for instance, found that all nine placements of sibling groups in homes that already had biological children resulted in disruption. Barth and Berry observed no disruptions among 47 children who were placed in sibling groups when no other children were in the home. Rosenthal's group (1988) found that among children younger than about age 9, sibling placements were somewhat more prone to disruption than were placements without siblings. Among children older than 9, the opposite pattern was observed.

Services for the adoptive family. Adoptive parent support groups appear to be a particularly effective vehicle for preventing disruption and helping the family (Feigelman & Silverman, 1983; Elbow & Knight, 1987). Gill (1978), for instance, emphasizes the key role of a postplacement parent support group at a private agency. She reports that only 5 disruptions in 900 placements occurred over a five-year period. Tremitiere (1979) describes a group study process for prospective special-needs parents and reports that many participating families form lasting friendships through this process. The overall pattern of findings from five studies shows that multiple-agency (and/or multiple-county) involvement is associated with disruption (Partridge et al., 1986; Boneh, 1979; Rosenthal et al., 1988;

Boyne et al., 1984; Barth & Berry, 1988). Multiple agencies are often involved in placements of difficult high-risk children.

Adoptive parent concerns regarding inadequate history and background information have also been linked to increased risk in at least four studies (Urban Systems, 1985; Barth & Berry, 1988; Schmidt et al., 1988; Nelson, 1985). For instance, four of the five families that experienced dissolutions in Nelson's study reported inadequate background information about the child.

Some studies identify parents' perceptions of agency and worker emphasis on permanency planning, which manifests itself in pressure to choose adoption even when it may not be the best plan. With the shortage of infants and young children, some families may be coaxed into adopting children with characteristics different from those that they desire. Valentine, Conway, and Randolph (1988) interviewed disrupted families who "felt the adoption worker was really in the business of 'selling' children" (p. 141). One client reported, "She [the caseworker] talked me into it. I knew I shouldn't. Deep down inside you know what's wrong or right" (p. 141).

Barth and Berry (1988) recommend behavior management training to help parents deal with problematic behavior on the child's part. Tutoring services were associated with reduced risk of disruption in one study (Partridge et al., 1986).

Other factors. Findings regarding the presence of other children in the home are complex and contradictory. Two studies show reduced risk when other children—biological or adopted —are present (Rosenthal et al., 1988; Groze, 1986), four demonstrate no association (Boyne et al., 1984; Zwimpfer, 1983; Festinger, 1986; Barth & Berry, 1988), and two studies show increased risk (Davis & Bouck, 1955; Barth & Berry, 1988, interview study). Kadushin and Seidl (1971) identify several studies from the 1960s that demonstrate increased risk for the second adoptive placement in a family. In contrast, two recent studies found reduced risk when there were other adoptive children in the home (Partridge et al., 1986; Rosenthal, 1985). Boneh (1979) found that the presence of biological children in the home was related to increased risk of disruption.

Other predictors of disruption include the amount of time in previous out-of-home placement (Partridge et al., 1986; Kagan & Reid, 1986), the number of placements prior to adoption (Rosenthal, 1985; Boneh, 1979, Kagan & Reid; Festinger, 1986), younger age of the adoptive parents (Rosenthal et al., 1988; Zwimpfer, 1983), physical and/or sexual abuse prior to adoption (Partridge et al., Kagan & Reid), and having experienced a prior disruption (Barth & Berry, 1988; Partridge et al.; Nelson, 1985; Boyne et al., 1984). Religious attendance, having relatives nearby, and having friends who are adoptive or foster parents may also mitigate risk (Barth & Berry).

While prior disruption is a risk factor, many children experience a successful second adoptive placement (Schmidt et al., 1988; Festinger, 1986; Kadushin & Seidl, 1971; Rosenthal et al., 1988). For instance, in a Colorado study 16 of 57 children who experienced disruptions were adopted again prior to the conclusion of the study (Rosenthal et al.). In Oklahoma, 126 of 170 children who experienced a disruption were successfully adopted by another family. Trial adoptions that terminated very shortly after the placement were counted as disruptions in this study (Rosenthal et al.).

Intact Special-Needs Adoptive Families

In contrast to the proliferation of disruption studies in the 1970s and 1980s, fewer studies focused on outcomes in intact special-needs families. In general, however, the research shows positive results among intact families with special-needs adoptive children. Many of the same social and demographic factors that figure into the research on disruption are also the focus of study for intact families.

Nelson's (1985) important study of 177 intact special-needs families demonstrated high levels of parental satisfaction among approximately three-quarters of those interviewed. Only 48 percent of respondents indicated that the information provided by the agency regarding the child was both accurate and sufficient. While most were satisfied with social work services, many reported unmet service needs, particularly regarding counseling for the child and special education services. Predictors of parental satisfaction included the child's not being emotionally isolated from peers and family members, adequacy of agency preparation, frequency of church attendance, adequacy of agency information about the child, and the child's not having been previously placed for adoption. Parents who had adopted girls expressed somewhat greater satisfaction than did those who had adopted boys.

Age of child. Several other studies show good outcomes for children adopted when older. Triseliotis and Russell (1984) compared perceptions of adults who were adopted at an older age (mean age 3.5 years) with those of adults who were raised in foster care. The adoptees indicated more satisfaction with how they were raised and higher life satisfaction (happiness). Tizard's (1979) study of 30 children adopted at age 2 years or older showed that 84 percent of parents were well satisfied with the children's progress. Smith and Sherwen (1983) found that 82 percent of 33 adolescents, most of whom were adopted at age 3 or older, described at least some good things about their adoptions. Lahti (1982) found that adoptive placements disrupted less often than did foster care placements or foster children returned home. Caretaker ratings of the child's well-being, however, did not vary according to type of placement.

Child handicaps. Several research studies have focused on outcomes of adoptions for children with handicaps, that is, vision, hearing, or other physical handicaps, mental retardation, and serious medical conditions. Although severity of handicap may adversely affect adoptive family functioning, good adoptive outcomes have been demonstrated for handicapped children. Franklin and Massarik (1969a, 1969b, 1969c), for instance, reported that more than three-quarters of parents adopting children with medical handicaps were well satisfied with their adoptions. The literature on children with handicaps is reviewed in greater depth in Chapter 9.

Family structure, ethnicity, and socioeconomic status. Several studies demonstrate good outcomes for adoptions by single parents (Shireman & Johnson, 1976; Shireman & Johnson, 1985; Shireman, 1988; Feigelman & Silverman, 1977; Branham, 1970), although these parents may encounter resistance from agencies and communities and often adopt older, more difficult children (Feigelman & Silverman, 1983).

Transracial adoption is a controversial topic. The practice expanded greatly in the late 1960s (Feigelman & Silverman, 1983), leading to a 1972 statement by the National Association of Black Social Workers expressing its "vehement opposition" (cited in Feigelman & Silverman, 1983, p. 235). In addition, Chestang (1972), Jones and Else (1979), Small (1984), and Chimezie (1975) raised a variety of political and child development concerns about transracial placements. While some studies identify problems in child adjustment, the balance of studies demonstrate good psychosocial outcomes for transracial adoptees. (This research is described in greater detail in Chapter 8.) Though transracial adoption has decreased greatly since the early 1970s, the overrepresentation of minority and biracial children in the child welfare system as well as the substantial number of interracial couples and biracial children ensure that some transracial placement will continue.

Following the same pattern as do findings from disruption studies, several studies of intact families show modestly better outcomes when applicants are from lower socioeconomic status (Jaffee & Fanshel, 1970; McWhinnie, 1967, cited in Zwimpfer, 1983; Davis & Bouck, 1955; Ripple, 1968). In contrast, Kraus (1978) observed less problematic child adjustment in 7-year-old adoptees whose fathers were of higher rather than lower socioeconomic status. Ripple (1968) found higher education and economic status to be modestly associated with worse outcomes in her sample of white families. Among black adoptive parents, a trend in the opposite direction was observed. Hockey (1980) noted that middle-class as contrasted with working-class adoptive parents experienced greater difficulty in adoption of mentally handicapped children. Goetting's (1986) review of the general parental satisfaction literature suggests that educational level and parental satisfaction are negatively correlated; those with higher educational attainment tend to report lower levels of satisfaction.

Type of adoption. Good outcomes are also reported for foster parents who adopt (Meezan & Shireman, 1982) although some foster parents may feel pressured into adoption by agencies (Proch, 1981). Some states and agencies grant preference to foster parents in adoption. This practice may lead to "adoption by default" (Proch, p. 622). Adoption by default occurs when foster parents are able to adopt "because they are given preference, not because they are the best available resource" (Proch, p. 622–623). Proch recommends careful screening of foster care placements that have the potential to evolve into adoptions.

Other. Feigelman and Silverman (1983) compared the emotional adjustment of children adopted by preferential and nonpreferential parents. The preferential parents were predominantly fertile couples who were adopting by choice rather than because of infertility. On average, better adjustments were noted for the nonpreferential parents. Yet the children adopted by the preferential parents were more often older and of a different racial background from their parents. When statistical techniques were used to control for these and other differences, better adjustments were observed among the children of preferential adopters.

Special-needs adoption presents distinctive challenges for both children and families. Barth and Berry (1988) argue convincingly for the lifetime advantages of adoption for the child who might otherwise reside in foster care. Taking into account such factors as the value of parent-child relationship and the higher anticipated earnings for those reared in adoptive rather than foster homes, they calculate the financial value of adoption to the child as in excess of $500,000. These authors, along with three colleagues, state that "when older child adoptions succeed they may be the most complete and beneficial intervention in all the human services" (Barth, Berry, Yoshikami, Goodfield, & Carson, 1988, p. 233).

Chapter 2

Study Design and Sample

This study, conducted in 1988, explored the adoption experiences of 799 families who adopted children with special needs from agencies in Oklahoma, Kansas, and Illinois. The adoptive parents completed mailed questionnaires covering such areas as support from family and friends, handicaps and disabilities, the perceived helpfulness of social work and supportive services, school attendance and grades, behavioral problems, family functioning and relationships, parent-child relationships, and the impact of the adoption on the family. Factors such as age, gender, out-of-home placement history of the child, and type of adoption, for instance, adoptions by foster parents, adoptions by single parents, and adoptions of sibling groups, are analyzed. This chapter reviews the survey methods and describes the characteristics of the responding families and their adopted children.

METHODOLOGY

Sampling Techniques

Families of children placed by four different adoption agencies compose the sample, which totaled 1,413. Sampling procedures differed across agencies. A sample from the caseload of the Oklahoma Department of Human Services comprised 434 children placed in adoptive homes from March 1983 to December 1987 and whose adoptions had been finalized by March 1988. Only children age 4 or over at the time of placement and age 17 or younger at the time of mailing (March 1988) were included. Identical sampling procedures were used at Project Adopt ($n = 37$), a private Oklahoma agency. This mailing was in April 1988.

A sample from the caseload of the Kansas Department of Social and Rehabilitation Services (KDSRS) comprised 335 children placed by that agency or by a private agency contractor between July 1984 and June 1988. There was no minimum age of placement; children 18 or older at the time of mailing (October 1988) were excluded. A small number of nonfinalized placements were included in the Kansas sample but disruptions and dissolutions were excluded. In the Oklahoma and Kansas agencies, a maximum of one eligible child per family was selected. Where more than one child was in the home, a random method was used to select one for the study.

A sample from the caseload of the Illinois Department of Children and Family Services (IDCFS) was chosen from the subsidized adoption list in effect for November 1988. For a small percentage (less than about 10 percent) of children, the subsidized families received medical coverage only. Via systematic sampling, every fifth child (a total of 607 children) was selected for the study. This eliminated the inclusion of multiple adopted children from a single family except where there were more than five subsidized adoptees in the home. The survey was mailed in November 1988. Some Illinois children had entered their adoptive homes as many as 17 years prior to the survey. Some Illinois placements were made by IDCFS while others were made by contracting agencies.

At each agency, one follow-up mailing was made to families that did not respond initially. Response rates were excellent. Mailings were returned marked "address unknown" for about 60 families, suggesting that 96 percent of families (1353) were successfully contacted. Approximately 25 questionnaires were returned indicating that the child had moved permanently out of the home. These were dropped from the sample since the intent of the study was to survey intact families. The response rate among successfully contacted families with children at home was 60 percent (799 of 1328). The sample of 799 cases includes 267 (33 percent) families from Oklahoma Department of Human Services, 18 (2 percent) families from Project Adopt, 184 (23 percent) families from Kansas, and 330 (41 percent) families from Illinois.

A small percentage of sample children do not meet any of the most frequently used criteria that define special needs. For instance, 4 percent (35 of 799) were not of minority or biracial status, placed with biological family siblings, age 3 or older at the time of adoptive placement, or handicapped. (The working definition of handicapped as used in the study includes vision and hearing impairments, physical disability, mental handicap or mental retardation, and chronic or life-threatening medical problems.) The percentage of children who did not meet any of the special-needs characteristics increases to 7 percent (59 of 799) when minority or biracial status is excluded as a criteria. Even though some children may not have special needs, all are included in most analyses.

The full sample is diverse and, given the participation of agencies from several states, at least somewhat representative of public agency adoptions in the midwestern United States. Further, the large sample size provides an opportunity to focus on the needs and outcomes for older children, who are a cohort of special concern to adoption professionals. In some instances, results were analyzed for the subsample of 516 children who were age 4 or older when they first entered their adoptive homes. Results for this distinct and interesting subsample can be compared with those for the full sample.

Variables and Measures

The large sample size facilitated analysis of various types of adoptions and a host of variables pertaining to the child and the adoptive families. In addition, the survey included several standardized instruments and scales to assess different aspects of family life.

Among the variables examined, the survey identified different types of adoptions, such as those by foster parents, relatives, and single parents. Outcomes for subsidized and nonsubsidized adoptions were also compared.

The analysis of family variables included income and educational levels, the occupations of the parents, whether the mother worked out of the home, the presence of other children in the home, the type of residence of the adoptive family, and the size of the community in which the family resided.

A significant number of variables relating to the child also were examined. The child's age at entry into the home and at the time of the survey are important independent variables, as is the child's gender. Other variables analyzed were handicaps and disabilities of the child, sexual abuse prior to adoption, prior out-of-home placement history, sibling placement, and contacts of the child with the biological family.

Findings were reported in relationship to the race of both the adopting parents and the child and for transracial adoptions. In most analyses, race was presented as a dichotomous variable with the categories of white and minority or biracial.

The questionnaire consisted primarily of close-ended questions. Of critical interest are those questions that probe the responding parent's perception of the overall impact of the child's adoption on the family. In addition, several other measures of adoptive outcome were used. A five-item scale, termed the parent-child relationship scale, assessed the quality of and closeness of parent-child relationship. The questionnaire also asked about school attendance and grades and the child's enjoyment of school. Finally, the children's and parents' participation in various services and their degree of satisfaction with those services was studied. (All of the above responses are presented in the overview of study findings in Chapter 3.)

In addition, two standardized instruments were included with the questionnaire to explore child behavior and family functioning. The behavior problems section of the Child Behavior Checklist (CBC) allowed comparisons of the study sample with two normative groups, a clinical sample composed of children in mental health treatment and a nonclinical sample of typical children (Achenbach & Edelbrock, 1983). (See Chapter 10 for further description of the CBC). The Family Adaptability and Cohesion Scales, version 3 (FACES III), permitted comparisons of family functioning with a representative sample of families (Olson et al., 1985; see Chapter 6).

Finally, the survey posed several open-ended questions to probe for parents' views on the rewards and difficulties of special-needs adoption. These responses were content-analyzed and are presented in Chapter 4.

Limitations of Data

All data reflect parent reports and may differ from data in agency records. For instance, reports of the number of placements prior to adoption should be viewed as approximate. Similarly, the percentage of children with learning disabilities, mental retardation, and similar conditions is based on parent perceptions rather than on formal diagnostic criteria. Parent reports of certain dates may not be precise, particularly in Illinois, where children entered their homes up to seventeen years prior to the mailing. Data regarding the date of entry into the home, the date of adoptive placement, the child's age at entry into the adoptive home and at adoptive placement, and the length of time that the child had been residing in the home at the time of the survey should be viewed as accurate to within about a year.

The date of adoptive placement was problematic for children who were adopted by foster parents. Respondents attached different meanings to "adoptive placement": Some reported the day that the child entered the home, while others provided the date of finalization. Since the intent had been to capture the date that plans to adopt the child were made, a somewhat arbitrary operational definition was developed. Where it appeared that parents had listed either the date of entry or the date of finalization, the date of placement was calculated to be one year prior to finalization. The rationale was to make the date of placement in adoptions by foster parents roughly comparable with that in adoptions by "new" parents, for example, in new placements one year is a fairly typical period of time for the adoption to progress from placement to finalization. Due to the problem just mentioned, the child's age at initial entry into the home rather than age at adoptive placement was used more frequently in various analyses that are presented. In the authors' opinion, age at entry may be the more important variable affecting the progress of the adoption.

Even with the described limitations, the data set was well suited for the planned analysis. Fanshel (1972) and Kadushin (1970) used parent reports in adoption studies and demonstrated that these reports possess adequate reliability and validity.

Checks for Sampling Bias

Two procedures were used to check for possible sampling bias. First, at two agencies the characteristics of respondents and nonrespondents were compared on selected variables. In the Oklahoma Department of Human Services sample, no significant differences between respondents and non-respondents were observed with respect to gender and age of the child and single-parent versus two-parent family structure. In Illinois, a comparison between the sampling frame (the subsidized adoption list) and responding families did not reveal significant response bias with respect to gender and race of the child. For instance, 52 percent of children on the subsidized adoption list were of minority or biracial status compared to 53 percent of the children of the respondents.

The second procedure involved examining assessments of the impact of the adoption on the family in relationship to two variables: (1) whether the respondent responded to the first or the second mailing and (2) the number of days to respond to the first mailing. The investigators had anticipated that those who delayed or had to be "nudged" into responding with a second mailing would be more negative in their assessments of impact. If so, it could have been inferred that those who did not respond would have been even more negative. This pattern was not observed. The mean score on perceived impact did not vary between the first- and second-mailing respondents. Similarly, the correlation between the number of days to respond to the first mailing and impact was very weak and did not reach significance; those who delayed in responding were only slightly more guarded in their assessments ($r = -.06$, $N = 564$). These results suggest the possibility that respondents and nonrespondents may be similar with regard to their perceptions of adoptive outcome.

Notwithstanding the two just-mentioned checks for bias, two potential biases may be present in the sample. First, given the normal pattern of survey response, we advance the "educated guess" that those who responded to the survey may have experienced, on balance, more positive adoptive outcomes than those who chose not to respond. Second, the complexity of the questionnaire may have deterred those with low reading or writing skills from responding. Whether this second potential bias would have substantially changed the results is unclear.

SAMPLE CHARACTERISTICS

The sample may be described from different perspectives, including the type of adoption, the characteristics of the families and the respondents, and the traits of the adopted child.

Types of adoptions. Over half of the adoptions involved foster parents or relatives. Specifically, 43 percent (343 of 791) had previously been foster parents to the child named in the questionnaire, though 52 percent of respondents (415 of 792) had been foster parents at some time. About 10 percent of placements (78 of 788) were relative placements, including 29 placements with grandparents and 42 with aunts, uncles, or cousins. Subsidized adoptions outnumbered nonsubsidized, with financial assistance going to 60 percent of respondents (467 of 773). Thirty-seven percent of the children (290 of 778) had biological family siblings placed with them in the home. This percentage is lower than it would have been if the sampling methodology had not limited participation in the study to one sibling per family. Sixteen percent (122 of 773) of the placements were with single parents.

Characteristics of the families and respondents. The vast majority of the respondents (85 percent, 680 of 797) were adoptive mothers. They reported their marital status at the time of the survey as: married, first marriage, 59 percent (467 of 793); married, second or later marriage, 20 percent (158); separated or divorced, 8 percent (67); widowed, 6 percent (44); single, never married, 7 percent (54); and living with partner but not legally married, 0.4 percent (3).

The responding families presented diversity with respect to educational level and income. Among adoptive mothers, 13 percent (102 of 768) had not finished high school, 26 percent (202) had earned a high school diploma or GED, 33 percent (252) had attended some college, 16 percent (125) had graduated from college, and 11 percent (87) had earned a master's degree or above. Among the fathers, 12 percent (78 of 645) had not finished high school, 25 percent (163) had earned a high school diploma or GED, 28 percent (179) had attended some college, 20 percent (130) had graduated from college, and 15 percent (95) had earned a master's degree or above. The median yearly income from all sources of responding families was

$32,000, while the mean was $35,653 ($SD$ = $22,247, n = 657). Twenty-one percent (141 of 657) of families reported earning $50,000 or more per year. Unfortunately, 18 percent (142 of 799) of families left the question on income blank, so the data in this area are less than complete.

The fathers' occupations were categorized according to the Classified Index of Industries and Occupations (1982) developed for the 1980 Census. These classifications were: managerial and professional specialty, 40 percent (213 of 529); technical, sales, and administrative support, 18 percent (97); service occupations, 6 percent (30); farming, forestry, and fishing, 4 percent (22); precision production, craft, and repair, 17 percent (88); operators, fabricators, and laborers, 13 percent (67); and self-employed, occupation unspecified, 2 percent (12). Sixty percent of adoptive mothers (457 of 758) and 89 percent of adoptive fathers (573 of 645) were employed at the time of the survey.

The families resided primarily in single-family dwellings, but in communities of varying sizes. Fully 75 percent (588 of 787) lived in single-family houses, 14 percent (107) on farms or ranches, 5 percent (42 of 799) in apartments, 3 percent (22) in duplexes, condominiums or cluster homes, and 4 percent (28) in some other residence. Regarding the population of the city or town of residence, 28 percent (210 of 760) responded that it was less than 5,000; 16 percent (122), 5,001 to 15,000; 20 percent (153), 15,001 to 40,000; 13 percent (99), 40,001 to 100,000; and 23 percent (176), more than 100,000.

Characteristics of the children. Eleven percent of children (87 of 799) were age 5 and younger at the time of the survey, 48 percent (381) were age 6 to 11, and 41 percent (331) were age 12 or older. Boys outnumbered girls by a small margin (415 to 382, 52 percent to 48 percent). Selected data on the ages of the children and their adoptive parents and on the numbers of children in the home are presented in Table 2.1. Thirty-nine percent (307 of 795) of respondents indicated that at least one son or daughter (adopted, biological, or stepchild) lived outside of their home at the time of the survey.

The reported racial background of the children in the sample was 62 percent (489 of 793) white, 22 percent (176) black, 1 percent (6) Asian-American, 5 percent (36) Native American, 4 percent (35) Hispanic, and 6 percent (51) biracial. The racial background of respondents was similar to that of the children, although a larger percentage were white (72 percent). The Illinois sample was distinguished from the other two state agency samples by the higher percentage of minority children: 53 percent (173 of 325) children in the Illinois sample were of minority or biracial status compared to 31 percent (82 of 266) in the Oklahoma sample and 21 percent (38 of 184) in the Kansas sample, p < .01. Eleven of the 18 (61 percent)

Table 2.1
Ages of and Numbers of Children in the Home

				Percentile	
Age/number	N	Mean	Median	15	85
Age					
Adopted child					
When entered home	796	5.52	5.33	1.08	9.75
At adoptive placement	799	6.81	6.58	2.83	10.50
At time of survey	799	10.84	11.00	6.75	15.00
Adoptive parents					
Mother	755	42.67	41.00	34.00	52.00
Father	644	43.86	43.00	35.00	53.00
Number of children in adoptive family home[a]					
Total children[b]	787	2.96	3.00	1.00	5.00
Adopted children[b]	787	2.04	2.00	1.00	3.00
Biological children	787	0.56	0.00	0.00	2.00
Foster children	787	0.29	0.00	0.00	0.00
Number of children including those outside of the home	776	4.05	3.00	2.00	6.45

[a]Includes only children residing in home at time of survey.

[b]Includes child to whom survey pertains.

children adopted through Project Adopt were of minority or biracial status. Several (perhaps two or three) of the Project Adopt children were born outside of the United States.

A substantial number of children had developmental or physical handicaps. Parents reported the following percentages of handicaps: blindness or vision impairment (minor vision problems excluded), 1 percent (8 of 799); deafness or hearing impairment, 4 percent (30 of 799); physical handicap, 8 percent (64 of 799); mental retardation or mental handicap, 11 percent (84 of 799); chronic medical problem, not terminal or life threatening, 6 percent (46 of 799); chronic medical problem, terminal or life threatening, 2 percent (16 of 799); and other, 0.3 percent (2 of 799). These conditions defined the category of children with handicaps, who represented 20 percent (163 of 799) of all children (see Chapter 9 for detailed analysis regarding children with handicaps).

Many children had experienced out-of-home placement prior to adoption. Ninety-four percent (483 of 514) had experienced family foster home placements, 10 percent had previously been in group home or residential treatment (50 of 514), and 6 percent (31 of 514) had been in psychiatric hospitals. Twelve percent (61 of 514) of children had experienced an adoption disruption. Counting all of the just-listed categories as placements, the median number of placements was 1.00, while the mean was 2.27 ($SD = 2.02$, $n = 514$). Sexual abuse prior to adoption was confirmed or suspected for 34 percent (166 of 494) of children, including 41 percent (102 of 247) of girls and 26 percent (64 of 246) of boys. The percentage for boys was higher than the authors had anticipated. (The data on the number of placements and on sexual abuse were gathered only for the Kansas and Illinois samples. Hence, the sample size is smaller.)

Chapter 3

An Overview of Findings: Promise and Optimism

For families and their adopted children who stay together, special-needs adoption represents a future of promise framed with the realism that parenting and growing up are never easy processes. On balance, the families in this study reported good and positive outcomes, close parent-child relationships, and a favorable impact of the adoptions on their home and family life. Particularly promising were the results reported by minority parents, single parents, grandparents, and lower-income families, who assessed their special-needs adoption experience even more favorably than the sample as a whole.

This chapter reviews and summarizes the overall study findings. First, we examine the parents' perceptions of how their families and friends supported them during the adoption process and how helpful the social work services and agencies were. Second, we explore how parents evaluated the outcome of the adoption in terms of their child's school performance, their child's behavior and the family environment, and their overall assessment of the adoption's impact on the family. Third, we consider and analyze which variables seem to be predictive of whether the parents viewed the adoption more or less favorably. Finally, we offer some interpretations of the findings and their importance for social work and adoption practice.

PERCEPTIONS OF SUPPORT AND SERVICE

Support from Family and Friends

Almost all respondents reported significant support from extended family and friends regarding their adoption of a special-needs child (See Table 3.1).

Table 3.1
Parent Perceptions of Support from Family and Friends

Question and response	Full sample		Child aged 4 or older at entry into home	
	Freq.	%	Freq.	%
Do your relatives approve of the adoption?				
Yes, very much so	617	78	385	75
Yes, somewhat	157	20	116	23
No, not really	17	2	11	2
Do your spouse's relatives approve of the adoption?				
Yes, very much so	467	69	295	68
Yes, somewhat	169	25	117	27
No, not really	36	5	22	5
Have your friends been supportive of the adoption?				
Yes, very much so	644	81	408	79
Yes, somewhat	128	16	93	18
No, not really	19	2	13	3

In the full sample, about 80 percent of respondents reported very strong support. This percentage drops hardly at all when attention is focused on the subsample of families whose children were age 4 and up when they entered the home. The respondents reported somewhat lower levels of approval with regard to their spouses' relatives.

Social Work and Agency Services

Parents were asked to evaluate the services, information, and support activities of the agencies from which they adopted children. While most respondents were satisfied with agency services, more than one-third (35 percent, 264 of 757) reported that background information on the child was insufficient. Fifty-eight percent (418 of 726) reported that the background information was accurate or almost always accurate. When asked whether services provided by the adoption workers were helpful, 55 percent (409 of 749) responded "Yes, very much so." Responses to selected questions about services are presented in Table 3.2.

Table 3.2
Parent Perceptions of Services of Adoption Agency Social Worker(s)

Question and response	Full sample		Child aged 4 or older at entry into home	
	Freq.	%	Freq.	%
Since adoptive placement, would you say you had ...				
More visits with social worker than necessary	22	3	13	3
About the right number	550	78	369	79
Not enough visits	132	19	86	18
Did your social worker(s) provide you with ...				
Too much information on the child's background and possible problems	7	1	5	1
About the right amount	486	64	309	62
Not enough information	264	35	183	37
Was the information provided regarding the child's background and characteristics ...				
Accurate or almost always accurate	418	58	265	55
Mostly accurate but sometimes inaccurate	227	31	164	34
Mostly inaccurate	81	11	56	12
Are your child's problems and/or handicaps, if any,				
More serious than described to you	178	27	129	28
About as described	386	58	260	57
Less serious than described	101	15	67	15
Think about the services provided by your social worker. Were these services helpful?				
Yes, very much so	409	55	256	53
Yes, somewhat	231	31	159	33
No, not really	109	15	70	14

Table 3.3
**Number of In-Person Meetings with Adoption Agency Social Worker(s)
Concerning Child**

Number of meetings	Full sample		Child aged 4 or older at entry into home	
	Freq.	%	Freq.	%
Total				
None	169	22	76	15
One to three	209	27	140	28
Four to nine	211	27	164	32
Ten to nineteen	97	12	74	15
Twenty or more	95	12	53	10
Since adoptive placement				
None	239	30	111	22
One to three	265	34	184	36
Four to nine	180	23	141	28
Ten to nineteen	59	8	48	9
Twenty or more	41	5	23	5
Since legal finalization				
None	543	71	321	66
One to three	162	21	119	24
Four to nine	38	5	31	6
Ten to nineteen	13	2	10	2
Twenty or more	10	1	8	2

Table 3.3 presents the number of in-person meetings with adoption
agency social workers concerning the child. Surprisingly, substantial percentages of respondents reported that they did not meet with their social
worker at any time during the adoption process. For instance, 31 percent
reported no meetings with their workers since the date of the adoptive
placement. While some respondents may have forgotten meetings that
actually took place, the data suggest that follow-up services were not carried
out systematically. Clearly, at least some of these placements reflect the
philosophy of nonintrusion into the family's affairs after the placement. As
mentioned earlier, some of the Illinois placements were made as many as
17 years prior to the date of the survey, a time when there was less emphasis
on postplacement services. Hence an analysis was conducted that was
restricted to children who had been in their homes for five years or less.
In this subgroup, the percentage of parents reporting no contacts since the

time of placement, 19 percent (85 of 454), is distinctly lower. Among those in this subgroup whose children were four or older when adopted, this percentage decreases still further, to 16 percent (57 of 359). Thus, the data do suggest a trend towards increased visiting in the more recent adoptions.

Table 3.4 presents the percentages of families receiving selected services such as individual therapy (counseling) for the child, family therapy, and adoptive parent support groups. Contact with other special-needs adoptive parents, whether formal or informal, was also viewed as a service. Among the different services, participation in support groups was least common, while individual therapy for the child was most common.

On balance, the services listed in Table 3.4 were perceived as helpful, with 80 percent or more of the respondents evaluating each service area as very or somewhat helpful. Participation in support groups and contact with other special-needs families were rated distinctly more helpful than individual and family therapy. The less favorable evaluations for individual and family therapy may reflect that these services are frequently provided in

Table 3.4
Counseling and Supportive Services Post-Adoptive Placement

Service	N	Receive service %	Was service helpful? yes, very %	somewhat %	no %
Full sample					
Individual therapy for child	775	36	36	49	15
Family therapy	780	26	39	47	14
Adoptive parent support group	782	19	47	45	7
Contact with other special needs families	780	31	52	42	6
Child age 4 or older when entered home					
Individual therapy for child	505	43	34	50	16
Family therapy	507	32	38	48	14
Adoptive parent support group	507	23	49	44	7
Contact with other special needs families	506	34	57	37	6

very difficult situations where the prognosis for change is limited. Where respondents had been in contact with other parents, the questionnaire probed for the frequency of contact. Responses were: daily or almost daily, 11 percent (26 of 236); about once a week, 13 percent (30); about once a month, 28 percent (65); every three or four months, 27 percent (63); and about once a year or less, 22 percent (52).

ADOPTION OUTCOMES

The survey explored the impact of the special-needs adoption on all major facets of the child's and the family's life. In particular, questions probed to assess outcomes related to school attendance and performance, child behavior, family functioning, and parent-child relationships.

School Life

School-related findings were positive, particularly with respect to attendance. Ninety-two percent of children (731 of 795) were attending school at the time of the survey. Almost all children age 6 to 17 (99 percent, 695 of 703) were attending. Among teenagers (ages 12 to 18) fully 98 percent (322 of 329) of children were attending. The children's attendance surpassed expectations and may well represent the most positive finding of the study.

Twenty-eight percent of parents (227 of 799) reported that their children had learning disabilities. Among those attending school, 40 percent (287 of 719) were enrolled in some special education courses. Among children enrolled in special education, 30 percent (83 of 280) were enrolled exclusively in special education and 70 percent (197) were in a mixture of special education and regular classes. Of those with children enrolled in "mixed" classes, 62 percent (123 of 197) of the parents reported that the majority of their child's classes were regular classes. The following percentages of parents reported that their children attended given types of special education classes: learning disabilities, 20 percent (145); speech or language difficulties, 16 percent (117); emotional or behavior problems, 8 percent (57); mental handicap or retardation, 9 percent (66); deaf or hearing impairment, 1 percent (8); blind or vision impairment, 1 percent (8); physical or orthopedic handicap, 3 percent (20); and other 6 percent (45). The percentages pertaining to type of special class are based on the sample of 731 children who were attending school.

Among families whose children were attending school, 84 percent (606 of 724) reported that their children attended the local public school. Among those not attending the local public school, 6 percent were in another public school (6 of 96), 45 percent (43) were in private school, 39 percent (37)

were in a specialized school for children with handicaps, and 10 percent
(10) were in some other type of school. A fairly high percentage (40 percent,
272 of 681) of those attending school had been retained at least once, either
prior to or subsequent to adoption.

Overall, 67 percent of parents (489 of 730) reported that their child
"enjoys school," 28 percent (204) reported that their children "like it and
dislike it about the same," and 5 percent (37) reported that they "dislike
school." Similar responses were noted for the subsample of children age 4
or older when they entered the home; these percentages were, respectively,
62 percent (312 of 502), 32 percent (160), and 6 percent (30). Such
responses suggest that many children are actively and meaningfully involved at their schools. Student grades in the most recent semester, reported
in Table 3.5, indicate solid performance, with B and C grade averages
reported most frequently.

Table 3.5
Parent Reports of Child's Grades in Most Recent School Semester

Grades for full sample

Letter grades (n = 580)			Pass-fail grades (n = 279)		
Grade	Freq.	%	Grade	Freq.	%
A average	75	13	Passed all courses	162	58
B average	229	40	Passed most courses	91	33
C average	204	35	Failed most courses	22	8
D average	62	11	Failed all courses	4	1
F average	10	2			

Grades for those age 4 and older at entry into home

Letter grades (n = 435)			Pass-fail grades (n = 186)		
Grade	Freq.	%	Grade	Freq.	%
A average	55	13	Passed all courses	109	59
B average	174	40	Passed most courses	61	33
C average	158	36	Failed most courses	13	7
D average	42	10	Failed all courses	3	2
F average	6	1			

Note. Some parents responded to questions pertaining to both letter and
pass-fail grades.

Child Behavior

The Child Behavior Checklist (Achenbach & Edelbrock, 1983), a standardized checklist, has separate norms by age group and gender for both a clinical sample of children in mental health treatment and a nonclinical sample of "typical" children. Table 3.6 compares the percentage of children in these samples and in the adoption sample who score in the clinical range. While percentages vary for the different age/gender subgroups, the clinical range is defined as approximately the 90th percentile or higher with respect to the nonclinical sample. Hence, a score in the clinical range indicates that a child has more pronounced behavioral problems than about 90 percent of his or her peers. Table 3.6 reports percentages in the clinical range on the internalizing, externalizing, and total problems scales. The internalizing scale captures acting-out and aggressive behaviors, while the internalizing scales measure withdrawn, inhibited behaviors. The total problems scale is essentially a sum of all behavioral problems noted.

Among those age 4 and 5 at the time of the survey, the percentages of children in the adoption and nonclinical samples who score in the clinical range are similar, particularly for boys. This suggests that as a group, the adoptees in this age range demonstrate fairly typical behavior. Among 6- to 11-year-olds and 12- to 16-year-olds, the percentages of adopted children scoring in the clinical range greatly exceed those in the nonclinical sample. Hence, the data suggest serious behavioral problems for many adoptees in these age ranges. Behavioral problems are evident for both boys and girls and on all three scales. The comparison between the full sample and the subsample of children who entered their homes at age 4 or older is interesting. For most age-and-gender categories, the percentages in the clinical range are quite similar. The expectation had been that the scores of the subsample would be elevated considerably more than those in the full sample.

Considering the full sample, 41 percent (286 of 702) of children scored in the clinical range on the total problems scale. More in-depth analysis of behavior problems is presented in Chapter 10.

Family Functioning

The Family Adaptability and Cohesion Evaluation Scales (FACES III) measure adaptability and cohesion, two major dimensions of family functioning posited in the Circumplex Model (Olson et al., 1985). Adaptability is defined as "the ability of a marital or family system to change its power structure, role relationships, and relationship rules in response to situational

Table 3.6
Percentages of Scores in Clinical Range on Child Behavior Checklist in CBC and Adoption Samples

| | Ages 4 and 5 | | | | Ages 6 to 11 | | | | Ages 12 to 16 | | | |
| | CBC | | Adoption | | CBC | | Adoption | | CBC | | Adoption | |
	Clin-ical	Non-clin.	Full sample	Age 4 and up[a]	Clin-ical	Non-clin.	Full sample	Age 4 and up[a]	Clin-ical	Non-clin.	Full sample	Age 4 and up[a]
Girls	(n=100)	(n=100)	(n=26)	(n=5)	(n=300)	(n=300)	(n=185)	(n=120)	(n=250)	(n=250)	(n=121)	(n=99)
Internalizing	68	9	15	20	69	9	25	33	58	5	26	27
Externalizing	42	6	19	40	72	9	42	50	52	4	26	28
Internalizing and/or externalizing	69	12	27	40	82	14	45	55	68	7	33	35
Total problems	73	12	23	40	75	10	43	53	74	10	45	45
Boys	(n=100)	(n=100)	(n=2)	(n=3)	(n=300)	(n=300)	(n=177)	(n=119)	(n=250)	(n=250)	(n=159)	(n=125)
Internalizing	59	11	12	0	68	10	27	34	62	10	42	42
Externalizing	62	10	15	0	70	8	35	42	66	9	38	39
Internalizing and/or externalizing	74	14	19	0	83	14	44	53	76	12	50	51
Total problems	72	10	15	0	77	9	40	48	71	10	45	46

[a]Age refers to age at time of entry into adopted home.

and developmental stress" (Olson et al., p. 3). Cohesion is defined as "the emotional bonding that family members have toward one another" (Olson et al., p. 3).

The adoptive families score modestly higher with respect to adaptability (Mean = 24.9, N = 728, SD = 5.1) than do the "typical" families that comprise the normative sample for FACES III (Mean = 24.1, N = 2453, SD = 4.7). This suggests that the sample families are flexible with respect to roles, rules, and tasks and are able to alter interaction patterns in times of stress.

The adoptive families also score slightly higher on cohesion. Their mean score was 40.3 (N = 742, SD = 5.4) while that of the normative sample was 39.8 (N = 2453, SD = 4.7). This suggests that the majority of special-needs families experience a strong sense of family closeness and bonding. A selected item from FACES III conveys this closeness. Families were asked to describe how often "family members feel very close to each other." Fifty-six percent (428 of 765) responded "almost always"; 30 percent (226), "frequently"; 11 percent (86), "sometimes"; 3 percent (22), "once in a while"; and 0.4 percent (3), "almost never." In the subsample of children who entered the home at age 4 or older, 54 percent (272 of 501) responded "almost always" to this question, while only 0.6 percent (3) responded "almost never." This subsample scored very much like the other adoptive families on the two scales, with mean scores of: adaptability, 25.0 (N = 484, SD = 5.1) and cohesion, 40.2 (N = 490, SD = 5.4).

On balance, then, the family measurements indicate that special-needs adoptive families may be modestly more cohesive and more adaptable than typical families. A detailed explication of the Circumplex Model as well as additional findings and discussion are presented in Chapter 6.

Parent-Child Relationship

Six questions probe various aspects of parent-child relationship (See Table 3.7). Most respondents report close, satisfying relationships with their adopted children. For instance, in the full sample, 58 percent (463 of 795) responded "Yes, very much so" to the question "Do you feel close to your child?" Responses in the subsample of families that adopted children who were age 4 or older are somewhat less positive; for instance, only 48 percent (246 of 513) responded "Yes, very much so" on the just-mentioned question. The less positive responses in this age group are in part due to the fact that a higher percentage of these children were in adolescence, 51 percent versus 43 percent in the full sample, at the time of the survey.

Table 3.7
Relationship Between Parent and Child

Question and response	Full sample		Child aged 4 or older at entry into home	
	Freq.	%	Freq.	%
How do you and your child get along?				
Very well	521	66	294	58
Fairly well	241	30	192	38
Not so well	24	3	19	4
Very poorly	7	1	6	1
How would you rate the communication between you and your child?				
Excellent	321	40	160	31
Good	349	44	255	50
Fair	99	12	77	15
Poor	25	3	22	4
Do you trust your child?				
Yes, very much so	281	36	142	28
Yes, for the most part	381	49	274	54
Not sure	45	6	33	6
No	78	10	62	12
Do you feel respected by your child?				
Yes, very much so	401	51	220	43
Yes, for the most part	305	39	225	44
Not sure	49	6	41	8
No	33	4	26	5
Do you feel close to your child?				
Yes, very much so	463	58	246	48
Yes, for the most part	260	33	207	40
Not sure	35	4	29	6
No	37	5	31	6
How often do you and your child spend time together which you both enjoy?				
Just about every day	538	68	309	61
Two or three times a week	167	21	128	25
About once a week	55	7	46	9
About once a month	18	2	14	3
Less than once a month or not at all	12	2	11	2

A five-item scale measuring parent-child relationship (alpha = .90) was developed by combining responses to the questions probing communications, trust, respect, closeness, and how the parent and child "get along." The range of possible scores is from 1.0 to 4.0; the higher the score, the better the parent-child relationship. The mean scale score, 3.34 (n = 773, SD = 0.65), indicates good parent-child relationship. Figure 3.1 presents the mean score by the child's age at entry into the home, by the child's age at the time of the survey, and by the number of years the child resided in the home.

As expected, the closest parent-child relationships were observed for those who entered the home when they were young. As age at entry increases, the mean score decreases through age 10 and then levels off. With respect to age at the time of the survey, the mean score decreases steadily as age increases. This pattern was expected. A similar pattern, conveying greater closeness for younger children and less for older children would most probably be found also in nonadoptive families.

The results based on the years of residence in the home were somewhat disappointing. We had hoped to see a discernible improvement in mean scores over the first several years. Yet, no such trend was evident, suggesting that parents should not expect dramatic improvements in parent-child relationships over this time period. The reader should remember that a longitudinal design would have been preferable and that some of the reasons that the relationships do not appear to grow closer have to do with the normal process of separation between parents and children that takes place as children become older.

Figure 3.1
Parent-Child Relationship by Child's Age and Years in Home

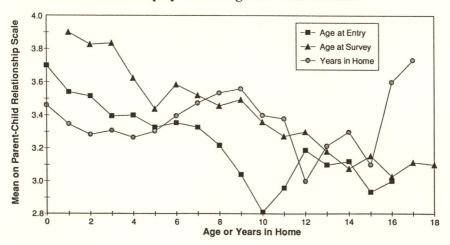

The Impact of Adoption on the Family

The central outcome measure for the study, the impact of the adoption on the family, is assessed by the question: "Overall, has the impact of this child's adoption on your family been . . . very positive, mostly positive, mixed (positives and negatives about equal), mostly negative, or very negative." Overall, three-quarters of respondents (583 of 780) responded "Very positive" or "Mostly positive." Twenty-one percent (163) chose the "Mixed" category, while 4 percent (34) responded "Mostly negative" or "Very negative." Response patterns were similar to Nelson's (1985) and Kadushin's (1970) studies, both of which showed that 75 percent or more of parents who adopted special-needs or older children were well satisfied. In the subsample of children age 4 and up at entry into the home, 68 percent (344 of 505) responded "Very positive" or "Mostly positive." Table 3.8 presents responses to this question.

A second outcome measure probed the "smoothness" of the adoption. About one-third chose each response category: 32 percent (254 of 789) responded "Smoother than expected"; 35 percent (277), "About as expected"; and 33 percent (258), "More ups and downs than expected." With the subsample of children age 4 and up at entry into the home, more parents described the adoption process as being more difficult than expected. The percentages for the subsample are 29 percent (146 of 511), 31 percent (157), and 41 percent (208) respectively. In both the full sample and the subsample, about two-thirds of respondents indicated that they had either fewer or more difficulties than had been anticipated. This may suggest that it is difficult to predict whether a special-needs adoption will steer a smooth or "rocky" course. On the other hand, with more in-depth preparation, the percentage

Table 3.8
Parent Perception of Overall Impact of Adoption on Family

Response	Full sample		Child aged 4 or older at entry into home	
	Freq.	%	Freq.	%
Very positive	365	47	194	38
Mostly positive	218	28	150	30
Mixed; positives and negatives about equal	163	21	133	26
Mostly negative	24	3	20	4
Very negative	10	1	8	2

of families whose experiences are congruent with expectations may increase.

PREDICTORS OF THE IMPACT OF ADOPTION

Just as the previous disruption research has looked for clues to what factors may foretell the possibility of disruption, so too this analysis explored those demographic and socioeconomic criteria that may be associated with more favorable outcomes in special-needs adoptions. The analysis covers the age of the child at different points in the adoption process, parent education and family income, community setting, race of the child and parents, and various types of adoptions.

Age and Time in the Home

Children. Table 3.9 presents parents' assessments of the adoption's impact by the child's age when he or she first entered the home, when adopted, and at the time of the survey. Focusing first on entry into the home, responses were most positive for those age 0 to 5. Even so, many parents of older children reported positive impacts. Responses are encouraging regarding adoptees who entered the home as adolescents; they are quite similar to those for children who entered the home in their latency years. Given that adolescence is often a time of conflict between parent and child, our expectation had been for more negative impacts in the adolescent adoptions.

Focusing on age at the time of the survey, the most positive results are for those in the youngest age group, while the least positive reports pertain to adolescents. These results are in accord with expectations and, we believe, similar to those that would be observed in nonadoptive families.

Figure 3.2 presents the percentage of "Very positive" responses in relationship to children's ages and time in the adoptive home. This figure highlights the very positive responses for children adopted younger than age 2. While the trend is modest, the percentage of "Very positive" responses increases across the first three years that children are in the home. In contrast with the parent-child relationship findings (see Figure 3.1), this trend suggests that at least in some instances, parents' perceptions of the adoption's impact may improve over this time period. A less optimistic interpretation is that the improvement reflects the effects of adoption disruption. Over the course of the first three years many of the less successful adoptions may have disrupted, rendering families ineligible for this study of intact families. The apparent improvement may reflect this dropout rather than a real change.

Table 3.9
Age of Child and Impact of Adoption on Family

Age	N	Percents			
		Very Positive	Positive	Mixed	Negative/ Very Negative
At entry into home	777				
0 to 5 years	435	54.5	27.8	14.9	2.8
6 to 11 years	307	37.1	27.0	29.3	6.5
12 to 18 years	35	37.1	34.3	22.9	5.7
At adoptive placement	780				
0 to 5 years	337	56.1	25.5	15.1	3.3
6 to 11 years	377	39.3	30.0	25.7	5.0
12 to 18 years	66	42.4	28.8	22.7	6.1
At time of survey	780				
0 to 5 years	86	68.6	17.4	12.8	1.2
6 to 11 years	372	48.1	32.0	16.9	3.0
12 to 18 years	322	39.4	26.1	27.6	6.8
All respondents	780	46.8	27.9	20.9	4.4

Figure 3.2
Impact of Adoption on Family by Child's Age and Years in Home

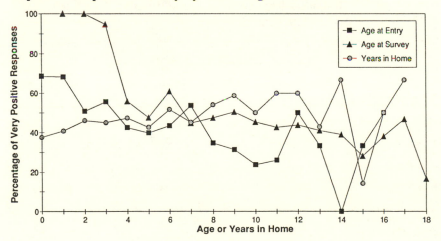

Table 3.10 presents the percentage of "Very positive" responses in relationship to both age at entry into the home and age at the time of the survey. By reading down the columns, one can compare responses for children of similar ages at the time of the survey who entered the home at different ages. As expected, such a comparison reveals that children placed at age 2 or younger experience the best outcomes. The comparison for 3- to 5-year-olds is of interest. Where these children entered the home at age 2 or younger, 72 percent of parents responded with "Very positive." In contrast, for those who entered the home as 3- to 5-year-olds, this percentage, 28 percent, was markedly lower.

Reading across the rows allows comparisons of children who entered the home at similar ages but were in different age groups at the time of the survey. The comparison for 12- to 14-year-olds is of most interest. The adoptions of children who are still in this age group at the time of the survey are evaluated much more positively than are those of children who are in the 15-to-18 age group (71 percent versus 26 percent). Given the small sample sizes, sampling error or "chance" may be the best explanation for this difference.

Parents. Age of the adoptive mother at the time of the survey showed a modest but interesting association to impact. Outcomes in families with younger mothers (34 or younger) and older mothers (45 or older) were more positive than those mothers between the ages of 35 and 44. The percentages of "Very positive" responses by age of the mother were: 34 and younger, 55 percent (67 of 122); 35 to 44, 42 percent (156 of 375);

Table 3.10
"Very Positive" Responses Regarding Impact of Adoption by Child's Age at Entry into Home and at Time of Survey

| Age at entry | Age at time of survey | | | | | | | | | | | | All Ages | |
| | 0-2 | | 3-5 | | 6-8 | | 9-11 | | 12-14 | | 15-18 | | | |
	%	n	%	n	%	n	%	n	%	n	%	n	%	n
Birth to 2 years	100	12	72	60	58	59	71	45	53	30	38	21	64	227
3 to 5 years	--		28	14	48	79	41	69	45	29	53	17	44	208
6 to 8 years	--		--		35	20	43	86	48	63	36	22	43	191
9 to 11 years	--		--		--		21	14	27	75	33	27	28	116
12 to 14 years	--		--		--		--		71	7	26	19	38	26
15 to 18 years	--		--		--		--		--		67	3	67	3
All Ages	100	12	64	74	50	158	47	214	41	205	38	111	47	780

and 45 and older, 49 percent (118 of 243); $p < .05$. This pattern weakened considerably in the subsample of children who entered the home when age 4 or older. Percentages in the subsample were: 34 and younger, 43 percent (34 of 79); 35 to 44, 34 percent (91 of 264); and 45 and older, 40 percent (54 of 135); $p > .05$. The particularly good outcomes observed for younger mothers may in part be explained by the more frequent placement of younger children with this group.

Education and Income Level

Educational level of the adoptive parents is negatively related to the impact of the adoption; in other words, lower educational levels are associated with more positive assessments. Table 3.11 demonstrates a steady decline in the percentage of very positive responses as the respondent's educational level increases. The correlation of the impact of the adoption with educational level was: $-.16$ ($n = 753$) for adoptive mothers, $-.12$ ($n = 639$) for adoptive fathers, and $-.16$ ($n = 776$) for the questionnaire respondent. In the subsample of children age 4 and older at entry into the home, the very low percentage of "Very positive" responses for parents with master's degrees (or above) stands out.

A similar pattern is observed for income level. As family income increases, the percentage of "Very positive" responses decreases. Yet, as Table 3.12 shows, this association is not a simple one. While the percentage of "Very positive" responses (60 percent) in the lowest income group is much higher than that in the highest (32 percent), this percentage changes

Table 3.11
"Very Positive" Responses Regarding Impact of Adoption on Family by Education Level of Respondent

Education level	Full sample		Child aged 4 or older at entry into home	
	%	n	%	n
Did not finish high school	56	97	52	44
High school diploma or GED	52	192	42	109
Attended college	47	247	36	166
College graduate	44	133	42	99
Master's degree or above	36	107	29	85

Table 3.12
**"Very Positive" Responses Regarding Impact of Adoption on Family by
Annual Income from All Sources**

Income	Full sample		Child aged 4 or older at entry into home	
	%	n	%	n
$0 to $14,999	60	77	49	37
$15,000 to $24,999	47	129	41	74
$25,000 to $34,999	44	143	36	94
$35,000 to $44,999	47	131	36	85
$45,000 to $59,999	45	93	45	75
$60,000 and up	32	77	26	62

hardly at all in the middle four groups (income range $15,000 to $59,999). For the subsample of children age 4 and older, outcomes are most problematic in highest income group.

Given the negative association of income to the impact of the adoption, it was anticipated that those families where fathers were in professional occupations would more often experience negative outcomes. Only a hint of such a pattern emerged. While positive outcomes were reported slightly more often in families where fathers were employed in service and operator/laborer jobs or were self-employed, the perception of impact did not vary significantly according to occupation (see Tables 3.13 and 3.14).

Type of Residence and Size of Community

Some interesting patterns were evident with respect to type of residence; however, they are not easily interpreted. Surprisingly positive assessments were reported by those residing in apartments. Those reporting very positive impacts by type of residence were: apartment, 72 percent (26 of 36); duplex, condominium, or cluster home, 38 percent (8 of 21); single-family home, 48 percent (276 of 579); farm or ranch, 37 percent (40 of 107); and other, 29 percent (8 of 28). These differences reached statistical significance, $p < .01$. The same pattern was observed in the subsample of children who entered the home when age 4 or older. These percentages were: apartment, 76 percent (10 of 13); duplex, condominium, or cluster home, 24 percent (4 of 17); single-family home, 39 percent (143 of 365);

Table 3.13
"Very Positive" Responses Regarding Impact of Adoption by Occupational Classification of Adoptive Father

Occupation	Full sample		Child aged 4 or older at entry into home	
	%	n	%	n
Managerial and professional specialty	42	212	33	153
Executive, administrative, and managerial	40	89	31	64
Professional specialty	42	123	35	89
Technical, sales, and administrative support	39	97	37	70
Technicians and related support	48	25	44	18
Sales	40	35	38	29
Administrative support including clerical	32	37	30	23
Service occupations	62	29	41	17
Private household	0	2	0	2
Protective service (police, fire, etc.)	50	12	29	7
Service, not protective or household	80	15	63	8
Farming, forestry, fishing	27	22	21	19
Precision production, craft, and repair	47	88	38	53
Operators, fabricators, and laborers	55	66	44	41
Machine operators, assemblers, and inspectors	54	26	40	20
Transportation and material moving	58	19	60	15
Handlers, equip. cleaners, helpers, and laborers	52	21	17	6
Self-employed (occupation unspecified)	67	12	60	10

Note. No differences reach significance in ANOVA.

Table 3.14
"Very Positive" Responses on Family Impact Question by Selected Case Characteristics

Case characteristic	Case has characteristic		Case does not have characteristic	
	N	%	*N*	%
Demographics, family structure				
Adoptive mother is respondent	663	47.7	115	40.9
Adopted child is female	373	46.4	406	47.0
Respondent or spouse a (biological) relative to child	72	55.6	697	46.2*
One-parent (vs. two-parent) family (status at survey)	155	54.8	623	44.8
One-parent (vs. two-parent) family (status at placement)	112	58.9	646	44.1*
Child minority or biracial (vs. white)	291	56.7	485	40.8**
At least one adoptive parent minority or biracial (vs. white)	241	55.6	531	42.7**
At least one parent same race as child	702	45.9	67	53.7
Adoptive mother has paid job outside of home[a]	386	42.7	242	44.6
Adopted mother graduated from college	212	38.2	541	50.1**
Father in managerial or or professional occupation	212	41.5	314	46.8
Other children in the home				
Other children in home at time of survey	623	45.7	152	50.7
Biological children of adoptive parents in home at time of survey	273	40.7	495	50.1
Other adopted children of adoptive parents in home at time of survey	436	46.3	332	47.3
A biological child in home within one year of age	49	30.6	731	47.9*
Another child in home of same sex within one year of age	121	42.1	653	47.5
Foster children in home at time of survey	106	53.8	662	45.6*
Adoptive family has other children who live outside of the home	300	41.3	476	50.2*
Child placed as part of sibling group	283	45.2	477	47.6

44

Table 3.14 (continued)

Case characteristic	Case has characteristic		Case does not have characteristic	
	N	%	*N*	%
Child and service factors				
Child placed as part of sibling group	283	45.2	477	47.6
Child experienced a disruption prior to placement[b]	61	44.3	434	51.2
Group home or psychiatric placement prior to adoption[a]	66	33.3	429	52.9**
Group home placement prior to adoption[a]	50	32.0	445	52.4**
Psychiatric placement prior to adoption[a]	30	26.7	465	51.8**
Sexual abuse prior to placement (actual or suspected)[b]	163	36.2	317	57.4**
Child participated in individual therapy post-adoptive placement	276	27.9	486	56.8**
Family participated in family therapy post-adoptive placement	196	27.6	571	52.5**
Parent(s) participated in adoptive parent support group post-placement	147	38.8	622	48.4**
Parent(s) in contact with other special-needs parents post-adoptive placement	240	42.9	527	48.2
Child is handicapped	156	47.4	624	46.6
Child has learning disability	223	38.6	557	50.1**
Financial subsidy provided	452	46.5	305	46.9
Child had contact with member of biological family after adoption	265	42.3	508	49.2
Adoptive parent previously a foster parent to child	331	51.1	441	43.3**

Note. Test of mean score on family impact used for all significance tests.
[a]Includes only two-parent families.

[b]Variables not included in questionnaire sent to Oklahoma and Project Adopt families, hence the smaller sample size.

*p<.05, **p<.01

45

farm or ranch, 32 percent (27 of 84); and other, 25 percent (5 of 20);
$p = .01$.

With respect to size of community, modestly more positive impacts were observed in small towns and in urban areas, while reports in middle-sized communities were less positive. The percentages of "Very positive" reports by population of community were: 15,000 or lower, 47 percent (154 of 328); 15,000 to 100,000, 39 percent (97 of 246); and greater than 100,000, 55 percent (94 of 171); $p < .01$. Similar findings were observed in the subsample of children who entered the home when age 4 or older: 15,000 or lower, 40 percent (93 of 231); 15,000 to 100,000, 31 percent (50 of 160); and greater than 100,000, 46 percent (44 of 95); $p < .05$.

While the questionnaire did not specifically probe for whether the respondent's residence was in a suburban, urban, or rural community, one is tempted to conclude that those with suburban residences experienced less positive outcomes. A cautious interpretation of these findings is advised, since the just-described associations may reflect the influence of factors other than type of residence or size of community.

Other Children in the Home

Under some circumstances, the presence of other children in the home showed modest associations to adoption outcome (see Table 3.14). For instance, the adoption's impact was evaluated less positively when there was a biological child of the adoptive parents within one year of age of the adopted child. The presence of any biological child (regardless of age) approached significance as a predictor of negative outcome. Those families with children (biological, adoptive, or step-) living outside of the home also reported more negative outcomes. This finding was unanticipated. We had thought that the experience of raising other children would have been helpful to the adoptive parents, and that this experience might have been associated with positive outcome. Table 3.14 also presents findings pertaining to several other questions regarding other children.

Adoptions of Minority Children

The impact of the adoption was perceived more positively by respondents who adopted minority or biracial children and by respondents in families where at least one parent is of minority status or biracial (see Table 3.14). In part, the particularly good outcomes for children in minority families may be explained by the fact that these children differ in key characteristics from other children in the study. For instance, children in minority families were, on average, younger at adoptive placement and had less often experienced group home or psychiatric placement. Nonetheless, the positive outcomes for these children are noteworthy.

Table 3.14 suggests that the match in race between child and parents is not an important factor affecting the impact of the adoption on the family. Chapter 8 provides greater detail contrasting transracial and inracial placements and includes analyses that focus on minority children rather than on the full sample.

TYPE OF ADOPTION AND SERVICE CHARACTERISTICS

Adoptions by relatives received some of the most favorable assessments in the study. Very positive outcomes were reported in 73 percent (19 of 26) of adoptions by grandparents, 48 percent (19 of 40) by aunts, uncles, or cousins, and 29 percent (2 of 7) by other relatives, $p < .05$. Similarly, foster parents experienced good outcomes (see Table 3.14), perhaps because they often choose to adopt after good bonding has developed. The questionnaire does not differentiate between fost-adopt placements, those in which foster parents intend to adopt when (and if) parental rights are terminated, and other foster parent placements, those in which adoption was not considered initially. Single-parent adoptions were evaluated positively, with 59 percent reporting very positive outcomes. These outcomes are discussed in more detail in Chapter 7. Unrelated to outcome were such factors as the availability of a financial subsidy, adoption as part of a sibling group, and contact with the biological family after adoptive placement (see Table 3.14).

More negative outcomes had been anticipated for adoptions where children had experienced a prior adoption disruption. This was not the case. The impact of the adoption did not show a statistically significant association to whether the child had experienced a prior disruption. While handicap status was unassociated with outcome, learning disabilities, sexual abuse prior to adoptive placement, and prior group home or psychiatric placement were predictors of more negative outcome. Similarly, outcomes were less positive in families that participated in individual and family therapy and in support groups. This association was anticipated, since problems lead families to use such services rather than the reverse.

Correlations with the Adoption's Impact

Table 3.15 presents correlations of selected variables with the impact of adoption. The two scales presented in Table 3.15 that are based on the CBC require explanation. The 20-item external problems scale (alpha = .91) is composed of those items common to all six CBC externalizing scales (e.g., both sexes in three age groups). The 18-item internal problems scale was developed using the same logic (alpha = .82). These scales were developed for the current study. Correlations of less than about .20 convey weak (modest) associations between variables, correlations between .20 and .50 convey moderate associations, while correlations greater than .50 convey fairly strong associations.

The strongest correlation presented in Table 3.15 is between the impact of the adoption on the family and the score on the parent-child relationship scale. This correlation is of such a magnitude ($r = .70$) that these variables may be viewed as nearly synonymous. While the external problems scale shows a strong negative association with the adoption's impact, the internal problems scale shows a more moderate relationship. In other words, acting-out, aggressive behavior bears more on a negative adoptive outcome than does inhibited, withdrawn behavior. As expected, the child's enjoyment of school is strongly associated with positive outcome.

Family closeness, as measured by the FACES III cohesion scale, predicts positive outcome. Flexibility in family functioning as measured by the adaptability scale is also positively associated with outcome; however, this association is quite weak.

Approval of the adoption and support from friends and, in particular, from relatives affects adoptive outcome positively. As discussed earlier, educational and income levels of the adoptive parents show modest negative relationships to outcome. Positive associations with outcome are evident regarding both the amount of and the accuracy of background information. Finally, the number of children in the respondents' family of origin is positively, though very weakly, associated with outcome.

MULTIPLE REGRESSION ANALYSIS

Given the number of different factors associated with the impact of the adoption, it is apparent that many associations are not causal; that is, they reflect the influence of other variables. For instance, the better outcomes for minority and biracial children in part reflect the fact that these children were younger, on average, when they entered their homes. Multiple regression, the preferred statistical procedure in a situation such as this, controls statistically for the effects of all variables entered in an equation. Hence, if a variable in a multiple regression is significantly associated with the dependent variable, in this case the impact of the adoption, the other variables in the equation are ruled out as possible explanations of that association.

Table 3.15
Correlations of Selected Continuous Variables with Family Impact

Variable	Full sample N	Full sample r	Child aged 4 or older at entry into home N	Child aged 4 or older at entry into home r
Demographic variables				
Age of child at time of survey	780	-.21**	505	-.08*
Age of child when entered home	777	-.26**	505	-.13**
Mean age of adoptive parents	769	.01	500	-.02
Family income (in thousands)	650	-.17**	427	-.14**
Mean educational level of parents[a]	776	-.14**	503	-.12**
Number of children in respondents' family of origin	767	.11**	499	.11**
FACES measurements				
Cohesion	731	.27**	482	.30**
Adaptability	720	.08*	477	.10*
CBC-derived measures				
External behavior problems[b]	751	-.58**	491	-.56**
Internal behavior problems[c]	742	-.38**	484	-.34**
Support systems/approval of adoption				
Approval of respondents' family[d]	775	.38**	502	.37**
Approval of spouses' family[d]	666	.31**	431	.34**
Support from friends[d]	777	.30**	505	.32**
Perceptions of social work services				
Amount of background information[d]	744	.20**	491	.18**
Accuracy of background information[d]	718	.18**	481	.16**
Overall helpfulness of adoption social worker service[d]	739	.17**	480	.18**
Other variables				
Child's enjoyment of school[d]	712	.36**	491	.34**
Importance of religion to respondent[d]	776	.05	765	.06
Parent-child relationship[e]	755	.70**	---	---

[a] Five-point response continuum utilized.
[b] 20-item scale, three-point response continuum for item.
[c] 18-item scale, three-point response continuum for item.
[d] Three-point response continuum utilized.
[e] Five-item scale, four-point response continuum for each item.

*p<.05, **p<.01

Three different multiple regressions are presented in Table 3.16. The first two regressions use objective variables only (i.e., those requiring little, if any, subjective judgment, such as age of child, race of child, family income, adoption by foster parents, etc.). These two regressions differ in that the second includes two variables—group home or psychiatric placement prior to adoption and sexual abuse prior to adoption—that were included only in the questionnaires mailed to the Kansas and Illinois samples. The third regression differs from Regression 1 because in addition to objective variables it also includes attitudinal variables, those requiring considerable judgment on the respondent's part (for instance, external behavior problems and family cohesion). This division was made because the attitudinal variables show markedly stronger associations to perceived impact and dominate the objective variables when they are entered together. (For a more technical explanation of the methodology as well as additional regressions, see Rosenthal & Groze, 1990). The betas in Table 3.16 are interpreted as correlations with the effects of other variables controlled for statistically. Similar to the interpretation of correlations, betas of less than .20 convey weak associations, while betas greater than .50 show fairly strong associations, and so on.

With some exceptions, the regressions affirm results already presented. In the case of the child's age at the time of the survey and at the time of entry into the home, the regression analyses were contradictory. Interestingly, in Regressions 1 and 2, the child's age at the time of entry into the home is not a significant predictor, but the child's age at the time of the survey is predominant. In contrast, in the third regression, the situation is reversed for these variables.

The regression analyses suggest only modest associations between adoption outcome and the sociodemographic variables of race, income, and education. The child's minority or biracial status was associated with positive impact in two of the three regressions. Adoption by foster parents, lower family income level, and lower educational level each predicted more positive impact in one regression. Clearly, none of these factors should be used to rule families in or out in the selection process. To cite a specific example from Regression 1, those with lower family incomes, when controlling for other variables, evaluate the adoption's impact slightly more positively than do those with higher family incomes. In other words, family income is only a weak predictor, and some wealthy families evaluated the impact quite positively while some poor families were negative in their assessments.

Regression 2 includes the variables prior group home or psychiatric placement and prior sexual abuse. Both of these variables, in particular group home or psychiatric placement, predict negative outcome.

Table 3.16
Three Stepwise Regressions on Family Impact

Variable	Regressions using objective variables				Regression #3: objective and attitudinal variables	
	Regression #1		Regression #2[a]			
	(N = 618)		(N = 371)		(N = 495)	
	B	β	B	β	B	β
Objective variables						
Child age in years when entered home	ns	ns	ns	ns	-.024	-.086**
Child age in years at time of survey	-.057	-.230**	-.043	-.203**	ns	ns
Child minority or bi-racial (vs. white)	.284	.140**	.349	.182**	ns	ns
Family income (in thousands)	-.0045	-.105**	ns	ns	ns	ns
Mean educational level of parents	ns	ns	ns	ns	-.069	-.077*
Adoption by foster parents	.193	.100*	ns	ns	ns	ns
Single-parent adoption (status at placement)	ns	ns	ns	ns	.304	.101*
Sexual abuse prior to placement[a] (actual or suspected)	--	--	-.211	-.112**	--	--
Group home or psych-iatric placement prior to placement[a]	--	--	-.535	-.202**	--	--
Attitudinal variables						
External behavior problems	--	--	--	--	-1.021	-.409**
FACES cohesion score	--	--	--	--	.028	.154**
Approval of respondents' family	--	--	--	--	.393	.200**
Amount of background information shared	--	--	--	--	.170	.086*
Child's enjoyment of school	--	--	--	--	.143	.087*
Adjusted R²	.097**		.141**		.441**	

Note. Dash ("--") conveys that variable not considered for equation. Number of children in respondents' family of origin and biological children of adoptive parents in the home were entered in each equation but did not achieve significance in any. FACES adaptability score and internal behavior problems were entered in Equation #3 but did not reach significance. Criteria to enter and remove variables was the .05 significance level. See Tables 3.14 and 3.15 for description of variables.

*$p<.05$, **$p<.01$

[a]Sexual abuse and group home or psychiatric placement questions included only in Kansas and Illinois samples, hence the smaller sample size for Regression #2.

Regression 3 identified several of the attitudinal variables that are predictive of positive impact. These include the amount of background information shared, the child's enjoyment of school, and family cohesion. Among all variables, external behavioral problems is the strongest predictor of negative impact. On balance, the regression analyses affirm those findings presented in earlier tables.

Regression analysis also was used to study the effects of individual and family therapy and participation in support groups. In these analyses, family impact is the dependent variable. Even when controlling statistically for four important variables—age of child at placement, age of child at survey, group home or psychiatric placement prior to adoption, and sexual abuse prior to adoption confirmed or suspected—the provision of counseling services was associated with negative impact (beta = −.24 for individual therapy; beta = −.21 for family therapy). A weak negative relationship was also observed with respect to participation in a support group (beta = −.10). These regressions suggest that individual and family counseling may sometimes be of limited value in dealing with the difficult problems that special-needs adoptive families may face.

INTERPRETATION OF FINDINGS

Parent reports were distinctly positive. About three-quarters (75 percent) of respondents reported that the adoption of a special-needs child had a positive impact on their family. Results were also positive in the subgroup composed of children who entered their adoptive homes at age 4 or older; in this group, about two-thirds of respondents (68 percent) reported positive impacts.

Parent perceptions are positive even though many children demonstrate severely disturbed behavior. Parent reports of acting-out, aggressive behavior emerged as the single strongest predictor of negative impact. Children who experienced group homes or psychiatric placement prior to adoption experienced, on balance, problematic outcomes. Serious behavioral problems were observed primarily among latency-age children and adolescents and not among children younger than age 6. Contrary to expectations, handicapping condition (vision, hearing, or physical handicap, mental retardation, or serious medical condition) was unassociated with outcome. More in-depth discussion of behavioral issues is in Chapter 10, while that for children with handicaps is in Chapter 9.

While a longitudinal design would have been preferable, Figures 3.1 and 3.2 do not suggest that dramatic improvements in either the impact of the adoption or the quality of the parent-child relationship take place in the first several years following the child's entry into the home. These findings suggest that families adopting special-needs children need to have a long-term focus.

The results bode well for the "nontraditional" adoptive family. For instance, single, nonwhite, less-educated, and lower-income parents all reported more positive impacts of the adoption. Good outcomes were observed in families where mothers were both younger than or older than the age of the once-typical adoptive parent. Similarly, those in non-middle-class residences, particularly those in apartments, reported excellent out-comes. We can only speculate as to the reasons for this. Perhaps the proximity of neighbors offers increased opportunity for support and friendship. The good outcomes for adoptions by foster parents were expected and are, in part, related to bonds formed prior to the adoption.

The findings indicate that no one factor compellingly predicts success in a special-needs adoption. Yet, on the other hand, the findings very strongly underscore that single-parent status, minority status, lower education level, lower income level, or adoption by foster parents in no way reduce the potential for successful outcome. Study findings point to the need to aggressively recruit families from diverse backgrounds and affirm that demographic and socioeconomic factors should not preclude families from consideration.

The excellent outcomes in minority families and those with lower socioeconomic status bear further comment. The strong kinship ties and extended family networks in many minority families and communities (Ho, 1987) are distinct assets in adoption. Minority communities have strong traditions of and experience in raising children away from the nuclear family. This experience and the reduced stigma attached to growing up outside the immediate birth family are also assets. The excellent results in minority families and families with lower socioeconomic status are in accord with those studies that suggest that these characteristics may mitigate the risk of disruption (Groze, 1986; Unger et al., 1981; Barth & Berry, 1988; Rosenthal et al., 1988; Urban Systems, 1985). The in-depth discus-sion of minority adoption in Chapter 8 suggests that the very positive outcomes in minority families are in part due to differences in the characteristics presented by minority and white children at the time of adoption.

In contrast with the results for minority families and those with lower socioeconomic status are the somewhat less positive outcomes reported by families with high incomes and education levels. These families may put too much pressure on children or hold expectations that may be too high or not in accord with the child's interests or aptitudes. Even if the family does not emphasize academic achievement, community pressure may impinge unduly on the child who has modest academic talent or interest.

The negative relationship between parental educational attainment and adoptive outcome parallels Goetting's (1986) conclusions based on her review of parent satisfaction in typical nonadoptive families. Goetting found that higher education of the parents was associated with lower levels of satisfaction. To some degree contradicting the findings pertaining to income and education level, the fathers' occupation, categorized as professional versus other, was unassociated with the adoption's impact on the family. This finding may reflect a central role of the mothers in child-rearing tasks, notwithstanding the societal trend away from gender-defined household roles and towards shared familial responsibilities.

The survey underscores the importance of flexible family patterns in special-needs adoptions. Families adopting special-needs children are fairly adaptable in terms of rules and decision making. Flexibility is an asset, if not a necessity, in special-needs adoption. If families are not flexible as the adoption begins, those that remain intact are likely to become so as it proceeds.

The findings related to family cohesion are encouraging for special-needs adoption. Even with the behavior problems demonstrated by some children, the majority of families report cohesive, close family relationships. Additional discussion of adoptive family functioning is found in Chapter 6.

The more negative reports of parents whose adoptees were in adolescence at the time of the survey study should, perhaps, be viewed largely as normal rather than as related to special-needs adoption. For instance, Goetting's (1986) review reveals less parental satisfaction when children reach adolescence. It had been expected that parents who adopted adolescents would report more negative outcomes than parents who adopted latency-age children. However, the outcomes reported for these subgroups are quite similar. Compared with the child adopted in latency, the child adopted in adolescence may have a more realistic perspective of events and may therefore be better equipped to separate emotionally from the birth family and adjust to a new home. Hence, study findings support efforts to adopt adolescents, with one cautionary note in interpreting the results. The children adopted in latency were often in early adolescence at the time of the survey. In contrast, those adopted in adolescence were often in older adolescence at the time of the survey. Since early adolescence is traditionally a time of heightened parent-child conflict, the realities of the parent-child relationship at the time of the survey may have contributed to the less positive evaluations of the adoptions of latency-age children.

On balance, parents evaluated the services of their social workers positively, although an unexpectedly high percentage of families reported no contact with their worker following the adoptive placement. Study findings affirm the importance of accurate and detailed background information.

Many parents reported that background information was insufficient, a finding that has been replicated in numerous studies (Nelson, 1985; Urban Systems, 1985; Barth & Berry, 1988, Schmidt et al., 1988). The provision of detailed information helps the parent make an informed decision regarding whether to adopt and also prepares parents for what to expect following the adoption. Important information includes medical and social history, prior placements and residences, handicaps and limitations, significant people in the biological extended family, and interests and aptitudes. In-depth information and careful preparation are particularly critical for prospective parents who want to adopt infants but consider special-needs children as an alternative because the demand for healthy babies currently exceeds the supply. These prospective parents are clearly at high risk for dissatisfaction.

Parent support groups and informal contacts with other special-needs families were regarded as helpful by many parents. Results of this and other studies recommend these as important postadoption services for families (Gill, 1978; Tremitiere, 1979; Feigelman & Silverman, 1983; Elbow & Knight, 1987; Nelson, 1985). Individual and family counseling services were evaluated somewhat less positively. This may be because families who seek these services often experience difficult behavioral problems that are not easily remediated by any kind of intervention. Specialized training regarding individual and family dynamics in special-needs adoption is recommended for mental health professionals. More in-depth discussion of the kinds of services needed by special-needs families is provided in Chapter 12.

Study findings pertaining to school attendance and achievement were positive and exceeded expectations. Further, the child's enjoyment of school emerged as an important predictor of the adoption's impact. The special-needs adoptee may need a diversity of educational services, including specialized testing and evaluation, an individualized curriculum, tutoring, close communication between adoptive parents and school personnel, and advocacy. Further discussion is in Chapter 12.

Several of the predictors of negative outcome in this study of intact families have also been identified as predictors of adoption disruption. These include older age at placement, placement in a new (nonfoster) adoptive home, behavioral problems, and inadequate background information. The reader is reminded that survey designs are not well suited for drawing causal conclusions. For instance, this study informs us that negative outcomes are more likely when background information is inadequate but does not allow us to conclude that such inadequate information causes negative outcome. Longitudinal studies are better suited for addressing causal issues. Such studies can compare the relative contributions of family, child, and service factors and are greatly needed in the special-needs adoption field.

Many special-needs adoptions work well, notwithstanding the painful realities of adoption disruption and the prolonged periods of difficult parent-child relationship which many intact families experience. The current study justifies a cautious optimism and recommends enhanced outreach to families from all backgrounds and walks of life.

Chapter 4

Rewards and Difficulties: The Parents' Perspective

Quantitative methods used in the previous chapter do not convey the experiences—positive and negative, expected and unexpected—of the adoptive parents. The research design included four open-ended qualitative questions, calling for brief written responses, to probe the most rewarding aspect of the adoption, the most difficult aspect of the adoption, the advice that respondents would offer to persons considering special-needs adoption, and perceptions of adoption agency services.

Many responses resonate the normal joys and difficulties of parenting, while others call attention to the unique issues of special-needs adoption. This chapter identifies common patterns and themes in the diverse experiences of adopting families.

METHODS

Content analysis was used to analyze responses to the first three topics listed above. Responses to the fourth question, on agency services, often overlapped with responses to the other questions. Since perceptions of agency services are discussed in other chapters and in the preceding chapter, responses to this question are presented briefly and are not content-analyzed. The sample for this chapter consists of the Oklahoma DHS and Project Adopt families and Kansas families, a total of 469 families. Resources did not permit analysis of the Illinois responses.

A team of graduate social work students analyzed each question. In conjunction with the authors, the team leader developed coding categories to capture common themes and trained two other students for coding.

Working independently, two coders assigned each survey response to a category, with any coding disagreements resolved by the team leader. The just-described procedure was used for the Oklahoma DHS and Project Adopt samples. The Kansas responses were coded at a later date by only one reader using the previously developed categories.

Based on the percentage of agreements and disagreements between the two coders, the statistic kappa was calculated for each coding category. Kappa corrects for agreements by chance and therefore presents a conservative, unbiased measure of agreement. Tables 4.1, 4.2, and 4.3 present the kappas for each coding category. While the kappas vary considerably, the overall level of agreement is adequate for an exploratory analysis such as this. Kappas of less than about .50 suggest distinct differences in opinion between coders and recommend caution in interpretation.

Often responses fit into more than one coding category. Where this was the case, all appropriate categories were assigned; no attempt was made to develop exhaustive categories that would capture all responses.

REWARDS

Among the most rewarding aspects of the adoption, the parents' comments reveal the joys of parenthood, the development of bonds between

Table 4.1
What Has Been Most Rewarding about This Child's Adoption?

Coding category	Frequency	Percentage	Kappa
Change and growth			
Skills (including academics)	52	11	.73
Behavior and emotions	59	13	.59
Growth and development (and other than above)	52	11	.50
Bonding and family membership	61	13	.37
Love			
Receiving love from child	53	11	.72
Giving love to child	38	8	.74
Love (direction not specified)	27	6	.77
Other rewards			
Enjoyment of parenting	51	11	.43
Sibling interactions	17	4	.57
Environmental change (providing opportunity)	38	8	.88
Family making	40	9	.41
Finalization of adoption	21	4	.74

parents and children, the building of strong family units, and the satisfaction that comes with helping to change the course of a child's life. Twelve coding categories were developed (see Table 4.1). These categories were then grouped into three basic areas: change and growth, giving and receiving love, and other rewards.

Change and Growth

Change and growth comprised four coding categories that reflect the progress, sometimes exceeding expectations but at other times quite slow, that the children made. These subcategories were (1) skills, (2) behavior and emotions, (3) growth and development, and (4) bonding and family membership.

The *skills* category most often reflects progress in school skills and improved intellectual functioning. Typical comments are:

Watching him learn to read despite his handicaps.

Dan couldn't read when we got him and now he is reading at sixth-grade level. He tries so hard.

Previous to coming to us he was considered retarded. By the time he finishes public school, I think his IQ will be in the normal range of 100 to 120.

Learning to read and write.

IQ up by 10 points . . . mastering new skills . . . stuttering less often.

In the second category, *behavior and emotions*, responses most frequently describe observable progress in self-esteem and confidence.

Seeing him (very slowly) coming out of his shell.

Develop[ing] her self-esteem; occasionally changing a problem into an opportunity.

Seeing her blossom into a warm, loving, giving, confident, smart young lady.

She reaches out and tries to help more in just about anything she does.

Watching him grow in security and love year after year.

Perhaps less common than the just-mentioned changes are accounts of improvements in problem behaviors.

Change from a problem child to a more responsible caring child.

Learning to overcome peer pressure . . . [not] taking it out on someone else by fighting . . . [instead] to handle these feelings more constructively.

Some children are reported to have joined the mainstream of community life and thereby become "normal" kids.

I'm sure if you meet him today you would have a hard time distinguishing him from any other "normal" teenager.

As time passes he has become more argumentative and acts like a fairly normal teenager.

The third category, *growth and development*, reflects the child's reaching his or her potential. These satisfactions are most similar to those in a typical birth family setting.

Watching her grow and become a young lady full of energy and life.

Just watching him grow.

Seeing all three of my children grow up, accepting responsibility.

The *bonding and family membership* category reflects the child's integration into family life. Child and family bond to and "claim" one another. Representative comments include:

We talk, share experiences, and help each other as a real family.

Seeing them start to respond both to us as parents and friends.

I can't imagine life without him.

To see the new twinkle in her eyes and happiness in her face.

Seeing her accept us as Mom and Dad. When she looks at me now her eyes focus.

These comments often convey that the child has become a full-fledged family member with all rights and privileges. One parent stated, "He accepted his place and rights as a member of our family."

Giving and Receiving Love

The responses pertaining to love convey the happiness and joy experienced in parenting special-needs children. When parents identified the rewards of love, the responses fell into one of three categories: (1) love received from the child, (2) love felt for the child, and (3) an unspecified expression of love. For example, these comments reflect the expressions of love by the child towards the parents:

He tells me that he loves me all the time.

The huge return of love (that is not to say there is no temper, though).

By contrast, other comments reflect giving love to children:

Being able to show her that we care and love her.

The love I have for her.

Other Rewards

The other rewards expressed by parents fell into one of five categories, ranging from the joys of parenting and sibling relationships to the satisfaction of bringing about change, making a new family unit, and finalizing the adoption.

Enjoyment of parenting reflects varied aspects of parenting, most often those common to parenting in general rather than those unique to special-needs adoption. Representative responses include:

Having a daughter to share my life.

It feels so natural to be her mother.

To have a child call me Mom.

Having children, excitement at Christmas, Easter, holidays.

Comments on *sibling interaction* referred both to biological children of the adoptive parents and to other adopted children. Those pertaining to biological children frequently referred to companionship for the biological child. Comments include:

He is very good for his shy, insecure sister.

Donnie has mellowed our children and they are much more aware of others with handicaps.

Eric (now 5) and our daughter (age 9) are best buddies. We wanted our daughter to have a brother to grow up with. She has this with Eric.

Responses in the *environmental change* category most often express the satisfaction that comes from providing a permanent and loving family. Many were thankful that their children were no longer in the foster care system. One was able to say,

If it wasn't for my efforts, she would have ended up in numerous placements and probably finally been lost in the system forever.

Adoptions were clearly seen as opening up new opportunities. Parents expressed the joy of

Helping her do things that she never had the privilege of doing before.

Giving Dan a home he needed so badly.

Family making conveys the rewards that come from forming or completing a family unit or from strengthening the bond within the family unit.

It has brought our family closer—both parties—*child* and *parents*. Love needs were met and a need for a family bond.

He made our family complete.

He filled a gap in our lives.

The final category, *finalization of adoption*, expresses the emotional relief that came with finalization. With finalization the child became a permanent member of the new family.

The day the adoption was final the boy turned and yelled, "Mom, we did it" numerous times in the courthouse.

It is very rewarding to be able to answer Yes to the following question: Does this mean I will never have to move again?

I'm not sure I understand this, but the most rewarding thing about this adoption was when it was finally final.

DIFFICULTIES

Responses to the question on the most difficult aspect of the adoption fell into seven major areas, with two themes being dominant. First, children's behavioral problems are mentioned most frequently as the most difficult aspect of special-needs adoption. The second most common area of reported difficulties involves parenting issues and stresses. Though not as frequently mentioned, other important themes involved the child's difficulties in severing ties with the past, problems coordinating school or other needed services, financial concerns, and general frustrations stemming from uncertainty and delays in the adoption process.

Behavioral Problems

The behavioral categories were developed prior to detailed reading of comments and are based loosely on selected scales in the Child Behavior Checklist (CBC, Achenbach & Edelbrock, 1983, see Chapter 10). The content analysis of behavior problems largely confirms the quantitative analysis presented in Chapter 3. Behavioral problems cause major hardship for the families, with acting-out, aggressive behaviors mentioned more frequently than withdrawn, inhibited behaviors.

Table 4.2 shows the most frequently mentioned problems. Acting-out, aggressive behaviors are reported most frequently—in particular lying, stealing, destruction of property, and not following rules. Withdrawn, inhibited behaviors are mentioned far less often. In Table 4.3, ten typical responses were randomly selected from the first three categories that are listed in Table 4.2 and represent the acting-out behavior experienced most frequently.

Of particular note are those behaviors that are *not* listed in Tables 4.2 or 4.3. For instance, there were no reports of younger siblings being physically abused; only one instance of sexual abuse of a sibling was reported. Even though acting-out and aggressive behaviors caused the greatest difficulty, very few reports describe behavior that endangers the child or others. The low incidence of such behaviors in this sample of intact families may reflect that placements frequently disrupt in situations where these behaviors are present. Listed here are several of the most serious behavior problems.

Having things torn up or destroyed that was part of the family (example: screens cut on the windows, taking a club and beating fences, . . . or throwing rocks, sticks, toys . . . into the pond).

Recurrent, serious problems at school, with siblings and peers. Fights, stealing, sexual acting-out, destructiveness to persons and property.

A mentally retarded, emotionally disturbed, sexually and physically abused child is *very* difficult to parent. She almost destroyed our family.

Cost—destruction to property, medical bills (self-abuse: cuts, scrapes, broken glasses, accidents—attention getters), moodiness, clingy.

sexual abuse that he did to friends' children and other children in our home.

Given that the CBC revealed hyperactivity to be the behavioral subscale that most distinguished the children in this sample from typical children (see Chapter 10), we expected *hyperactivity* to be mentioned frequently in comments. Yet only six respondents noted this problem. A number of parents noted, however, that their children demanded a great deal of

Table 4.2
What Has Been Most Difficult?

Coding category	Frequency	Percentage	Kappa
Behavior problems			
All problems (generic or from a specific category below)	173	37	.63[a]
Destructive, aggressive, temper	22	4	.50
Lie, cheat, steal, delinquent	43	9	.80
No respect for authorities	18	4	.33
Withdrawn, shy, dependent	17	4	.90
Immature	16	3	.72
Sexual behavior or promiscuity	8	2	.67
Poor self-image	8	2	.21
Hyperactive, "can't sit still"	6	1	.80
"Habits" from child's past	14	3	.45
Does not reciprocate warmth	16	3	.74
Behavior problems at school	12	3	.79
Parenting issues			
"Normal" parenting frustrations	38	8	.37
"Stressful" parenting frustrations	21	4	.43
Amount of attention or time demanded	21	4	.71
Missed prior stages of development	23	5	.66
Needs help with discipline	25	5	.50
Problems with siblings	24	5	.65
Other difficulties			
Letting go of ties	15	3	.62
Learning problems at school	29	6	.45
Coordinating educational services	12	3	.71
Coordinating health and social services	13	3	.56
Counseling services	5	1	1.00
Money	6	1	1.00
Waiting and uncertainty	21	4	.91

[a]A computer program was used to identify cases where a specific behavior problem was coded but the "All problems" category was not. These cases were included in the frequency count but not in the calculation of kappa. Hence, the presented kappa is approximate.

Table 4.3
Ten Randomly Selected "Acting-Out" Problems

```
Destruction of property.

Teaching her respect for her possessions, respect for others feelings and
being truthful.

His rebellious nature.

She can be untruthful--especially to stay out of trouble and at times is
almost devious. . . . She is so bossy. . . . She does like to start up
trouble.

Lying, tearing up things, hiding things, doing what he's told not to do.
. . . Doesn't take punishment seriously, forgets.

Absolute disregard of any authority figure, diagnosed . . .
hyperactivity, can be pleasant one minute and totally out of control
approaching hysteria the next minute.

Fred is a very strong-willed, stubborn child.  It has been difficult to
help (force) him to follow rules and instructions and to grow up. . . .
He still works hard at failing much of the time.

Breaking old habits, lying, deceiving, destructive behavior.

The lying, stealing, hoarding of food, and manipulation we've had to
face.

Get him to stop hiding his dirty clothes.  And to get him to stop lying.
```

---

attention (see Table 4.2); this may indirectly convey problems stemming from hyperactivity.

Some parents noted *habits from the child's past* that were presumably due to experiences prior to the adoptive placement. For instance, one child had been deprived of food.

She would often hide food under her pillow and various places and would eat as though she may not get food again. It took about four months before she finally realized that food, home, and a mommy or daddy who would always love her was really for real!

Another child slept with a pile of blankets over her even on hot nights. She had been molested in her sleep when she was younger and the blankets, her mother surmised, gave her a feeling of safety.

These responses reflect the children's learning to take on the behaviors and attitudes that are valued in their new families and communities. They broke old habits and learned to take care of possessions, be neat, and carry through with responsibilities. "Having to completely start over with other values, discipline, habits in school, around the house, it was like raising another baby who is already eight," one parent stated.

The category *does not reciprocate warmth* most often describes children who have not bonded to the adoptive family. These children were perceived as disinterested in adoptive family life. Representative comments include:

Accepting the lack of closeness from her.

He don't like his real mother and he don't like me.

The barrier he puts up has been very difficult to accept. He has no desire to bond with us or accept our values.

These responses sometimes indicated that the formation of bonds had been difficult rather than that no bonding had occurred. Many described progress as the adoption proceeded.

Gaining her trust, showing her that we would not give her up. Overcoming her feelings of rejection by her foster family.

We had to wait for Keith to want to be part of us.

Our son had never had a positive experience with men. He was reluctant to trust his new father and grandfather at first. This was hard for them, but they soon won him over. He now idolizes them both.

Parenting Issues

Parents reported a number of parenting difficulties which fell almost equally among six categories: (1) normal frustrations, (2) stressful frustrations, (3) time and demands for attention, (4) missed developmental stages, (5) discipline difficulties, and (6) problems with siblings.

Responses in the *normal parenting* category echo the common experiences of parenthood.

Getting him to understand why rules must be obeyed.

Trouble to get a babysitter.

Keeping them busy.

Teenage years and puberty.

The *stressful parenting* category reflects the strain that special-needs adoptive parents feel as they deal with difficult behavior.

Constantly getting past one hurdle only to find another hurdle. I thought after two years we would be a normal family and [I] could treat them normally. . . . I am constantly on pins and needles waiting for the bomb to fall, ready to referee, and dole out the consequences. . . . If they are out I am always happy and relaxed. I am tired. . . . I am tired of feeling like a grinch.

Trying to keep my sanity and show this child that my family loves her.

The whole adjustment and the strain on the marital relationship.

Telling someone 12 or 13 years old basic principles for the 20th time.

Having to deal day and night with this child who really did not want to be here.

He brings a different kind of stress than the usual sibling disputes . . . nonstop talking, a lack of logical thinking because of being mildly retarded, attitude of know-it-all.

Related to the previous category, many commented on the *amount of attention or time demanded*. While these comments sometimes reflected the time realities of the children's physical needs (e.g., "caring for two severely handicapped, nonambulatory children"), they more often reflected the attention-seeking demands of the children. Parents report feeling "physically and emotionally drained." The high levels of hyperactivity and immaturity reported in the standardized behavioral testing undoubtedly are reflected here. For example, two responses are:

[Gets] attention by any means.

The most difficult part . . . has been to deal with this child's need to have constant positive reinforcement, praise, and be thought of as someone who knows everything, has been everywhere and does everything.

Several parents commented on the child's having *missed prior stages of development*, often expressing pain at the child's suffering prior to adoption. Some expressed resignation that they could not change the effect of prior events.

Sometimes I know she's acting the way she is because of something that happened to her before she joined our family. And it makes me feel strange that there are parts of my child's experiences that I can't understand.

Thinking about his life before us. The abuse, neglect—sometimes I feel cheated that we did not have him from birth. Those four and a half precious years of his life that we did not share.

Missing out on the first two years of his life and knowing what he has been through.

Responses coded in the *need help with discipline* category underscore the parents' difficulties in dealing with acting-out behaviors, a frequent source of frustration and problems. In the words of one parent, for example,

It has been difficult to help (force) him to follow rules and instructions.

The *problems with siblings* category relates problems with other children (adoptive, foster, or birth) in the adoption family home. These problems include settling fights and arguments, adjusting to a new family member, maintaining fairness among siblings, and dividing parental attention among siblings with competing or even contradictory needs.

Other Difficulties

A variety of other concerns were identified by parents as difficulties in the adoption process. Parents reported problems with schools and social services, financial stresses, and issues unique to placement or finalization of the adoption. The responses fell into seven categories.

The *letting go of ties* category expresses difficulties experienced in relationship to the birth family or foster family. Representative responses are:

Seeing her separated from her siblings.

Dealing with biological mother's contact at this time.

Overcoming the grief of leaving the foster family.

Learning at school is a persistent struggle for many special-needs children, and these difficulties are apparent in the parent responses. Some parents described their children as uninterested and difficult to motivate in schoolwork. Other children had experienced only failure in school and were convinced that this would not change; many lacked the basic skills necessary to succeed. One parent remarked,

This is our first experience at having someone who has missed out on all the BASICS in school and simply can't progress because of his lack of ability. . . . Lessons get pushed ON and ON. . . . [He] gets further and further behind.

Several parents related that their children are perceived by school faculty as intellectually slow or retarded when, in actuality, their delays stem predominantly from a lack of opportunity prior to adoption.

One of the most difficult tasks for many parents was *coordinating educational services*. One parent remarked,

Getting a proper diagnosis of his disabilities and then getting the support and help from the school system. It is an uphill battle.

Sometimes the search for specialized educational services is successfully resolved.

He could easily have "fallen through the cracks" if we had not been consistent.

Only one comment was entirely negative:

[School] administrators have been obtuse . . . the biggest hassle I have ever known.

Given the frequency and intensity of school issues, findings recommend that both the adoptive parent and the social worker need to advocate for the child's interests.

Fewer comments than expected were coded in the category of *coordinating health and social services* category. Many described everyday situations such as getting a ride to the doctor, locating and arranging services like speech therapy or medical tests, and getting a birth certificate. One parent commented on the lack of adequate medical information:

When the youngest one got hurt three weeks after we got them and we didn't have enough medical information to be sure of medication or surgery.

While only five comments pertained to *counseling services*, they frequently expressed frustration with finding a good therapist.

The comments on *money* often related general financial stress rather than the costs of specialized services needed by the child. Comments include:

Financially having to take time from him to meet the financial needs of the family.

Doubling our family size. . . . Quarrels and stretching the work load and budget.

Special-needs adoption involves *waiting and uncertainty*, which can be a source of difficulty for parents. Some parents expressed frustration with the slow progress of social and legal systems. Others expressed fears that their children would be taken away. For instance, one parent identified the most difficult aspect of the adoption as knowing for almost five years that authorities could take the child at any time.

ADVICE TO PROSPECTIVE PARENTS

The responding parents offered diverse advice to prospective parents thinking about special-needs adoption. Four themes dominated the suggestions, as they advised prospective special-needs parents to (see Table 4.4):

Get all possible background information on the child and family

Be assertive in dealings with the adoption agency

Adopt the child for who he or she is rather than for expectations of who they may become

Be realistic regarding both the child's and the family's capacities for change

The most frequently offered advice is to get all possible background information. Parents recommend medical and social information as well as the informal information that could be gathered from prior caretakers. Several comments stress that prospective parents have a right to all available information including that in the case file.

What I'm saying is *everyone* should be fully informed on all aspects of a child's background *before*, not after!

Table 4.4
What Advice Would You Offer?

Coding category	Frequency	Percentage	Kappa
Carefully examine motives	24	5	.66
Anticipate longer adjustment period	11	2	.25
Be patient	35	7	.45
Importance of love	40	9	.38
Importance of God, religion	16	3	.77
Adoption process too slow for child's interests	17	4	.96
Realism regarding child's development	19	4	.47
More background information	56	12	.73
More contact with previous caretaker	6	1	.50
Negative comments on adoption of sibling group	6	1	.55
Need for follow-up services			
Tutoring, school related	11	2	.31
Counseling, therapy for child	23	5	.50
Financial help	24	5	.84
Contact with other families	20	4	.62

Get as much information about child as possible. If I had it to do over, I would try to get more information about the child and his past.

Demand to be given a file on the child. What good does withholding information do? It only serves to handicap the child.

Sometimes needed information may not exist. Educational and psychological testing should be done prior to rather than following the adoption.

Assertiveness in dealing with the agency is stressed. At the same time, parent comments emphasize the importance of careful deliberation along with the need to "trust your gut." For example, parents wrote:

Demand that you get subsidy for your children's therapy and training for yourself.

Be careful that no one talks you into stretching more than you are comfortable with. (Stretching refers to adopting a child with characteristics different from those desired or decided on initially.)

I would strongly caution anyone considering doing this. It is *very* strenuous and can tear a family apart. If we had been aware of the problems, *deep* problems, we probably would never have attempted to adopt special-needs children.

Realism is encouraged in all aspects of the adoption, including the kinds of changes that the family can make. As one parent put it, "If you think your family is special, don't take on so much that you lose that specialness." Most of all, realism is needed regarding the child's capacities for change. Comments emphasize that emotional scars and destructive behavioral patterns do not disappear with love. Special-needs adoptive parents must focus on meeting the child's needs rather than their own. Some children will never open up and claim the adoptive family. As much as the adoptive parent may want a child to love, the child may not be able to reciprocate. Central to this issue, parents must love the child as she is now and not for who she may become.

The following comments suggest the disappointments that can accompany unrealistic expectations:

Parents must realize that adoption is something that you do for them [the children]—not vice versa! Any joys and love you get in return [are] pure pleasure. . . . Parents will be disappointed almost entirely if the children were adopted for the parents' pleasure, because these kids cannot give yet.

Older children are hard to change. Don't expect them to mold into what you think they can be, because it doesn't work. You must like and expect them to be nothing more or different than they are when you get them. If you don't like the child, your feeling probably will not change.

Examine your motives! Don't do it just because you think the child will appreciate a good home (she won't) or as a social duty. Don't expect the child to be grateful. More likely he/she will be angry—at you and the rest of the world—and will be plenty effective at letting you know about it.

You have to realize that you really never overcome the years that went by before that child is placed in your home. In spite of what idealistic social workers tell you, these children never catch up or overcome the years of neglect and abuse.

Realize some patterns are set at an early age; don't think you can change that person to think and feel as you do.

Be prepared that things might not go the way you expect. Do not have it already set in your [the parents'] heads that the children are going to accept things as they are right away (they might and they might not).

Adopt only when you are sincerely wanting a child and you can love the child for himself, not for what you want the child to be.

Clearly, parents recognize that there is wisdom in proceeding slowly. Several encouraged trial visits and opportunities for parent and child to get to know one another prior to placement.

The adoption of a special-needs child initiates change in family structure and relationships. Sometimes the needs of biological children are forgotten. Since the adoption may generate stress in the marital relationship, both husband and wife must be committed to the decision to adopt. The mutual support of husband and wife is paramount.

You and your husband's relationship . . . must be strong because you are going to need this support more than anything else and like you have never needed it before. You have to build the love and trust. . . . It's just not there immediately, so you can't be discouraged to the point of saying it's no use, believe me it will come, but it takes several years. . . . After four years I can only now say that we are finally a *real* family.

Few parents offered concrete suggestions for dealing with difficult behavior. The most common advice was for clear and consistent limits and discipline.

Never change the rules, never give in because you feel sorry for the child, and never, never, never make a useless threat.

Be firm. When you tell them something or anything, stand behind it.

Many comments emphasized the importance of a good support system.

Do not underestimate the value of having supportive people around you. The physical as well as emotional fatigue that sets in is impossible to imagine until you've lived through it.

Contacts with other special-needs families are particularly significant.

Don't depend on your agency for all of the support you need—make some friends who have adopted like you have and lean on each other, even daily if needed. Your new friends will be your lifeline—especially as your old friends and family may disapprove of your adoption.

Attend the workshops and meet as many adoptive parents as possible.

While the majority of just-presented quotations emphasize realism and the wisdom of proceeding slowly, these quotations do not reflect the tone of the most common advice: "Just do it." If love and patience do not solve all problems in special-needs adoptions, they are, at the very least, core qualities without which the adoption cannot succeed.

PERCEPTIONS OF SERVICES

In general, services were evaluated positively. Only two major criticisms were apparent. First, some parents expressed a desire for more follow-up, saying in essence that services simply stopped after placement or finalization. Second, parents conveyed dissatisfaction with background information, commenting that it was often incomplete or lacking. In the most extreme situations, parents felt that workers had misled or even lied to them.

The information we received prior to placement was poorly prepared, inaccurate, or nonexistent. At the initial meeting we were told that our son had few serious problems. This was totally inaccurate, although the worker was telling us all *she* knew. The child's foster care worker had *not* been honest or sent viable information about the child.

The red tape and screwups were a nightmare. We had much more trouble and spent much more time trying to correct the state's mistakes or misconceptions than in correcting any problems with our child.

Can't think of anything very helpful. The adoption went through because my wife and I persevered. Agency has too few people to provide adequate service.

These were some of the difficulties described. However, most agency workers were perceived as genuinely concerned about the children, and parents expressed appreciation for this. They referred to "emotional support," "availability in time of crisis," and "friendship" as important qualities in their relationships. Many workers clearly went beyond the call of duty.

When we started having trouble, we called our caseworker. She was so helpful. I asked if we had a support group. She said, "No, but we can start one." I believe in the next month we had one. She did almost all the work herself.

Good coordination of services by workers—concerning subsidy, courts, referral to needed testing and evaluation—was particularly noted. Pre-adoption training sessions and parent support groups drew positive responses. All of the parents encouraged participation in services.

Chapter 5

Voices of Adoptees:
Five Personal Stories

This chapter presents five summaries of in-person interviews with young adults adopted as older children. The interviews covered such topics as the problem leading to placement out of the home, birth and foster families, the initial meeting with adoptive parents, how adoption differed from expectations, what difficulties, if any, were encountered, school, community, friends, interests, contacts with the birth family since adoption, relationships with adoptive family members, and plans for the future. The adoptees also offer advice for social workers, children, and adoptive parents regarding things that they can do to help make older-child adoptions work.

The summaries portray adoption from the perspective of the adoptee. Particularly with respect to events in early childhood, say, ages 4 and 5, reconstructed memories rather than precise factual accounts are often presented. The sample was generated from suggestions of adoption social workers, so it should not be regarded as representative of any larger population. Names and some minor facts have been changed to disguise identities. The five stories are of Aaron, 17, adopted at age 4; Ashley, 19, adopted at age 16; Ron, 17, adopted at age 6; Andrea, 17, adopted at age 5½; and Daniel, 21, adopted at age 8. Ron is black and was adopted by a black family. Daniel is Native American and was adopted by a white family, the other three are white children adopted by white parents. All adoptions were in two-parent families.

Because of the small sample size and our intent to focus attention on the stories, we offer informal comments rather than formal interpretation. During childhood, the world was viewed with a child's eyes and mind. Basics and little things often made a huge impression, things like balanced meals, toys, money for shoes, and a clean-smelling house. Several adoptees recalled initial meetings with adoptive parents in clear, vivid, and positive terms. They seemed to know, right from the start, that their new homes would be good ones. Particularly for those who had experienced multiple foster care placements, the process of coming to believe and know that their new families were "forever" families was an important step forward.

AARON . . . FITTING RIGHT IN

Aaron, a relaxed and outgoing 17-year-old, was adopted with his older brother Zak as a sibling group just prior to Aaron's fourth birthday. With a wide smile and keen sense of humor, Aaron seems at ease in almost any setting, comfortable with his past and ready for his future.

Aaron and Zak were removed from the birth family when Aaron was 16 months old and placed in family foster care. Aaron has no memory of his birth parents, both of whom were addicted to inhalants. The two boys were often left alone and forced to scrounge for food. Aaron's birth mother had sexual relationships with many men; there is, therefore, doubt concerning the identity of his birth father. Though only a year older, Zak watched out for his younger brother's needs:

He basically just took care of me when I was real little. He kind of fathered me. He found food and stuff. I could never reach anything, I was always crawling, but he was able to climb up and grab whatever was there to eat.

Aaron remembers a mix of feelings about his foster family, with whom the boys stayed until Aaron was almost four. He enjoyed going for rides in the family cars and felt basically comfortable. Among his worst memories, he recalls an older foster sister sticking his head in the toilet, perhaps as part of toilet training.

By contrast, his earliest memories of his adoptive parents, the Andrews, are distinctly positive. Aaron remembers being picked up at the social services office by his adoptive parents.

I felt accepted right away. . . . They pulled up in a station wagon. It was loaded with toys. I kind of figured right then that this was a great deal. I liked this.

He remembers the "weird" smell of his new home, which he describes as "clean." He smiles broadly as he talks about food: "When I am hungry here, I just tell my mom. I go and get something to eat." The abundance of food contrasted distinctly with the malnourishment he experienced in his birth family.

The Andrews family also included two birth children, sisters age 13 and 10 at the time of the placement. Two previous adoptions had been difficult for the Andrews. A first son died following two open-heart surgeries. A second was profoundly retarded, a condition unknown to the Andrews at the time of the adoption. He was placed in a state institution.

Aaron and Zak were warmly accepted by family, extended family, and community.

I don't really remember anything being difficult. It was so good to have a home and get fed and have toys and be accepted and have brothers and sisters and aunts and uncles. All of the sudden there was a big family. I liked the big family part of it. We were just immediately accepted. It wasn't like we had to work our way into it. At the birth home there wasn't much of a family unit. The foster home was just a foster family, but here I had aunts and uncles.

We showed up here and we were two little prize fighters. Everybody was like "Oh!" My sisters were older by then, and they had friends. It was "Oh, look at the cute little boys." We used to play that up pretty good. . . . We would always sit on their laps through basketball games. One of my sisters was a cheerleader, so we were always getting in on the action.

Similarly, at church and at school he made friends easily.

Aaron does not recall any serious problems in adjusting to his new home. He missed his foster parents some, although he can not remember how much. He remembers his social workers and his adoptive parents talking to him about adoption.

About the time I finally felt comfortable [at the foster home], I was moved. And they kept telling me this is my real home, I get to stay, this is my mommy and daddy and I get to stay here, and these are my sisters, and I will stay here. I will never have to leave.

Aaron talks about the adjustments his parents had to make.

It wasn't so much that they complained . . . but going from having two girls who are older and suddenly two boys show up and they are rambunctious . . . if you have two boys running around, they are going to knock stuff over and things like that, and they are going to want to get into the food and they are going to want to sneak this and sneak that.

Family rules were relaxed at first, but became firm over time.

When the boys first arrived in the home, Zak was protective towards his younger brother, in particular by making sure that Aaron got enough to eat.

Even when we got here, he would give me stuff off his plate, thinking that there wouldn't be enough for me. I guess by doing that, he kind of malnourished himself at the birth home.

The sharing of food evolved into a game, sometimes with teasing. Food would be offered and then taken back. As the boys grew older, the protective pattern phased out and sibling rivalry set in.

Aaron enjoys being part of a group.

I have a lot of friends. . . . Wherever there is a group, I will just go join in and be a part of it. I am sitting here wearing Bugle Boys jeans and have a letter jacket on, but I have long hair, and I have a white shirt on underneath this one, so it is kind of like I can just suddenly blend in and change crowds. The group can just see whatever they want.

He enjoys sports and is one of the top swimmers on the varsity team at school. While Aaron does not enjoy school, he works hard. He likes his community, a town of about 40,000 in a rural area. He relates that his family is respected in the community. Mr. Andrews is vice president in a local bank.

Aaron feels close to both of his parents.

My mom is a good person. She is a caring person. She is the one who kind of wears the pants around the house. . . . Mom usually ends up talking to Dad and they make the rules, but Mom seems like the wicked witch sometimes because she has to enforce them. She is a good person. I like her. I love her. She is my mom.

My dad is more like the guy that made all the rules and then has somebody else enforce them. He is more like the general around the house. . . . My dad is more like the ball-game-type dad. . . . I don't do much athletic-type stuff with my mom. That is what my dad seems to be for, make the money, come home, and play around with him, a big old grizzly-type thing.

Mrs. Andrews sets firm rules. Yet any anger that is connected with wrongdoing dissipates quickly: "Nobody here really holds a grudge." Aaron's mother "is never too busy" to find the time to talk to him.

Five years after adopting Aaron and Zak, the Andrews became a foster family, eventually fostering 29 children. Aaron enjoyed the foster children and mentioned several favorites. He made a real effort to be a caring big brother, in part because he remembered the cruelty of an older sibling during his own foster placement. Aaron's foster siblings, in particular those who were eventually placed for adoption, helped him to better understand what it must have been like for him as a younger child.

Aaron offers suggestions to participants in the adoptive process. He advises social workers to move children out of foster care as quickly as possible. He adds that workers should focus on whether the family really wants a child, and if so, make the placement right away. Birth parents need to consider adoption earlier on as an option for their children, particularly when they do not have financial means to support a family. His advice for adoptive parents is straightforward:

Hang onto the kids. If something goes wrong, don't send them back to the [foster] home. If you are going to adopt them and give them a real home, make it stick.

He advises adoptive parents to treat the adopted child as one of the family, as no better than or worse than a birth child.

At the time of the interview, state championships in swimming and graduation from high school represented major upcoming milestones. Aaron smiles as he states that he won't get kicked out of the home when he turns 18. He plans to attend community college and is considering a career in mortuary science.

ASHLEY . . . FINDING THE RIGHT HOME

Now almost 19, Ashley's poised and outgoing demeanor belies a difficult and often unhappy childhood that included abuse by her birth father, several foster placements, and a disrupted adoption at age 15. Since age 16, however, she seems to have found the right home.

Ashley's birth mother, who was physically abused by Ashley's birth father, abandoned her 3-week-old baby at the welfare department. Two older sisters (eight years and five years older than Ashley) had previously been adopted, and Ashley's birth mother anticipated the same for her. However, with the aid of an attorney, Ashley's birth father gained custody and proceeded to raise her until age 12.

Ashley describes herself as unhappy in childhood ("a 3.5 on a 10-point scale"). She and her father moved frequently from place to place, sometimes to avoid child welfare authorities. She was beaten frequently.

My dad would get really angry at me and he would throw ashtrays at me, and throw pots and pans. Just anything he could pick up, he would throw at me. . . . I didn't know anybody but Dad, and I always thought he was doing right. All his friends did the same thing. They would whip their kids all the time and stuff like that. And so that is just the environment that I was in. Now I know that is wrong.

Ashley may also have been sexually abused by her father, although she is not sure about this. Supported primarily by a disability pension, the family was basically poor. Meals were not balanced, and Ashley was considerably underweight. She recalls several stepmothers although "they weren't ever there long enough to really remember anything about them." Ashley fondly remembers her paternal grandmother, whom she describes as loving and understanding.

I loved my grandma. She knew that my dad whipped me all the time, and she was really upset, and she liked for me to stay with her a lot. My fondest memory of my grandma is sitting with a towel in our laps and peeling apples and splitting them in fours. We would eat them like that, because that is how grandma and I always did it.

Ashley attended many different schools and made some friends. But she describes herself as "not very popular at all" because of the frequent moves, poor grades, and old clothes that showed that she was poor. Ashley confesses that she often stole things as a child and sometimes "got licks at school" for this. She sometimes helped her father with tasks. On one occasion, school authorities observed her helping him with a roofing project during school hours, causing her father to get into trouble. In anger, her father

beat me with a board with nails in it. He hit me with this board, and threw me to the ground beating me.

This incident led to her placement in a family foster home at the age of 12. She liked this home, enjoying both parents as well as having access to more material comforts. Nevertheless, there were drawbacks, including unusually strict discipline by the foster father and a slap to the face which led to termination of the placement. Following a brief placement in a youth shelter, she was placed in a second foster home. Again she enjoyed the placement—a large house, a horse to ride, newfound popularity at school—but it ended suddenly, in part because of a poor relationship with her foster mother.

Following two more foster home placements, Ashley was adopted at age 15. This adoption lasted only two months, disrupting when a biological child, about one year younger than Ashley, ran to his grandmother's house and announced that he would not return home until Ashley left. As with her other placements, she indicated that she was happy.

At age 16, Ashley found herself in a youth shelter for the second time. Along with another youth, she was invited for Friday-night pizza by the youth's child welfare worker. At the pizza supper, Ashley visited with the worker and his family and friends. Returning to the shelter, she indicated to the other youth that she thought that the family wanted to adopt her. She was right.

The Wilsons, in their thirties and with a 1-year-old adopted daughter, adopted Ashley. Ashley describes her first impressions:

[Mrs. Wilson] struck me as a very attractive young lady. She is only 33. So she is not very much older than I am. Well, quite a bit, but not really. So she struck me as a very attractive lady who would have a warm heart and be a loving mom. Of course, Dad was like this great big old teddy bear or something. I just love my dad to death. I don't know if I am a mom's girl or a daddy's girl. I am really not either one. I am both.

Just before the adoption's finalization, Mrs. Wilson became pregnant, a surprise, as the Wilsons had thought that they were infertile. This was the one time that Ashley worried about whether her adoption would remain intact. Now that the Wilsons would finally have a birth child, Ashley reasoned, they would no longer want her in the home. To her joy, her parents remarked, "Nothing is going to change our mind about you."

Just recently, the Wilsons adopted a sibling group of teens. The Wilson family now comprises Mr. and Mrs. Wilson, Ashley, and children age 16, 14, 13, 3, and 1. Ashley enjoys family life greatly—"9.8 on a 10-point scale." In her words, her parents are

very dedicated people. My mom and dad are very dedicated to each other. They will never be divorced, no matter what happens. They are very dedicated to God and they are very dedicated to each of us kids.

The Wilson's strong Christian faith has been instrumental in the building of a close-knit family. Ashley also describes herself as a devoted Christian, her faith beginning to take form during her shelter care placement, when she decided "to give this God person a chance" by praying for the perfect family, a prayer that she believes has been answered.

Asked about what helps make the family work, she describes her parents' commitment to the kids.

My mom is very important to every one of us because she is always there. Usually on applications you state that you contact a friend in an emergency because your mom or dad is not at home. My mom is always at home. My mom hardly ever leaves. . . . I love coming home and mom being there. . . because I never had a mom. That is what I always wanted.

Mr. Wilson helps Ashley with managing money and other responsibilities. Ashley acknowledges the enjoyments of a middle-class lifestyle.

I am a materialistic type of person. I never had anything. I have never had anything in my life, but now I do. I love it. I don't think people appreciate what they do have when they have it.

In addition to a rich family life, Ashley enjoys many friends, including a boyfriend who at the time of the interview was in Hawaii facing possible deployment to Saudi Arabia in the impending Persian Gulf war. She graduated from high school and was ready to begin a job as a sales clerk in a department store. Her career ambition, one that she has had since the age of 7, is to become a hairdresser. She describes herself as "loving, appreciative, [with an] outgoing personality."

Ashley has had very limited contact with either birth parent. Her birth father sent her a high school graduation card. Prior to her first adoption, she communicated with her birth mother regarding formal termination of parental rights.

Ashley advises social workers working with teens to listen carefully to the characteristics that they want in a home and match accordingly. She advises teens to "pray for the right home and God will send you to it. . . . Don't give up, because it may take Him a long time."

RON . . . FROM NEW YORK TO THE MIDWEST . . . TO THE NBA?

Ron, 17, a black tenth-grader with ambitions to play professional basketball, was adopted on his sixth birthday. Ron's adopted family, the Simons, includes an older brother, Clay, 22, who was adopted as an infant; Ron's mother, 48; and Ron's father, 54, all of whom are black. Born in New York City, Ron was placed for adoption in the Midwest by a private adoption agency. Dressed neatly in jeans, he has a relaxed manner and easygoing style.

Ron was born with a liver problem that resulted in extended hospitalization and influenced, he thinks, his mother's decision to place him for adoption. So far as Ron knows, he never actually lived in his birth family home. Ron's birth father was in the military and also unable to care for him. He does not know whether he has brothers or sisters from the birth family, and he thinks that his birth parents were not married.

Ron's liver problem had improved greatly by about the age of 6 months, and he was placed in a foster home at this time. He believes that he stayed in only one foster home prior to adoption. Ron liked his foster home and, in fact, never realized that his situation was any different from that of anyone else. In his mind, his foster home was simply home: "I thought they were my parents. It was pretty nice there. I went to school there, went to church, had brothers, and everything like that." He remembers that the house was quite big and in a city neighborhood. He particularly enjoyed rides on his foster father's motorcycle.

Shortly before his sixth birthday, Ron flew with an adoption worker to the Midwest for a preplacement visit with the Simons. He enjoyed the plane ride, including the peanuts and snacks that were served. He recalls meeting the Simons at the airport and, in particular, seeing his prospective brother Clay's cowboy hat. Like his foster parents, the Simons lived in a big house in a city neighborhood. It was equipped, to Ron's delight, with an air hockey game, train set, toy racing cars, and pool table. He recalls seeing the bunk beds in the bedroom that he and his brother would share.

Events were confusing for Ron. He did not fully understand the purpose of the trip and was not sure what it meant to be adopted. He flew back to New York and, several weeks later, returned to stay.

He felt comfortable early on in his new family and does not recall major changes in terms of rules. He remembers being scared of sleeping in the dark, a problem easily solved when his parents got a night light. Ron related one humorous anecdote:

One time I wanted to go to the park. But I guess that since I was from New York, they couldn't understand the way that I said "park." I guess that New York people talk a little bit different. They finally figured out where I wanted to go.

Ron joined in easily with a group of kids in his new neighborhood and church and started first grade in the fall following his adoption. He recalls being teased about being adopted by peers and says that this sometimes drew him into conflicts or fights. Ron thinks that he was about age 9 when he really figured out what it meant to be adopted.

Ron enjoys parts of school, including friends and some subjects, particularly history. A few of Ron's classes are in special education, while the others are mainstreamed. He has had some discipline problems and was suspended for three days shortly before the interview.

Ron and Clay have always been pals, playing together and competing with one another. In Ron's words:

Clay might be able to get [beat] me in running . . . but in basketball, I get him. He knows it, but he might not want to say it around people.

Clay's desire for a brother was one of the major motivations leading to the Simon's decision to adopt Ron.

Ron describes a close relationship with his mother: "She is pretty fun. She talks nice. She's someone [you can] talk to." When asked if his mother differed from other mothers Ron shrugged his shoulders noncommittally and stated simply that his mother cared a great deal about her family and kids. Mrs. Simon works in adult day care. Ron's father is a retired police officer who supplements his retirement pension with work as a security guard at a large corporation. At least at present, Ron and his father disagree about issues pertaining to authority and rules. Ron enjoyed the many camping and fishing trips that his family took while he was growing up. He wishes that he and his dad had spent more time together playing basketball.

Ron's passion is basketball. He brightens when this subject comes up in the interview. Basketball is much easier to talk about than subjects such as what it's like to be adopted, how one gets along with parents, and the like. Ron hopes to progress through the ranks to junior college, college, and then on to the National Basketball Association (NBA). This dream is reinforced by the fact that one of his brother's good friends has become a star in professional football. As of the time of the interview, Ron had recently quit his high school basketball team, in part because of a disagreement with his coach. He will rejoin the team as a junior.

Ron has not been in personal contact with his foster family since the adoption. They were in the Midwest when he was about 10 years old and inquired about visiting him, but plans could not be rearranged.

Ron would like to see his birth mother "to see what she looks like" and to ask why she placed him for adoption. The subject of transracial adoption of black children with white families came up during the interview. The very idea took Ron by surprise. "Do they really do this?" he asked with an amazed look on his face. "How do they work out?" Ron stated that he was glad that he was adopted by a black family. He said that he would consider adopting a child but that if he adopted it would be a black child. Ron experienced some teasing around his adoption and believes this would have been much worse if he had been adopted transracially.

Ron feels that he was adopted young enough so that his adoption worked well. He remarked that "10 is too old" and that adoption right after birth is best.

Ron describes himself as outgoing and happy. He recognizes the importance of school to his future and plans to apply himself towards graduation. As the discussion ended, he asked the interviewer to remember his name and follow his progress towards the NBA.

ANDREA . . . KNOWING THEY'LL BE THERE

Adopted at age 5½ along with a younger sister, Andrea exudes the energy, enthusiasm, and confidence of a 17-year-old ready to take on the world with a loving family to support her. In addition to her birth sister, Susan, two years younger, Andrea's family also includes her parents and a brother, Bobby, 12, adopted at age 5.

As infants and toddlers, Andrea and Susan were frequently neglected and left alone at night in their birth home. The girls were sometimes locked in their rooms, in closets, and in kitchen cabinets. Andrea often protected her younger sister and as a result the two have always been close.

When we would get locked in the room, she would cry and get scared. . . . I took care of her. When I was that young, there would be a bottle laying on the floor or a pacifier or something, and I would always feed her. I would always take care of her.

While Andrea does not remember being abused in her birth home, she knows that Susan was abused. The most serious incident occurred when the girls' mother, in anger, knocked hot grease onto Susan, severely burning her leg. Besides her sister, Andrea does not remember ever having friends while she lived in her birth home. She recalls that she "didn't have as many toys as you would see that children have on television" and that she often felt discouraged.

There were times when I wished that I could just run away, just walk away. There [were] a few times that I would wish that I just wasn't there. Why me?

Andrea is not sure of the identity of her birth father, although she does know that she and Susan have different fathers.

Susan's burn precipitated the girls' initial placement in foster care, when Andrea was almost age 4. In all, the girls experienced seven placements, although Andrea remembers only three.

Andrea has negative memories of her second placement, which lasted for about six months.

[My foster mother] was kind of distant from her kids and us. She never really paid any attention to us. If we did something wrong she was really mean. She got really outraged. She was horrible.

Andrea was once slapped so hard for not eating that she was knocked out of her chair and to the ground. There were only a few rules, so in some sense she had a lot of freedom. Yet if she did break a rule, she might be hit quite hard for having done so.

Andrea reflects on her experiences in foster care:

[I was] scared of what each home would be like. . . . You think of what your birth mother was like and how she treated you, and it seemed like every home just seemed to get worse. You got scared. Was there someone who was going to ever keep you, or are you going to be passed around for the rest of your life?

At one foster home, Andrea and Susan slept "inside the wall. No sheets, no covers. You never got cold. You curled up and slept. We liked it." Her final memories of foster care come from a third home where she and her sister stayed for only a couple of days preceding their adoptive placement. She liked this home. Although the mother was quite reserved and not interested in the girls, she remembers the foster father as "a nice man."

Andrea can describe her caseworker's red car coming to pick her up for adoptive placement. She recalls that the placement took place in a "big building" rather than at a home as had been the case for her foster placements. The official appearance of the building ("like somewhere you go to pay your water bills . . . It was really nice. It had marble floors.") and also the fact that the meeting did not take place at a home conveyed to Andrea that this placement was different from earlier ones.

Andrea vividly recalls meeting her parents for the first time:

I remember my mom and dad walking in. I remember my mom smiling at me [and saying,] "Oh, these are my daughters." She picked me up. . . . It was really weird, but it wasn't like with any other person that picked me up, she had this warm feeling. She was gentle and she had this warm look in her eyes. I knew, just something inside of me told me that I would be there forever. She told me, "I am going to be there forever."

Andrea also remembers her mom playing with her hair, getting lifesavers from her new parents, signing the papers, and going to a toy store where she and her sister both got dolls. Andrea still has hers today. Her initial impressions of the house were positive:

It was big to me. It had a warm feeling to it. It felt so different from all the other homes I had been in. Some of them had like a cold feeling. But this was real weird because it felt nice to be there.

Andrea describes "roaming" the house and yard, holding her sister's hand. Her room was painted pink, which soon became her favorite color.

Adjusting to the home required changes:

Adjusting was very difficult. I wasn't used to having rules. . . . I was scared to do anything wrong, but then I was scared to do something right, afraid of being wrong, afraid of getting hit again, I never wanted to be hit because I remember them [foster parents] doing that to me.

Other changes in routine included learning to make her bed and to stop sucking her thumb, keeping her parents informed of her whereabouts, and getting used to "set times. . . . There would be a time when you could go out and there would be a time when you had to come back in."

Andrea rebelled and tested her mother's authority. She remembers "feeling hate," wanting to see "someone get hurt because I had been hurt [by birth mother and foster parents]." One time, in an attempt to provoke her mother, she purposely folded socks incorrectly. Unable to elicit Andrea's cooperation, her mother stated: "You are going to be in here all day and I am going to make you do this all day until you get it right." Andrea responded by yelling, "I hate you." She remembers her mother dropping to her knees and bursting into tears:

Right then I knew that I hurt her. I knew that I had hurt someone because I had been hurt. I told her that I was sorry, and that I didn't mean to do it. From then on, it seems like I just changed around. I turned into the child I knew I could be, a good child. I just had to see someone hurt.

For all her rebelliousness, Andrea never worried that her adoptive placement might disrupt. She comments on how the adoption differed from her expectations:

They were nice. They were really good people. They fixed you cereal in the morning, and they would fix you lunch and supper. I can remember eating with them. It was a family, is what it was, something that I had never experienced. I didn't know what a family was. I didn't know what it meant to have one.

Andrea felt like part of the family within the first four to five months. Going to the movies together, long trips in the car to visit relatives, and swimming lessons from dad all helped to build a feeling of family.

Today, Andrea is outgoing and well liked by her peers. She is "pom-pom captain" at her high school and "that is a really big deal." In her words, "I don't wait for people to accept me. I accept them first before they can accept me. Then when I accept them, they accept me." She enjoys

cruisin' on 12th Street, you know, and just to go out and go to the mall . . . get a new hairdo or something, go over to each other's houses and really dress yourself up and go out. And just having fun.

Andrea has a best girlfriend as well as a boyfriend with whom she enjoys seeing movies, eating out, and talking.

She remains close to Susan, who is now bigger than Andrea and, consequently, protective of her. Bobby "is a good brother," although she acknowledges that "it is hard to get along when you are 17 and he is 12."

Andrea likes school but sometimes has trouble buckling down to study. Andrea was in a learning lab program for two years. Now she attends regular classes and is preparing for graduation. She is thinking about attending a community college and transferring later to a four-year school to study fashion merchandising.

Andrea is close with her mother.

She expects you to do the best you can do. . . . She will let you slide by and slack off a few times, but if you get too out of hand, she is going to tell you when enough is enough. She is basically the "hard ball" in the family. She keeps everything in line.

She is rewarding when you do something right. When you do it right [or if] she knows that you tried your hardest, even if you do it wrong . . . then she is a very rewarding person.

Andrea's mom "worries about me more than most moms do." In Andrea's words,

She feels that she wasn't lucky enough to have [give birth to] children [but] that she was lucky enough to get [adopt] children, [and] she would do anything to keep us out of harm.

Andrea's mom works part-time in food services at a local elementary school.

Andrea speaks affectionately of her dad: "If you want to get away with something, if you are grounded or something, and you want to get away with it, you ask your dad, because dad will let you off." Mr. Hill works as a skilled assembler and supervisor at an automotive assembly plant.

She advises birth parents to be honest about whether they can bring up a child and not to go ahead with adoption if they cannot. Andrea notes that she has not heard from her birth mother since her adoption and that she has no plans to contact her.

Andrea offers the following advice for parents adopting older children:

Do not be short-tempered with them; have a lot of patience . . . because what some of these kids have been through is beyond belief. You have got to give them a long rope because they have got a long climb.

Don't think about yourself first. . . . Always think of your children first. . . . If they have a bad day at school, or if they have trouble with their friends, or if they get into a fight . . . be there for them. Don't say we will take care of it after we go to the mall.

She describes herself as very happy, knowing that her parents will "be there" for her always.

DAN . . . NATIVE AMERICAN AT HEART

Contrasts and contradictions are apparent in the adoption experience of Dan, now 21, married for one year and with an 8-month-old daughter of his own. A Native American (by blood one-half Creek, one-quarter Cherokee, and one-quarter white), he was adopted at age 5 by white parents (a placement that disrupted three years later) and again at age 8. Interviewed at his apartment and dressed casually in a knit shirt and old jeans, he uses contradictory terms to describe himself: "obnoxious, understanding, caring, rebellious."

Dan, the youngest of four biological siblings, was 3½ when his biological father was jailed for writing bad checks as well as other offenses. Shortly thereafter, Dan's biological mother ran off with a boyfriend and abandoned her four children:

She didn't leave us with any food. My older brother Ken fed us out of the trash can of the neighbors next door. That is how we lived for seven days. . . . It was very hard.

Child welfare services intervened. Initially, the four siblings were placed in different foster homes. Shortly, however, they were reunited in one foster home, only to be separated again. Over the course of a year, Dan was placed in eight foster homes, running away at least once from each one. Dan yearned to be with his paternal grandparents, who were of Creek heritage, or with another member of his extended biological family.

I wasn't comfortable with the people that I was with. I belonged to a tribe; my natural heritage was important to me, but nobody else thought it was. I just wished that I would have been around an [extended] family member to keep in touch with, even though none of the other siblings besides myself cared.

Dan's biological family had lived with his grandparents for part of the time before the children were placed in foster care. When Dan was initially placed in foster care, several relatives, most notably his grandparents and an aunt, had indicated an interest in adoption. Dan is not sure why these options were not pursued, although he believes that the state agency was not willing to do so. While his memories of life in his nuclear family are largely negative, Dan remembers being particularly close to his grandfather.

We were buddies. I was told that every time I wanted to do something, all I would do is go up there and grab his two fingers and take off. And we were out. We were gone for the day. I remember going fishing with him, taking rides in his truck, being at the church, and basically doing everything with him really.

Dan cites his desire to be with his grandparents as part of the reason for running from foster care. Dan is not sure why none of his siblings were interested in adoption by relatives, although he acknowledges that they were older and better understood the events that were taking place. Eventually, all four children were adopted, initially into four different nonrelative homes.

Dan describes himself as rebellious and very hard to control. He traces much of his rebelliousness in foster care and adoption to the fact that he is Indian and did not want to be in a white home. He was severely abused in one foster home; his hands were scalded in hot water so badly that the skin peeled. Dan speaks fondly of one foster home where he stayed on more than one occasion. His biological siblings were all together in this home.

Dan initially was placed for adoption at age 5 with the Cox family in Dallas. Dan describes some positives. He had friends whom he enjoyed being with. Also, the family participated in a variety of outdoor activities. Yet he feels that he never fit in or had a sense of belonging. Dan describes his adoptive parents' expectations for him:

They wanted this little schoolboy, you know wear a hat and a suit and everything like that. Like you see on TV, the little boys who carry a sucker around with a sailor hat . . . socks up to their knees, little black shoes. . . . That wasn't me.

Dan once hid for about five hours from Mrs. Cox. He thought she was coming to punish him, when in actuality it was to compliment him for a task well done. This was one of the final events precipitating disruption.

Dan, now age 8, was taken by the Coxes to a social services office. The Bakers, who had adopted Dan's oldest brother, Ken, were contacted regarding their interest in adopting Dan. Without ever having met Dan, they picked him up and brought him into their home. The Bakers' household consisted of an older daughter (the biological child of Mrs. Baker), Ken, and Dan. Mr. Baker worked primarily as a janitor, while Mrs. Baker worked in various part-time jobs. Several years after adopting Dan, the Bakers became foster parents.

Dan continued his rebellious behavior in the Bakers' home. He got into trouble with the police on two occasions. At the age of 9, he broke into a house with some friends. At 16, he was involved in a minor shoplifting incident, although no charges were filed. Dan describes himself as somewhat below average in school and as having learning disabilities. His mother intervened on his behalf in junior high, helping him get into some special classes that he felt were helpful. He stated that he and his mother "had a real good relationship back then."

When asked what made him finally stop running away, Dan responded that he never did stay put. He ran away on many occasions, both in the years immediately following his adoption and in his teens. At about age 16, Dan moved away for two months before coming back to the home. Dan was suspended from school at around this time and did not earn a diploma.

Dan feels that the Bakers loved and cared for him and that they were a "real family." Sometimes, however, Dan felt on the outside looking in and wondered whether he really belonged. Dan's maintaining of emotional distance and ambivalence in the family reflects in large part his own choice. His emotional tie to his grandparents remained strong, although he rarely expressed these feelings to his parents. "I always wanted most to be with my grandparents," Dan notes.

Dan's yearning for freedom, activity, and independence rather than for closeness is evident in his comments about a family camping trip.

I was comfortable there [in the hills]. I could run all the way around the hills, but they [the rest of the family] couldn't keep up with me. They liked camping but not to the extent that I did. [If I could have planned a perfect trip,] I would have been looking for some deer or something. . . . I would rather have been running around chasing something rather than sitting around the campfire roasting marshmallows and telling stories.

At the time of the interview, Dan was working as a frame carpenter, which he enjoyed. He plans to complete a G.E.D. and fulfill his ambition to become a policeman. He has good relationships with both of his adopted parents, although he views these relationships as less close than those in many families. He concedes, however, that "we are much closer than what I expected. I never thought we would have a really close tie." His adopted father takes a special interest in Dan's new daughter. Both parents get along well with his wife. Dan enjoys interacting with two younger brothers whom the Bakers adopted about seven years after adopting Dan. Consistent with his desire for more freedom, he indicated that these boys have much more freedom than he did. They, for instance, get to take karate lessons, while he was never allowed to box.

About two months before this interview, Dan visited his grandfather, whom he had not seen for 17 years. At the time of the visit, his grandfather was hospitalized and terminally ill with cancer. At first, he and Dan could not communicate due to a language barrier—his grandfather spoke only

Creek and Dan only English. Dan was angry when his grandfather did not recognize him and did not know that he was his grandson. Dan's biological father, fluent in both Creek and English, arrived at the hospital about two hours after Dan. With father as interpreter, Dan and his grandfather talked; the grandfather, age 91, did indeed remember Dan.

Dan returned one month later for his grandfather's funeral. He plans to stay in contact with his biological extended family with whom he feels "at home" and to learn more about his Indian heritage.

Dan clearly wanted to be adopted by his grandparents or by others in his biological extended family. He advises social workers to keep children with their extended family whenever possible and questions the wisdom of transracial placement. Being separated from his biological siblings was quite painful for Dan, and he advises workers to try to keep siblings together. Finally, Dan expresses frustration that he was provided very limited and at times inaccurate background information about his extended family. For instance, Dan initially thought that he and his oldest brother were half brothers. Only after Dan searched for his biological family did he learn that they were full brothers.

Chapter 6

Focus on Family Functioning

Most research on families adopting children with special needs has focused on the problems experienced by these families. Less investigation describes typical family structure and processes. This chapter uses a family systems structural perspective to study day-to-day functioning. The structural approach identifies the rules and patterns that regulate family relationships and emphasizes the importance of family structure to the functioning of the family system and the well-being of its members (Walsh, 1982).

The importance of family functioning in special-needs adoptions has been touched upon only to a limited degree in prior research. Barth and Berry (1988) found that the characteristics of the child—behaviors, temperament, habits, academic skills, and so forth—are important to assess, but only in relation to family characteristics and patterns. This contention is supported by Bourguignon (1989b) who found that psychological profiles of adopted children were not predictive of adoption outcome. Analyzing data for 20 intact adoptions and 10 unsuccessful placements, 19 of 20 scales from a battery of psychological tests failed to discriminate between intact and disrupted adoptions. Bourguignon reports that the "main predictors of success in special-needs adoption are to be found in the partnership formed by the adoptive parents" (p. 48), emphasizing that success is related to systemic functioning rather than to individual psychological functioning.

Essential to the structural family systems model is the notion that family problems and difficulties are connected to developmental processes; in other words, families change as they deal with transitions (Olson, 1989). For example, family dysfunction or difficulties often may occur when a member is added or removed from the family system, when the structure of the family and the developmental requirements of a family member do not coincide, or when the pace of family reorganization is too fast or too slow (Falicov, 1988).

Adoption of a special-needs child is a unique event that most families do not encounter. Understanding how families accommodate this transition may be helpful to social workers and others who work with these families.

STRESSORS AND RESOURCES

Barth and Berry (1988) adapted a model of adjustment to special-needs adoption that emphasizes the influence of stressors on and resources of the special-needs family as it goes about the task of integrating a new child into the unit and building a family system that includes the new child. In following sections we identify and discuss selected stressors for and resources of families that adopt children with special needs. These resources and stressors influence the coping styles of the child entering the family system and of other family members and affect the family's success in the task of family integration or blending.

Stressors

The primary sources of stress in special-needs adoptive families involve the distinctive role played by adopting parents (as compared with biological parents), the involvement of the adoption agency, the gaps in information about the child, the child's specific needs, and the complications resulting from rigid roles and rules.

Parental role differences. Adoptive families must contend with difficulties and issues that biological families never encounter (Talen and Lehr, 1984; DiGiulio, 1987). For instance, they must assume a parental role without wide support and endorsement from the community. Katz (1986) speaks to the difficulties inherent in assuming a parental role for a disturbed, half-grown child for whom adoptive parents have little parental feelings, no gratification history, and no sense of entitlement. Some adoptive parents reject or deny that there are differences between adoptive and biological parenthood. Others acknowledge differences (DiGiulio, 1987; Kirk, 1984; Small, 1987). Kirk (1984) found that adoptive parents who acknowledged differences were more empathetic with their adopted children than were those who denied differences.

Those who adopt older and special-needs children acknowledge differences more readily than do those who adopt infants. In many instances, special-needs children have lived with their birth families for many years and thus come to adoption with a wide range of experiences that result in values, expectations, and behaviors that are much different from those of the adoptive family. These role differences accentuate the differences between biological and adoptive parenthood and challenge the adoptive family system.

The adoption agency. In addition to role differences, the adoptive family's dealings with the adoption agency over an extended period of time affect the family structure (Talen and Lehr, 1984). First, the agency recruits and studies the family to determine eligibility as adoptive parents, an experience which can be intimidating for families. Second, if a child is placed, a social worker makes periodic supervision visits until legal finalization. Lastly, for some families, agencies provide ongoing postlegalization services such as counseling for child or family, support groups, or training sessions. This prolonged involvement may undermine the inherent confidence and competence of some families and therefore become stressful to the family system. In addition, this involvement may accentuate the differences between biological and adoptive parenthood. Of course, agency involvement is a critical part of the adoption process; these issues are raised to highlight the uniqueness of adoptive parenthood.

Gaps in information. Inadequate or incomplete information about the child is a third source of stress (Nelson, 1985). For instance, interviews with parents who experienced disruptions frequently revealed gaps in information about the child's history (Schmidt et al., 1988). These gaps become apparent when children behave in ways that are incongruent with their known history. One clear example occurs when parents adopt children who were not reported to have been sexually abused but who behave in a sexually provocative or reactive manner. Parents have a particularly difficult time dealing with this issue when not told beforehand (Barth & Berry, 1988).

Information assists parents in cognitively preparing for the child's behavior. Information, like preparation, tempers the expectations of adoptive parents. If parents perceive the adoption as proceeding more smoothly than they had expected, this causes no problems. On the other hand, the opposite pattern, idealistic expectations that are not in sync with the child's needs and capacities, may create stress, anger, and disappointment and increase risk for disruption.

The child's needs. A fourth source of stress results from excessive internal demands on the family to meet the needs of the child (Smith & Sherwen, 1983). Children with special needs require a great deal of resources and energy. At times, children require more nurturance, structure, limit setting, or attention than parents can provide. Meeting children's needs can be overwhelming, particularly for parents who are adopting for the first time and have not parented other children (Nelson, 1985). Families that are not connected with community resources and social supports may also be stressed as they attempt to meet all of the child's needs within their primary family system.

Where the family presses too hard in responding to the needs of the special-needs child, the needs of other family members may be neglected. For instance, parents may spend less time with other children in the family. These children in turn may feel resentful or jealous towards the "problem" child. Similarly, the steady demands of parenting may be physically and emotionally draining to the parents, who may not, for instance, get adequate rest. The needs of the marriage may be neglected, as parents find no time to take a "night out away from the kids." The focus on the child's problems may create stress at work when parents are, for instance, called to the school for frequent conferences.

Rigidity. A fifth source of stress results from a lack of flexibility in family rules and roles (Boneh, 1979; Cohen, 1984). For the child with special needs, parents need to establish rules that the child can be successful in obeying and discipline that matches the child's level of development. For families with several children, this may require separate rewards and consequences for each child rather than general house rules that apply to all.

Effective parenting for any child requires collaboration between the parents. Given the high level of demands and needs of some special-needs children, a shared parental approach to teaching, nurturing, and disciplining becomes even more important. By sharing roles, the pressure on one parent, usually the mother, is redistributed and less likely to generate a family crisis. While clarity of roles is important, parents should not be limited in the assuming of various roles.

Resources

While the aforementioned stressors bring unique challenges to bear on the special-needs family, important resources can be tapped to enhance adoptive family functioning. Key resources include realistic expectations, flexibility, patience, and good social support.

Many special-needs children simply do not know how to develop effective attachments. Attempts at attachment in the birth family may have been rebuffed, leaving the child feeling angry or sad. For some children, feelings of attachment to birth parents are connected to crisis and reconciliation following a violent episode between parents or after physical abuse of the child. The family foster home, a temporary setting, is often not conducive to the development of secure attachments. The child's inadequate sense of attachment leads the child to behave in ways that create feelings of anger, bewilderment, and helplessness in the adoptive parents. For instance, the child may provoke a crisis, seek punishment, withdraw, exhibit pseudomaturity, or persistently crave attention. The parents' feelings can result in withdrawal from the child with the result that the child's inadequate sense of attachment is reinforced (Sack & Dale, 1982).

Given these dynamics, realistic expectations for and acceptance of behavioral and emotional problems is an asset in special-needs adoption (Smith & Sherwen, 1983; Cohen, 1984). The majority of special-needs children will manifest attachment difficulties at some point in the adoption process. After a "honeymoon" period, children often behave problematically as they begin to make attachments and to test the parents' sincerity.

Parents must learn to prepare themselves for the child's behavior with patience and flexibility. In addition, they will need to plan a course of action to deal with problematic behavior (Partridge et al., 1986), particularly so that they don't reinforce negative behavior patterns. Adoptive families should strive to maintain flexibility and patience when the child behaves in an irritating manner (Gill, 1978; Fanshel, 1962; Feigelman & Silverman, 1983; Groze, 1986; Kagan & Reid, 1986; Deiner, Wilson, & Unger, 1988). These resources, which are skills that can be developed, promote steadiness in the adoption.

Another resource is social support from family and friends (Nelson, 1985; Partridge et al., 1986; Barth & Berry, 1988). Nelson indicates that families rely on an extended network of family, friends, neighbors, and self-help groups for assistance. The parents' comments in this study clearly show the importance of support from other special-needs parents (see Chapter 4). Contacts with support systems outside the immediate family energize the primary family system. Social support provides parents with an outlet for ventilating their frustrations without jeopardizing the stability of the placement and with important respite from the demanding tasks of parenting.

THE CIRCUMPLEX MODEL

The structural model utilized in this analysis is the Circumplex Model developed by Olson (Olson, Russell, & Sprenkle, 1979, 1983; Olson, 1989). Integrating concepts articulated in family systems theory, practice, and research, the model describes a topology of family systems based on the dimensions of cohesion and adaptability (Walsh, 1982; Olson et al.; Olson).

Family cohesion is defined as the attachment or "emotional bonding that family members have toward one another" (Olson, 1989, p. 9). Families are classified on cohesion as disengaged, separated, connected, or enmeshed. Family adaptability is the ability of a family system "to change its power structure, role relationships, and relations rules in response to situational and developmental stress" (Olson, p. 12). The classifications for adaptability are rigid, structured, flexible, or chaotic. In the initial conceptualization of the Circumplex Model, the two middle levels on each dimension—separated and connected for cohesion and structured and flexible for adaptability—indicated healthy family functioning. On the other hand, the extreme levels—disengaged and enmeshed for cohesion and rigid and chaotic for adaptability—indicated dysfunction.

Over time, a different interpretation emerged that places greater emphasis on family members' satisfaction with functioning. In particular, extreme levels are viewed as dysfunctional only if family members are dissatisfied with family functioning (Olson et al., 1985). Conversely, extreme levels of functioning on one or both dimensions may be considered healthy as long as family members are satisfied (Olson, 1989). In the reconceptualization of the model there is no absolute level of functioning that is best. In other words, if family members in a family classified as enmeshed on cohesion and chaotic on adaptability are satisfied with the family's functioning, these extreme levels may not be problematic.

Sixteen distinct types of family systems are generated by combining the four levels of cohesion with the four levels of adaptability. Four of the 16 family types, termed balanced families, are moderate on both the cohesion and adaptability dimensions. Norms were developed for the major scales via a large-scale survey of "nonproblem" families.

An integration of a resource and stressor model of family with the Circumplex Model developed by Olson provides for a comprehensive understanding of special-needs adoptive families. Such a description of the functioning of intact families' children may assist practitioners and adoption workers in identifying effective family patterns for special-needs children. This knowledge can increase the understanding of how intact adoptive family systems work, decrease the risk for disruptions, and help parents gain more satisfaction from their experience (Deiner et al., 1988).

FACES III

Included in the questionnaire was a standardized self-report instrument examining family functioning, the Family Adaptability and Cohesion Evaluation Scales, version 3 (FACES III) developed by Olson and colleagues (1985) as a means of applying the Circumplex Model. FACES III consists of 20 items, 10 for each dimension. Through a survey of about 2,400 individuals residing in "nonproblem" families, separate norms were developed for several groups, including the total group (a combination of families at all phases of the family life cycle) and families with adolescents (ages 12 to 19) in the home. The "cutting points" that define the levels of adaptability and cohesion differ between these normative groups. For instance, a given score on the cohesion scale could classify a family as connected with respect to norms for all families but as enmeshed with respect to norms for families with adolescents.

FINDINGS AND INTERPRETATION

We begin by presenting the cohesion and adaptability scores of different types of families, including comparison of special-needs adoptive families with normative families and two-parent adoptive families with single-parent adoptive families. For both cohesion and adaptability, comparisons are made for all families and then specifically for families with adolescents. Figure 6.1 presents percentages of families classified at each of the four levels of cohesion, while Figure 6.2 presents the same for adaptability.

Cohesion

Comparisons for all families. Special-needs families demonstrate modestly higher levels of cohesion than do normative families. For instance, in the two highest levels of cohesion (connected and enmeshed) the percentages of adoptive families are higher than are those of normative families. The converse is true at the two lowest levels (see Figure 6.1). The difference in mean scores on cohesion between adoptive families (mean = 40.3, $SD = 5.4$, $n = 742$) and normative families (mean = 39.8, $SD = 5.4$,

Figure 6.1
Family Cohesion: Comparing Adoptive and "Normal" Families (Percentages)

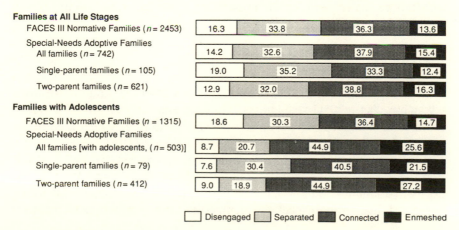

| | Disengaged | Separated | Connected | Enmeshed |

$n = 2453$) is small but achieves statistical significance, $t = 2.21$ (3193), $p < .05$, primarily due to the large sample size.

Single-parent adoptive families demonstrate slightly lower levels of cohesion than do two-parent families as evidenced by, for instance, the higher percentage of single-parent families that are categorized as disengaged (19 percent versus 13 percent; see Figure 6.1). A t-test of the difference in means bordered on significance, t (724) $= -1.93$, $p = .055$. The mean cohesion score in single-parent families was 39.4 ($SD = 5.6$, $n = 105$), while that in two-parent families was 40.5 ($SD = 5.3$, $n = 621$).

Comparisons for families with adolescents. Special-needs adoptive families with adolescents demonstrate markedly higher scores on cohesion than do normative families. For instance, 19 percent in the normative group but only 9 percent in the adoptive group were classified as disengaged (see Figure 6.1). The difference in mean cohesion scores was significant, t (1816) $= 8.96$, $p < .01$. The mean score in adoptive families was 39.7 ($SD = 5.3$, $n = 503$), while that in the normative sample was 37.1 ($SD = 6.1$, $n = 1315$). Single-parent (mean $= 39.1$, $SD = 5.7$, $n = 79$) and two-parent adoptive families (mean $= 39.9$, $SD = 5.3$, $n = 412$) with adolescents are similar with respect to cohesion, t (489) $= -1.15$, $p > .05$.

Interpretation. On balance, the special-needs families demonstrated close relationships among family members. In particular, many families with adolescents where characterized by higher-than-expected levels of cohesion. These families seem to postpone the task of launching their children towards independence and instead direct greater attention towards the development of bonding between child and parent. This is a functional family system reaction that may be in response to the child's psychosocial immaturity, the child's desires to compensate for the lack of close parental ties in previous settings, or the need to integrate the child into the family system before beginning the task of separation.

Adaptability

Comparisons for all families. Special-needs adoptive families are more adaptable than normative families. For instance, 24 percent of adoptive families in contrast to 16 percent of normative families were classified as chaotic (see Figure 6.2). T-tests of mean differences reach significance, t (3179) $= 3.78$, $p < .01$. Mean adaptability scores were 24.9 ($SD = 5.1$, $n = 728$) for adoptive families and 24.1 ($SD = 4.7$, $n = 2453$) for the normative families. Single- and two-parent adoptive families, on balance, appear similar with respect to adaptability, although the percentage of

Figure 6.2
Family Adaptability: Comparing Adoptive and "Normal" Families
(Percentages)

Families at All Life Stages

	Rigid	Structured	Flexible	Chaotic
FACES III Normative Families (n = 2453)	16.3	38.3	29.4	16.0
Special-Needs Adoptive Families				
All families (n = 728)	13.3	33.1	29.4	24.2
Single-parent families (n = 104)	8.7	38.5	26.0	26.9
Two-parent families (n = 608)	14.0	32.1	30.3	23.7

Families with Adolescents

	Rigid	Structured	Flexible	Chaotic
FACES III Normative Families (n = 1315)	15.9	37.3	32.9	13.9
Special-Needs Adoptive Families				
All families [with adolescents, (n = 492)]	13.2	33.3	33.3	20.1
Single-parent families (n = 78)	5.1	38.5	35.9	20.5
Two-parent families (n = 403)	14.9	32.3	33.3	19.6

Rigid   Structured   Flexible   Chaotic

two-parent families that are classified as rigid is higher, 14 percent versus 5 percent (see Figure 6.2). This t-test did not achieve significance, t (710) = 1.46, p > .05; mean = 25.6 (SD = 5.0, n = 104) for single-parent families and mean = 24.8 (SD = 5.1, n = 608) for two-parent families.

Comparisons for families with adolescents. The same patterns as just described for all families are evident for families with adolescents. Adoptive families (mean = 24.9, SD = 5.1, n = 492) are more adaptable than normative families (mean = 24.3, SD = 4.8, n = 1315), t (1805) = 2.26, p < .05. Among families with adolescents there was a slight trend towards greater adaptability for single-parent families. This trend bordered on significance, t (479) = 1.65, p = .09; mean = 25.8, (SD = 4.8, n = 78) for single-parent families and mean = 24.7 (SD = 5.2, n = 403) for two-parent families.

Interpretation. On balance, adoptive families with special-needs children are more adaptable than normative families. Flexibility as contrasted to rigidity facilitates the integration of the child into the family system, enabling the child and parents to learn about one another in a climate less apt to precipitate a major crisis. Highly adaptable families can tolerate a wider range of difficult behavior in children entering the family system. By allowing some troublesome conduct and not rejecting children who test the limits of parental acceptance, the flexible family system allows parents and children to adjust to differences in experiences and expectations.

Family Topology

Figure 6.3 presents the percentages of families classified in each of the 16 FACES III family types. Special-needs adoptive families, more often than normative families, are classified in the four family types located in the upper right quadrant of Figure 6.3. This quadrant represents scores higher than the mean of the normative group on both the cohesion and the adaptability dimensions and is termed the flexibly connected quadrant. With respect to all families, 23 percent of normative families and 32 percent of adoptive families are in this quadrant. Among families with adolescents, the difference in percentages is greater; 40 percent of adoptive families in contrast to 25 percent of normative families are in this quadrant. These findings suggest that both family cohesion and flexibility are distinguishing characteristics of families that adopt children with special needs.

Underlying Dimensions of Cohesion and Adaptability

Recognizing the increased adaptability and cohesion of special-needs adoptive family systems when compared to biological family systems, attention now focuses on the underlying dimensions of adaptability and cohesion.

In addition to adaptability and cohesion scales, nine brief subscales measure specific aspects of the major dimensions. The five subscales related to cohesion are emotional bonding, supportiveness, family boundaries, time and friends, and interest and recreation. The four subscales associated with adaptability are leadership, control, discipline, and roles and rules (Olson et al., 1985). These subscales are similar to the concepts employed in other system models used to understand and treat families (Minuchin & Fishman, 1981; Beavers, 1976, 1982; Beavers, Hulgus, & Hampson, 1988). There are no norms for the subscales to facilitate comparisons to normative families.

Table 6.1 presents the cohesion subscales for single- and two-parent families, while Table 6.2 presents the adaptability subscales. Two sets of statistical significance tests, one assessing differences in means and the other differences in variability, are presented in these tables.

Cohesion subscales. The cohesion subscales clearly indicate the high value placed on close emotional bonding and recreation by adoptive families. For instance, over 70 percent of families responded "Almost always" on the question regarding the importance of family togetherness. These responses suggest that a majority of families expect to focus considerable activities around each other. There is more diversity in the

Figure 6.3
FACES III Family Types for Special-Needs Adoptive and "Normal" Families (Percentages)

ADAPTABILITY \ COHESION	Disengaged	Separated	Connected	Enmeshed
Chaotic	F3 = 3.0 A = 2.8 F3A = 3.0 AA = 1.4	F3 = 4.7 A = 6.7 F3A = 3.3 AA = 2.7	F3 = 5.4 A = 9.6 F3A = 4.8 AA = 9.0	F3 = 2.9 A = 5.3 F3A = 2.7 AA = 7.2
Flexible	F3 = 4.7 A = 3.1 F3A = 5.1 AA = 2.7	F3 = 10.0 A = 9.5 F3A = 9.9 AA = 7.0	F3 = 11.3 A = 12.7 F3A = 12.6 AA = 13.8	F3 = 3.5 A = 4.2 F3A = 5.3 AA = 9.7
Structured	F3 = 5.8 A = 5.4 F3A = 6.5 AA = 3.3	F3 = 13.3 A = 11.7 F3A = 11.3 AA = 7.2	F3 = 14.1 A = 10.9 F3A = 14.7 AA = 16.2	F3 = 5.0 A = 4.6 F3A = 4.9 AA = 6.6
Rigid	F3 = 2.9 A = 2.7 F3A = 3.8 AA = 1.4	F3 = 5.7 A = 5.2 F3A = 6.0 AA = 3.9	F3 = 5.7 A = 4.5 F3A = 4.3 AA = 5.7	F3 = 2.1 A = 1.1 F3A = 1.8 AA = 2.3

F3 = FACES III Normative Families (All, *n* = 2453)

A = Special-Needs Adoptive Families (All, *n* = 716)

F3A = FACES III Normative Families with Adolescents (*n* = 1315)

AA = Special-Needs Adoptive Families with Adolescents (*n* =487)

Balanced

Mid-Range

Extreme

Special-Needs Adoption

Table 6.1
Cohesion Subscales for Two-Parent (2) and Single-Parent (1) Families (Percentages)

Subscale and items	Almost never		Once in a while		Sometimes		Frequently		Almost always	
	2	1	2	1	2	1	2	1	2	1
Emotional bonding										
11. Family members feel very close to each other.	0	1	3	2	10	17	30	29	56	52
19. Family togetherness is very important.	0	1	1	3	5	3	22	16	71	78
Supportiveness										
1. Family members ask each other for help.[+]	0	2	5	12	27	23	49	39	19	24
17. Family members consult other family members on their decisions.[*]	3	3	9	16	26	36	42	31	20	14
Family boundaries										
7. Family members feel closer to other family members than to people outside the family.	3	5	4	5	18	17	25	26	50	47
5. We like to do things with just our immediate family.[+]	2	4	7	11	28	27	48	42	16	16
Time and friends										
9. Family members like to spend free time with each other.	1	2	5	4	25	30	47	43	21	22
3. We approve of each other's friends.[+*]	2	4	2	6	21	36	36	22	40	32
Interests and reaction										
13. When our family gets together for activities everybody is present.	1	1	4	5	20	22	34	32	41	40
15. We can easily think of things to do together as a family.	1	2	4	5	16	16	38	32	40	45

[+]$p<.05$ for variability (standard deviation) of responses

[*]$p<.05$ for difference in means

responses for the subscales of supportiveness, family boundaries, and time and friends.

Comparing single- and two-parent families, the responses demonstrate that two-parent families are more likely to consult other family members on decisions and to approve of each other's friends. Three responses demonstrated greater variability in single-parent families.

Adaptability subscales. Responses to the adaptability subscales showed considerable diversity with no clear pattern evident regarding the aspects of discipline, control, and rules and roles. Only the leadership subscale showed a distinct response pattern; almost 70 percent of respondents said they "almost never" had difficulty identifying the family's leader. These findings suggest that adoptive families maintain a clear leadership structure but that there is fluidity with respect to the other dimensions.

Single-parents indicated greater involvement of children in decision making and more frequent changes in rules than did two-parent families. Two questions demonstrated greater variability in the responses of single-parent adopters.

Interpretation. The emphasis on close emotional bonding and family activities together mirrors previous research, which identified the importance of parent-child attachment in special-needs adoption (Ward, 1981; Melina, 1986). It is not surprising that family boundaries do not show the same high-cohesion pattern as does attachment. Elbow (1986) discusses how family boundaries are challenged by the essential, although sometimes intrusive, involvement of the agency. Also, relatively open boundaries are needed to facilitate interaction and mutual support from other families.

The strong leadership pattern in special-needs families clearly establishes parental authority, a necessity for those children who were leaders in their birth family systems or who experienced no sense of leadership in the birth family. Also, the firm leadership pattern is well suited to deal with issues of behavioral management. From this position of leadership, the special-needs adoptive parent nurtures a flexible family system with considerable opportunity for input from the children.

Some interesting differences between single- and two-parent families emerged. Children in single-parent families were more involved in decision making, a pattern that may help in preparing them for adult roles. The tendency towards less consultation in family decisions in single-parent families is a means of providing emotional distancing and may be therapeutic since single parents often adopt children with difficult problems (see Chapter 7). The indication that single-parent households do not require approval for each other's friendships suggests that this is an area in which adopted children are given more autonomy.

Resources and Adoptive Outcome

Findings. Many of the resources alluded to earlier in this chapter showed positive associations to adoptive outcome as measured by the respondent's perception of the impact of the adoption on the family. These include the amount of approval of the adoption by the respondent's and spouse's

Table 6.2
Adaptability Subscales for Two-Parent (2) and Single-Parent (1) Families (Percentages)

Subscale and items	Almost never		Once in a while		Sometimes		Frequently		Almost always	
	2	1	2	1	2	1	2	1	2	1
Leadership										
6. Different people act as leaders in our family.	28	39	27	19	25	24	18	12	3	7
18. It is hard to identify the leader(s) in our family.+	69	69	15	7	11	11	4	5	1	8
Discipline										
4. Children have a say in their discipline.	13	12	22	24	46	43	15	14	4	7
10. Parents and children discuss punishment together.	6	8	13	15	33	38	30	17	17	22
Control										
12. The children make the decisions in our family.+*	44	37	42	34	12	23	1	3	0	4
2. In solving problems, the children's suggestions are followed.	4	4	21	16	60	66	13	12	2	3
Roles and Rules										
8. Our family changes its way of handling tasks.	8	9	22	23	44	46	21	17	4	5
16. We shift household responsibilities from person to person.	12	8	17	17	31	27	26	28	13	20
20. It is hard to tell who does which household chore.	51	55	24	23	18	13	5	5	3	5
14. Rules change in our family.*	22	16	33	32	38	41	5	8	2	4

+p<.05 for variability (standard deviation) of responses

*p<.05 for difference in means

extended families, the level of support from friends, the amount of and accuracy of background information, and the helpfulness of the adoption agency social worker (see Table 3.15). Cohesion shows a moderate positive association to the adoption's impact on the family, r (729) = .27, p < .01, while adaptability evidences a very weak positive relationship, r (718) = .08, p < .01.

Interpretation. These findings reinforce the importance of family closeness in special-needs adoption. Parents need to maintain a sense of closeness even when children engage in disruptive, provoking behaviors. To do this they need to separate their feelings about the child's behavior from their feelings about the child. The child's provocative behaviors test the parent's commitment and answer the question: "Will my parents stick with me through tough times or will this be a temporary 'home' like all the rest?" Special-needs parents need to remember that many dysfunctional habits in the new family system, such as hoarding of food, stealing, bad manners, hitting of siblings, setting oneself up for punishment, assuming a parental role, were functional (or at least tacitly accepted) in the birth family system.

Families that received adequate background information reported more positive adoptive outcomes. Adequate information allows preparation for potential difficulties. Without in-depth knowledge of the child with regard to habits, temperament, strengths and weaknesses, and behavioral issues, the parent may simply expect that the child will fit automatically into the existing family system, an expectation that may be beyond the child's capacities. Parents who are fully informed about the child's prior experiences are more likely to be flexible and accommodating during the initial phases of the placement.

The findings emphasize the importance of support from extended family and friends for effective adoptive family functioning. Hence, the sense of closeness between family members should not isolate the family from sources of support and help. Interactions with family and friends may be particularly important for single-parent adoptive families (see Chapter 7).

Brief Test of Circumplex Model

The Circumplex Model postulates (with some exceptions as discussed earlier) that families functioning at moderate levels of cohesion and adaptability experience fewer problems than do those at extreme levels, in other words, that cohesion and adaptability show curvilinear relationships to healthy family functioning. To test this hypothesis, we computed the distance from the center score for each respondent according to procedures outlined by Olson and colleagues (1985). This score measures the total "distance of an individual's cohesion and adaptability score from the center of the model" (p. 28), that is, from a point on a two-dimensional space that indicates the mean of the normative (all families) group on both cohesion and adaptability.

We hypothesized that those families with lower distance scores, that is, those close to the center, would report greater smoothness and fewer "ups and downs" in the adoptive process. This hypothesis was not supported. The distance from the center score showed essentially no relationship to smoothness of the adoption, $r(711) = -.04$, $p = .12$. Similarly, no meaningful relationship was observed in a regression analysis that included also adaptability and cohesion scores, beta $= -.02$, $p > .05$. In addition to the just-described statistical tests, we conducted a t-test contrasting balanced families (those in the two middle levels on both dimensions) with all other families. While the "unbalanced" families reported reduced smoothness, the difference in means was exceedingly small and did not reach significance, t (709) = .31, p > .05.

These analyses perhaps do not provide a fair test of the Circumplex Model, as our data set does not include a variable focused directly on satisfaction with family functioning. We carried out some other selected regression analyses, using both smoothness and family impact as dependent variables and using separate terms to assess possible curvilinearity for each dimension. These analyses provided weak support for the curvilinear hypothesis with respect to adaptability and even less support with respect to cohesion; neither trend reached significance.

IMPLICATIONS FOR PRACTICE

Little information from a family systems perspective has been developed for special-needs adoptive families (Berman & Bufferd, 1986). A systems perspective focuses on the family patterns that emerge as a reaction to adoption rather than on chronic dysfunctional patterns. Family difficulties are examined in the context of the relationship of a child's problems to the family organization rather than viewed as the product of a child's internal pathology or history (Hartman, 1984; Talen & Lehr, 1984;). Bourguignon's (1989b) findings as summarized earlier as well as Katz's writings (1986) further emphasize the need to target intervention on family or marital dynamics rather than on child psychopathology or parental psychological functioning.

It is important to keep in mind that adoptive families are judged to be functional and appropriate during the home study. Subsequent difficulties that a family may encounter are less a function of enduring patterns of dysfunction and more reflective of new demands including precipitous life-style changes and alterations in the structure of the family relationship system (Hartman, 1984). In addition, reciprocal impacts involving the child, family, and larger systems (schools, courts, social services, etc.) are often present. For example, a child's misbehavior in school may bring about conflicts between the school and the family as well as difficulties between the child and the family. Therefore, practitioners may find an ecological framework helpful for understanding the adoptive family and its interactions with other systems (see Imber-Black, 1988, for instance).

A growing body of knowledge suggests differences between biological and adoptive families (Kirk, 1984; Hayes & Jennings, 1989; Small, 1987). These differences need to be acknowledged rather than ignored or denied.

The current study provides empirical evidence of differences between normative and special-needs adoptive families on the dimensions of cohesion and adaptability. Adoptive families, on balance, are both adaptable and cohesive.

Many adoptive families place a high emphasis on closeness and family-based activities. Such an atmosphere, if encouraged rather than demanded, can facilitate the child's bonding and perhaps allow the child to compensate for nurturing not provided in birth or foster families. If the family demands closeness, however, this may be a precipitant to disruption.

Adaptability helps integrate the child into the family system. It allows the family system to tolerate a wide range of difficult behavior and assists parents in responding to the unique needs of each child. The increased cohesion of adoptive families with adolescents attests to the resiliency that enables adoptive families to function in ways that meet the child's needs rather than in accordance with prescribed rules.

The child adopted during adolescence faces a dilemma with respect to developmental tasks. On the one hand, the child attempts to bond to the family, a task that promotes cohesion. On the other hand, the hallmark of adolescence is the development of independence and, eventually, separation from the family. As we have mentioned, one solution to this dilemma is to postpone adolescence. Clearly, the competing demands of bonding and separation create unique challenges for family and child, who must strike a precarious balance between these competing demands. As Olson (1989) asserts, family functioning should be viewed within the context of family satisfaction rather than according to descriptions or labels. Unfortunately, terms such as chaotic and enmeshed too easily conjure up negatives such as dysfunctional family and unhealthy functioning. Our findings further challenge the use of these terms in a narrow manner. High levels of cohesion and adaptability are both common and healthy in special-needs adoptive families.

Family therapists may be able to use study results to guide them in their practice with families adopting special-needs children. Where the family is not particularly flexible, they may want to encourage more flexibility. Conversely, therapists should not be particularly alarmed if adoptive families appear to be chaotic, as such a high level of flexibility can be functional in special-needs adoption. Where leadership is not well developed, the therapist may want to explore ways to enhance this.

The level of family cohesion is closely related to the parents' view of adoptive outcome. The therapist's task is to facilitate cohesion while at the same time helping parents to realistically appraise the level of closeness that children can handle, given their unique backgrounds. The goal is to develop close relationships between family members while at the same time keeping the family system open to help and support from other systems. Finally, therapists should recognize that what appear to be overly close relationships between adopted adolescents and their parents may indeed be functional in meeting the needs of both parents and adolescents.

Chapter 7

Focus on Single Parents

Historically, single people have not been considered as the most desirable candidates for adoptive parenthood. Singles are usually approved for adoption as a last resort and are more often pressured to accept children with significant emotional and behavior problems. Increasingly, however, those in the adoption field are recognizing the viability of single-parent adoption. Studies conducted in the 1970s and 1980s show a steady increase in the percentage of adoptions by singles from 0.5 percent reported by Branham in 1970, to 2 percent in 1974 (Grow & Shapiro, 1974), 4 percent in 1979 (Boneh, 1979), 8 percent in 1983 (McRoy & Zurcher, 1983), 20 percent in 1984 (Boyne et al., 1984), 23 percent in 1986 (Kagan & Reid, 1986), to a high of 34 percent reported by Festinger in 1986.

Several studies report on attributes of single adoptive parents. As with one-parent households in the general population, most single adoptive parents are female (Branham, 1970; Feigelman & Silverman, 1977; Dougherty, 1978; Shireman & Johnson, 1976, 1985). For example, Branham (1970) reports that 97 percent of single adoptive parents are female; Festinger's (1986) study reports 88 percent. Branham (1970) indicates that single parents have a high level of emotional maturity, have a high capacity to tolerate frustration, and are not overly influenced by the opinions of others. Other studies (Jordan & Little, 1966; Shireman & Johnson, 1976) note the enjoyment and personal fulfillment that single parents receive from interactions with their children.

Single-parent adoptive families tend to have lower incomes than do two-parent adoptive families (Shireman & Johnson, 1976; Feigelman & Silverman, 1977; Shireman, 1988). The higher incomes in two-parent families are in part the result of dual incomes. Yet the lower incomes in single-parent families also reflect the lower earning power of women. Even when performing similar jobs, women, on average, earn less than men.

While incomes are lower, single adoptive parents tend to be more educated than married adoptive parents (Feigelman & Silverman, 1977). Single mothers tend to be older than mothers in two-parent families, while single fathers are similar in age to married fathers (Feigelman & Silverman). Also, adopting singles are more often members of minority groups (Branham, 1970; Shireman & Johnson, 1976; Feigelman & Silverman).

Several studies report on selected characteristics of children adopted by single parents. Reid and colleagues (1987) and Feigelman and Silverman (1977) indicate that single parents more often wish to adopt older children than infants. Barth and Berry (1988) indicate that single parents are more likely than couples to adopt older children and boys, and less likely to adopt sibling groups or those who were previously their foster children. In contrast to Barth and Berry, Branham (1970), Shireman and Johnson (1976) and Feigelman and Silverman suggest that singles tend to adopt children of the same sex as themselves. Since the majority of single parents in these studies were female, the studies show that singles more often adopt girls. Historically, agency policy has emphasized same-sex placement. It is unclear whether this pattern of placement also reflects the preferences of parents.

In summary, single-parent placements represent an increasing percentage of special-needs adoptive placements. Most single parents are female. They are more likely to adopt older children and less likely to adopt sibling groups or their own foster children. Furthermore, there is some indication of demographic differences (income, age, education level) between singles and couples. Of particular concern to adoption workers and potential adoptive parents is whether single-parent adoptive homes are more prone to difficulties than two-parent homes. Following is a discussion of one indicator of adoption adjustment, that is, adoption disruption. What is known about single-parents and disruption?

ADOPTION DISRUPTION AND SINGLE PARENTS

Most studies have found that single parents are equally represented in both disrupted and intact adoptions (Boyne et al., 1984; Urban Systems, 1985; Festinger, 1986; Kagan & Reid, 1986; Barth & Berry, 1988). Urban Systems reports that single parents comprised 8 percent of all adoptive placements and 9 percent of disruptions. Boyne and colleagues indicate that 20 percent of placements and about 26 percent of disruptions involve single parents, a difference that is not statistically significant. Festinger reports that 34 percent of special-needs children in New York were placed with single parents. Placements with singles represented 37 percent of disruptions, again a difference that did not achieve significance.

Kagan and Reid (1986) reported no significant difference in adoptive outcomes between single and married adoptive parents. Their results, however, demonstrate an interaction between parent gender and child gender. Single women who adopted boys often experienced negative adoptive outcomes; only one of six boys placed with a single mother remained in adoptive placement at the time of the study. Finally, in Barth and Berry's (1988) California study, single parents represented 15 percent of the placements and 14 percent of the disruptions. Overall, these studies suggest that marital status is unrelated to risk of disruption.

However, in two studies (Boneh, 1979; Partridge et al., 1986) placements with single parents were more likely to disrupt. Analyzing case records, Boneh reports that five of six single-parent adoptions in her sample disrupted, a rate of 83 percent. As she indicates, this result should be viewed cautiously due to the small sample size. Partridge and colleagues report that 28 percent of the disrupted adoptions but only 10 percent of intact adoptions involved single-parent families. Given this finding, they conclude that married couples experience fewer disruptions.

Although these two studies suggest the possibility of less stable placements for single parents, the preponderance of research indicates that marital status has little, if any, effect on risk for disruption. It is important to examine the experiences of single adoptive parents to understand the uniqueness of this type of nontraditional adoptive placement.

EXPERIENCES OF SINGLE ADOPTIVE PARENTS

Several studies focus on the experiences of single adoptive parents. Jordan and Little (1966) interviewed adoption workers to examine the adoptions of eight children by single mothers. The workers expressed distinctly positive opinions about single-parent adoptive homes. Branham (1970) examined case records of 36 one-parent families. She was also positive in her assessment of single-parent placements for special-needs children. Feigelman and Silverman (1977) compared the overall social adjustment of children adopted by two-parent and single-parent families using a mailed questionnaire with a national sample. Fifty-eight single adoptive parents were compared to an unspecified sample of couples. No significant differences regarding adjustment were reported. Six years after the initial study, Feigelman and Silverman (1983) recontacted 60 percent of their original sample ($n = 35$). They continued to report that the familial experiences of adoptive single parents were similar to those of adoptive couples. Dougherty (1978) mailed a questionnaire to 131 single adoptive mothers. Sixty-seven percent responded, and she reached positive conclusions about their social adjustment, indicating that they achieved a high level of stability and success in parenting. Finally, Shireman and Johnson (1976, 1985, 1986; Shireman, 1988) conducted a longitudinal study of single adoptive parents, interviewing parents and children approximately every four years after placement (when the children were about ages 4 to 5, 8, and 14). Results again indicated that adoption by singles provides a constructive alternative for children who cannot grow up with biological parents. The single-parent adoptive homes provided continuity and stability. Family systems showed strength and changed appropriately to meet the needs of the child. Most children adjusted well. Family relationships were largely positive. Children were beginning the process of separation from the family in early adolescence. Peer relations were an area of strength, and there were no noticeable self-esteem difficulties.

In summary, the studies reviewed here indicate that single-parent families are a nurturing and viable resource for adopted children. Adoption outcomes are quite good and appear to compare favorably with those observed in two-parent families.

Employing a psychosocial framework for analysis, this chapter builds on previous research in several ways. Most important, it contrasts and compares the experiences of one- and two-parent families. Areas covered include parent-child relationship, educational functioning, ecological functioning, school functioning, child behavior, and adoption outcome.

FINDINGS

Characteristics of Children and Families

The sample includes 122 single-parent families (15 percent) and 651 two-parent (85 percent) families. Five parents who were single at adoption subsequently married; these families are considered as single-parent families in this discussion. Status of the adoption at the time of the survey could not be determined for 26 families; these families were not included in the analysis. The following analysis is based on the responses of 773 families.

Statistically significant relationships between family structure and the child's race, age, and handicap status were observed. Single parents were more likely to adopt older children (12- to 14-year-olds versus 9- to 11-year-olds for couples), nonwhite children (69 percent versus 31 percent for couples), and children with mental retardation (16 percent versus 9 percent for couples). (It is noted that mental retardation was according to the parent's description rather than a formal diagnostic criteria.) Single parents were also more likely to adopt girls (60 percent versus 45 percent for couples). This finding should be considered in the context that most (84 percent) of the single parents are women and singles tend to adopt children of the same sex as themselves (Shireman & Johnson, 1976; Feigelman & Silverman, 1977). The indication that older children often reside in one-parent homes is consistent with findings from other studies (Barth & Berry, 1988; Reid et al., 1987) while the finding that single parents more often adopt girls is in contrast to one other study (Barth & Berry, 1988). In our sample, 106 single mothers adopted 36 boys (34 percent) and 70 girls (66 percent) while 14 single fathers adopted 12 boys (86 percent) and 2 girls (14 percent).

Single adoptive mothers are older than their counterparts. Mean ages at the time of the study were 48.04 years for single mothers and 41.46 years for mothers in two-parent families, a difference of about 6.5 years. Adoptive fathers are about the same age in both single-parent (mean age is 43.95 years) and two-parent families (mean age is 43.77 years), findings consistent with the research of Feigelman and Silverman (1977).

There is also a statistically significant difference in education level; 26.2 percent of single adoptive mothers in contrast to 10 percent of mothers in two-parent families did not graduate from high school ($p < .01$). In contrast, Feigelman and Silverman (1977) found singles to be more educated.

Differences in ethnicity were observed between single- and two-parent families. Most single mothers (55.6 percent) and a substantial minority of single fathers are black (33.3 percent). In contrast, most parents in two-parent families are white (79.7 percent of mothers and 78.5 percent of fathers). These results are similar to those of the other studies reviewed (Branham, 1970; Shireman & Johnson, 1976; Feigelman & Silverman, 1977).

Lastly, single-parent families have lower incomes than two-parent families, a finding that is also consistent with other investigations (Shireman & Johnson, 1976; Feigelman & Silverman, 1977; Shireman, 1988). On average, they earn about $21,000 per year, while couples earn about $38,000.

Behavioral Functioning

Ratings of children's behaviors were obtained by the Child Behavior Checklist (CBC) developed by Achenbach and Edelbrock (1983). Behavior scores for children adopted in single- and two-parent families were compared to those of clinical and nonclinical normative groups as presented by Achenbach and Edelbrock. (See also Chapters 3 and 10.)

As presented in Table 7.1, the percentages of adopted children in the clinical range in both single- and two-parent families exceed the corresponding percentages for the nonclinical sample, suggesting that many children in both family forms exhibit behavioral difficulties. Differences between the special-needs sample and the nonclinical CBC sample are modest among 4- to 5-year-olds but more pronounced among the 6- to 11- and 12- to 16-year-old children. (See Table 3.6 for CBC norms.)

Comparisons between single- and two-parent adoptions suggest that children in single-parent families may experience fewer behavioral problems. For both boys and girls in all three age groups, the percentage of scores in the clinical range is lower in single-parent families. This holds for all three scales that are presented. Among latency and adolescent boys in single-parent families, internalizing problems seem to predominate. Among boys in two-parent families, internalizing and externalizing problems are equally common.

What explains the modestly more problematic behavior in two-parent families? Perhaps the intensity of relating to two adults on an intimate basis generates greater difficulties. It is unlikely that couples adopt more difficult children, given that older children and subsequently more "damaged" children are quite often adopted by single parents (mean age of child at placement is 5.9 years for single parents and 5.5 years for couples).

Table 7.1
Scores in Clinical Range for Children in Single- and Two-Parent Families (Percentages)

Gender and scale	Ages 4 and 5		Ages 6 to 11		Ages 12 to 16	
	Single-parent	Two-parent	Single-parent	Two-parent	Single-parent	Two-parent
Girls						
Internalizing	0	17	18	27	18	26
Externalizing	0	21	39	42	21	26
Total problems	0	25	39	44	36	47
n	2	24	28	153	38	87
Boys						
Internalizing	0	12	22	28	40	42
Externalizing	0	16	17	38	25	41
Total problems	0	16	17	43	45	46
n	1	25	18	155	20	138

Note. See Table 3.6 for comparison to CBC clinical and non-clinical samples.

Bourguignon (1989a) suggests while many single adopters enjoy taking care of children, they do not themselves have high needs to be nurtured. Consequently, they set up emotional boundaries between themselves and the children. This provides a safe environment for the child who has previously experienced failure in attempts at close emotional relationships with adults. The decreased demands for intimacy perhaps result in reduced behavioral difficulties for the child and fewer unmet needs for the parent. In addition, single parents may evaluate the behavior of their adopted child differently than do couples. There may be increased flexibility in accepting certain behaviors in single-parent households as well as the failure to observe certain behaviors, since only one and not two adults are available for supervision and monitoring. Whatever explanation the reader accepts, the single parents in this study experienced less difficult behavior than did couples, although both reported many behavior difficulties for adopted children.

Parent-Child Relationship

Table 7.2 displays results for five questions probing parent-child relationship. While most parents report getting along well, having good or excellent communication with their child, trusting their child, feeling respected by their child, and feeling close to their child, there is a modest tendency towards more positive reports in single-parent families. The responses to these questions suggest that even though many adopted children manifest behavioral and emotional difficulties, most singles and couples maintain good relationships with their children.

Educational Functioning

Excellent educational outcomes were observed in both single-and two-parent families. Among children age 6 to 17, 97 percent (108 of 111) of children in single-parent families and 99 percent (561 of 566) of children in two-parent families were attending school. Fifty-one percent (48 of 95) of children in one-parent families and 53 percent (246 of 465) of children in two-parent families earned grades of "B average" or better in the semester preceding the survey. Seventy percent (80 of 114) of children in single-parent families and 66 percent (390 of 591) of children in two-parent families "enjoy school," according to their parents' reports. None of the just-mentioned findings regarding educational functioning revealed statistically significant differences between single- and two-parent families.

Table 7.2
Relationship Between Parent and Child

Question and response	Single-parent family Freq.	%	Two-parent family Freq.	%
How do you and your child get along?				
Very well	87	73	412	64
Fairly well	29	24	208	32
Not so well	3	2	22	3
Very poorly	1	1	6	1
How would you rate the communication between you and your child?				
Excellent	55	45	251	39
Good	52	43	291	45
Fair	13	11	82	13
Poor	2	2	22	3
Do you trust your child?				
Yes, very much so	48	41	219	34
Yes, for the most part	54	46	319	50
Not sure	3	3	40	6
No	12	10	64	10
Do you feel respected by your child?*				
Yes, very much so	73	62	310	48
Yes, for the most part	35	30	267	41
Not sure	6	5	40	6
No	4	3	27	4
Do you feel close to your child?				
Yes, very much so	78	65	367	57
Yes, for the most part	35	29	220	34
Not sure	2	2	32	5
No	5	4	30	5

Note. T-test of difference in means used in significance testing.

*$p<.05$

Ecological Functioning

The concept of ecological functioning examines the resources and stressors available in the total family environment, including the network of social services available to the family and the social support from family and friends. This section focuses on the parents' perceptions of those resources.

Social work and other services. Singles report fewer visits by social workers after adoptive placement (see Table 7.3). Fifty percent of single parents but only 27 percent of parents in two-parent families reported no visits after placement.

The lower level of contacts for single-parent adopters is partially explained by factors other than family structure. In particular, the number of contacts varied by participating state (these differences being at least partially attributable to differences in sampling methods) and ethnicity of child (minority children were visited less often; see Chapter 8). When controlling for such factors, the association between single parenthood and lower visiting weakened in strength and only bordered on significance ($p = .13$).

There are no statistically significant differences between how single-parent and two-parent families evaluate the appropriateness of the number of visits with their social worker, the amount of information provided, the accuracy of the information, or the helpfulness of services. About 20 percent of respondents in both types of families indicated that their social workers did not visit often enough in the postplacement period. A significant minority of respondents, 39 percent in single-parent families and 35 percent in two-parent families, indicated that they had not received enough background information on the child. Yet 89 percent of respondents in both types of families indicated that the information provided was accurate or almost always accurate.

Patterns of postplacement services differed in one- and two-parent families (see Table 7.4). Single parents were more frequently involved in family therapy, 32 percent versus 25 percent. On the other hand, two-parent families were more often in contact with other families who had adopted special-needs children, 32 percent versus 26 percent. While both family types evaluated parent support groups and contacts with other families as more helpful than individual or family therapy, single parents were much more likely to report that parent support groups had been very helpful, 72 percent versus 44 percent.

Social support. Social support from family and friends is particularly important in special-needs adoption. About four-fifths of respondents in both one- and two-parent families report that relatives approve of the

Table 7.3
Reported In-Person Visits with Adoption Agency Social Worker(s) by Marital Status

Post-placement visits	Single-parent family Freq.	%	Two-parent family Freq.	%
None	50	43	173	27
One to three	31	26	227	35
Four to nine	23	20	155	24
Ten to nineteen	6	5	53	8
Twenty or more	7	6	33	5

Note. Test of significance by t-test using five-point ordinal response scale reached significance at .05 level

$*p<.05$

Table 7.4
Services and Support Received Since Adoptive Placement and Assessment of Helpfulness of Service (Percentages)

Service/support	Single-parent family Received service	Responded "Very helpful"	Two-parent family Received service	Responded "Very helpful"
Individual therapy for child	35	40	37	35
Family therapy	32	44	25	36
Adoptive parent support group	18	72*	20	44
Contact with other special-needs families	26	50	32	51

Note. Receiving of service tested by chi-square. Helpfulness of service tested by t-test using three-point response scale.

$*p<.05$

adoption "very much" and that friends support the adoption "very much." Thus the level of social support appeared high for both types of families and did not vary according to family structure.

The authors speculated that support and approval from others might be particularly important for single parents, as they cannot draw upon a marital relationship for additional support. Following this line of reasoning, we hypothesized that support from friends and approval from relatives would be associated more strongly with adoptive outcome in single- as contrasted with two-parent families. The data analysis provided tentative support for this hypothesis with respect to approval from relatives. Where respondents reported that relatives did "not really" approve or approved only "somewhat" of the adoption, there was little difference in reports regarding the adoption's impact on the family, with 18 percent (4 of 22) in single-parent families and 20 percent (24 of 119) in two-parent families responding "Very positive." Yet where relatives approved "very much," 69 percent (60 of 87) of the single-parent families but only 52 percent (261 of 501) of the two-parent families responded that the adoption's impact was "Very positive." Statistical significance tests of this interaction by two different methods bordered on significance ($p = .09$ and $p = .15$). These findings affirm the particular importance of support from the extended family for single parents. This interpretation is consistent with the observation that single adoptive parents often engage the assistance of extended family and friends to assist with the responsibilities and duties of child rearing (Feigelman & Silverman, 1977).

Adoption Outcome

Single-parent families evaluated the adoption's impact on the family more favorably than did two-parent families, with 59 percent versus 44 percent responding "Very positive" (see Table 7.5). Table 7.6 presents perceived impact on the family controlling for selected variables. Single-parent adoptions are assessed more positively for both boys and girls, although the difference is more pronounced for boys. Single-parent adoption appears to have been an excellent alternative for children whose entry into the home was at age 6 or older. In this group, the difference in percentages is particularly large; 53 percent in single-parent families versus only 34 percent in two-parent families responded "Very positive." The degree of difference in assessment of impact also varied according to ethnicity. For white children, assessments of impact were much more positive for single-parent adoptions. In contrast, for minority children assessments did not vary according to family structure. The largest difference presented in Table 7.6 pertains to children who were placed in group home or psychiatric

Table 7.5
**Impact of Adoption and Smoothness of Adoption in Single- and
Two-Parent Families**

Question and response	Single-parent family		Two-parent family	
	Freq.	%	Freq.	%
Overall, has the impact of this child's adoption on the family been . . . *				
Very positive	66	59	285	44
Mostly positive	24	21	191	30
Mixed; positives and negatives about equal	18	16	142	22
Mostly negative	1	1	21	3
Very negative	3	3	7	1
Overall, has the adoption gone . . .				
Smoother than you expected	38	32	206	32
About as you expected	48	40	218	34
Had more "ups and downs" than you expected	34	28	221	34

Note. T-test of difference in means used in significance testing.
*$p<.05$

settings prior to adoption. Among this group, 56 percent of respondents in single-parent families in contrast to only 28 percent of those in two-parent families responded "Very positive."

This last finding suggests that single-parent adoption may be an excellent option for children who have experienced prior psychiatric or group placements. Formal tests of the statistical interaction of prior placement and family structure bordered on significance when impact on family was dependent, $p = .07$, and reached significance when mean score on the parent-child relationship scale was dependent ($p = .02$). This finding, while encouraging, should be considered as tentative due to the low number of children with placement histories who were placed in single-parent homes.

Table 7.5 also reports on parents' perceptions of the smoothness of the adoptive process. While responses favor single parents by a modest amount, the difference between one- and two-parent families does not achieve

Table 7.6
"Very Positive" Responses Regarding Family Impact by Marital Status and Selected Factors

Factor	Single-parent family %	Single-parent family n	Two-parent family %	Two-parent family n
Gender of child				
Female	54	67	45	292
Male**	66	44	44	354
Gender of respondent				
Female (mother)**	60	98	45	545
Male (father)	50	14	40	99
Age of child when entered home				
Younger than six years	64	53	52	364
Six years or older**	53	58	34	280
Minority status of child				
Minority or biracial	60	72	55	198
White	57	37	40	447
Minority status of respondent				
Minority or biracial	57	61	52	131
White*	60	50	42	513
Transracial adoption?				
Yes	60	10	53	57
No**	59	97	43	583
Adoption by prior foster parent?				
Yes*	62	61	47	258
No	55	47	42	385
Group home or psychiatric placement prior to adoption?				
Yes	56	9	28	54
No	58	67	51	347

Note. Test of significance by chi-square test with impact treated as dichotomous variable, very positive versus any other response.

*$p<.05$, **$p<.01$

significance. Clearly, the findings pertaining to adoptive outcome, while good for both types of families, are particularly encouraging for single-parent adopters.

DISCUSSION AND PRACTICE IMPLICATIONS

These findings suggest that recruitment and adoption policies should target single parents. Single-parent adoption emerges as a good plan for providing permanent homes for many children in need. As one single parent wrote, "Special-needs children are a challenge but can be a very positive aspect of your life."

Singles make up a significant portion of the population, and many are raising children on their own. They are a feasible and largely untapped resource for children with special needs, a recommendation made by Kadushin in 1970.

While single-parent adoption has increased, the percentage of single-parent adoptive families remains lower than that in the general population. In the 1980s, approximately 26 percent of all households were single-parent families (Maris, 1988). Only three of the adoption studies conducted in the 1980s show a similar percentage (Boyne et al., 1984; Festinger, 1986; Kagan & Reid, 1986). The lower percentage of single-parent adoptive households may indicate that recruitment efforts focused on single adults have not been as successful as efforts to recruit two-parent families. As a result, many children remain in foster or group care with no permanent adoptive home.

While the two-parent adoptive family is usually considered the best possible choice, such a family may be unavailable. Moreover, a single parent may be best equipped to meet the needs of some children. A single adult, unencumbered by the demands of a marital relationship, can give the kind and amount of involvement and nurturing that some children with severely damaging experiences need (Mendes & Roberts, 1979). These children require a parent who is skilled in "therapeutic parenting" and who has the time, energy, and patience to help a child with serious emotional and/or behavioral problems. Therapeutic parenting requires the provision of consistent structure and limits without becoming too rigid or too emotionally involved with behavior difficulties. At the same time, the therapeutic parent needs to provide emotional support, nurturing, and love. The balance of these conflicting demands is perhaps the central task in parenting these children. A couple may confront competing demands, meeting the needs of a special-needs child and continuing to develop and nurture the marital relationship. As one single parent remarked, "There is only so much of me to go around." For children who need therapeutic relationships with an adult, single-parent homes may be particularly appropriate.

In addition, one of the survival behaviors demonstrated by children who have been in the child welfare system for extended time periods is manipulation. The children learn to manipulate and to play adults against each other in order to get some of their needs met (Donley, 1990). Placement in a single-parent home decreases the opportunity to engage in such maladaptive behavior.

Single-parent adoption effectively meets the needs of children and adults who would otherwise miss the joys and challenges of a family environment. In almost all situations, single-parent adoption offers benefits far beyond those found in foster or group home placement. Study findings, corroborating those of previous research, show distinctly positive adoptive outcomes and lead to the recommendation of enhanced recruitment of single adoptive parents for special-needs children.

Chapter 8

Focus on Minority Children and Families

Children from minority backgrounds are greatly overrepresented among those in foster care placement and those awaiting adoptive placement. In fiscal year 1985, black children represented 38 percent of the population of children in substitute care and awaiting adoptive placement. In contrast, only 23 percent of children who were adopted through public agencies were black (Tatara, 1988). Some argue that this disparity reflects the reluctance of minority persons to come forward as adoptive applicants; alternatively, others cite the barriers to minority adoption within the child welfare system.

Because of the overrepresentation of minority children in foster care and other factors that will be explored in this chapter, the adoption worker often experiences difficulty in finding an adoptive home for the minority child. These difficulties are compounded for the older or handicapped minority child. The large number of minority children among those awaiting adoption provides minority applicants greater opportunity to adopt a younger child or one with minimal handicap. Thus the older or handicapped minority child loses in a supply-demand market and may face delay in adoption or the possibility of not being adopted at all.

The search for a home also involves difficult choices. A two-parent family with a middle-class income that matches in race—once viewed as the ideal family—may not be available. On the other hand, the child's foster family, perhaps white and of moderate financial means, may be an alternative. But how does this alternative compare with the possibility that a family of the same race, perhaps a single-parent family of modest means, may also be interested in adoption? Finally, a two-parent, educated, and middle-class family that does not "match" the child in ethnicity may be considered.

This chapter addresses ethnicity and cultural patterns as factors affecting adoptive practice and outcome. Three types of adoptions are identified and compared: inracial adoptions by white parents, inracial adoptions by minority parents, and transracial adoptions. Strengths of minority families in the context of special-needs adoption as well as issues specific to transracial adoption are examined.

The research on adoptive outcomes in different types of placements provides helpful clues for shaping adoptive practice. We, however, cannot offer a placement formula that is right for every child. Ultimately, the child's best interests and individual needs, not race, income, or family structure, must guide the placement decision.

ISSUES IN MINORITY ADOPTION

Most professionals in the adoption field support inracial adoption whenever this is possible. For instance, the adoption standards of the Child Welfare League of America (CWLA, 1988) state: "Children . . . have a right to be placed into a family that reflects their ethnicity or race" (p. 34). The CWLA standards recommend that transracial placements be implemented only when "aggressive, ongoing recruitment efforts are unsuccessful in finding families of the same ethnicity or culture" (p. 35). Existing research suggests some possible barriers to minority families in the adoption process, and other studies explore disruption rates among minority adopting families.

Barriers to Minority Families

Barriers to minority applicants may develop at several points, including the earliest stages of the adoptive process. Day (1979) cites a 1966 study (District of Columbia Department of Welfare, tables 4, 8A, and 8B) demonstrating that disproportionate numbers of black birth mothers who desired adoptive counseling were not granted interviews. In a Texas study, a lower percentage of Hispanic family applications as contrasted with white family applications resulted in adoptive placement (Camarata, 1989, p. 23). A National Urban League study found that only two of 800 applications from black families were approved ("Black Children Facing Adoption Barriers," NASW News, April 1984, p. 9, cited in Simon & Alstein, 1987, p. 9).

The relatively low numbers of minority workers in adoptions appears to function as a barrier to the recruitment of minority families. As of 1984, about 83 percent of child welfare workers in the United States were white ("Black Children Facing Adoption Barriers," NASW News, April 1984,

p. 9, cited in Simon & Alstein, 1987, p. 8). Fliegenspan (1979) found that black adoption workers were more likely than white workers to approve black adoptive applicants. Day (1979) found that the percentage of agency social workers who were black was strongly correlated ($r > .80$) with the number of black placements implemented by 16 adoption agencies. Surprisingly, Day's study also found that agency workers with strong identification with the social work profession were less likely to implement placements of black children. Professional identification was measured by factors such as membership in professional organizations, attendance at professional meetings, and use of the professional literature or other information sources.

The low number of minority workers and the limited knowledge of minority cultural patterns can lead to misunderstandings that discourage worker and minority applicant. For instance, Day (1979) describes the black church as a center of community life: "The storefront church probably offers a warmer, more accepting, new community for an adopted child than the homogeneous, competitive suburbs. Unfortunately, white workers [are] put off by religious behavior they do not understand" (p. 63).

Notwithstanding the barriers just discussed, Gershenson (1984a) found that black families adopt children from public child welfare agencies at a rate that is 3.5 times greater than that among white families. Among two-parent families, the rate for black families is about 4.5 times greater. In Gershenson's view, the higher rate for black families shows that the black community is motivated to and successful in adopting minority children. Gershenson contends that the greater difficulty encountered in implementing placements of black children is primarily due to the disproportionate number of black children in the foster care system. Hence, even though minority families are overrepresented among adopters, this overrepresentation does not offset the even greater overrepresentation of minority children in the foster care system.

Disruption Rates in Minority Families

Several studies focus on whether race (of parents or child) affects risk for adoption disruption. Lower disruption rates for minority families have been observed in two studies. A five-state study found that placements with minority parents represented 36 percent of all placements ($n = 143$) but only 18 percent of disruptions (Urban Systems, 1985). In a Colorado study, 35 percent of mothers in a sample of intact adoptions ($n = 23$) but only 11 percent in a sample of disrupted adoptions ($n = 27$) were of minority status (Rosenthal et al., 1988). In contrast to these studies, several studies with larger samples, including a California study of more than 900 placements, show no association between race and disruption rate (Boyne et al., 1984; Festinger, 1986; Barth & Berry, 1988). A study in the northeastern United States found higher disruption rates for minority parents, but factors other than minority status may explain the higher rate (Partridge et al., 1986). A New Zealand study found higher disruption rates for families that were of non-European background (Zwimpfer, 1983).

TRANSRACIAL ADOPTION

Transracial adoption was most popular in the 1960s and early 1970s. Transracial black/white adoption, for instance, peaked in 1971 at about 2,500 adoptions, but had declined to less than half that number by 1975 (Feigelman & Silverman, 1983). The exact number of adoptions in the United States, inracial or transracial, is uncertain as official records have not been available since 1975 (Simon & Alstein, 1987). The issues surrounding transracial adoption have, however, attracted a great deal of attention in social work research.

Psychosocial Adjustment

Numerous studies assess transracial adoption from the perspective of the child's psychosocial adjustment. The overall pattern of findings is distinctly positive, with outcomes similar to those observed in inracial placements. Research studies demonstrate good social adjustments by transracially adopted black children (Grow & Shapiro, 1974), equal levels of satisfaction among white parents adopting white children and white parents adopting black children (Zastrow, 1977), equal levels of self-esteem for black inracial and transracial adoptees (McRoy, Zurcher, Lauderdale, & Anderson, 1982), no difference in the social adjustment of black transracial adoptees and white adoptees when controlling for age (Silverman & Feigelman, 1981), equal levels of self-esteem in Hispanic inracial and transracial adoptees (Andujo, 1988), good adjustments by transracially adopted Native American children (Fanshel, 1972), and good self-esteem and social adjustment among Korean adoptees in United States homes (Kim, 1978). Feigelman & Silverman (1983) found excellent emotional adjustments among transcultural adoptees from Colombia, although many had health problems. Korean adoptees in this study experienced adjustment problems at a lower rate than did white adoptees.

Three British studies also show good outcomes. In Gill and Jackson's study (1983), the great majority of transracial adoptees experienced good outcomes in family relationships, peer-group relationships, level of self-esteem, and in the absence of behavioral disorders. Results of the British

Adoptive Project, an effort to find homes for minority children, usually with white families, were distinctly positive, with few of the children evidencing serious adjustment difficulties (Raynor, 1970, cited in Gill & Jackson, 1983; Jackson, 1976). The final study describes a sample of young (average age 7), predominantly mixed-race children as making good social adjustments in white homes (Bagley & Young, 1979, cited in Gill & Jackson).

Simon and Alstein's longitudinal study (1977, 1981, 1987) presents solid evidence in support of transracial adoption. Their initial sample in 1972 consisted of 204 families. About two-thirds of these families responded to a mailed questionnaire seven years later. Eighty-one percent were judged to be well satisfied with the adoptions, a percentage similar to that found in inracial adoptions. By 1984, about half of the original families had dropped out of the study. At this time, most adoptees were in adolescence. In addition to transracial adoptees, many families also included white (inracial) adoptees and/or birth children. Reports from both parents and children were obtained on a diversity of measures. Parents reported on school grades, relationships with the children, anticipated future relationships, and sibling interactions. Reports regarding the white and transracial adoptees were quite similar. While these reports were largely positive, parent reports for the birth children were more positive still. The child-based reports showed similar self-esteem scores for all three groups of children. The birth children and transracial adoptees indicated greater emotional closeness and commitment to their families than did the white adoptees, who were somewhat older and perhaps more engaged in the adolescent task of separation from family.

While most studies of transracial placement show positive outcomes, some identify problems. Shireman (1988) found predominantly similar social adjustments among transracially adopted black children and four other groups of children. Yet the transracial adoptees, particularly boys, were more likely to experience serious school problems. Falk (1970) found that white parents of black adopted children were less likely to recommend adoption to others and less likely to adopt again than were white parents who adopted inracially. One study of adoption disruption found a higher disruption rate for transracial placements (Groze, 1986), while two found no association to disruption rate (Barth & Berry, 1988; Partridge et al., 1986).

The transracial adoptee and family is more likely to experience hostility or nonsupportive attitudes from relatives and neighbors. Falk (1970) found less support from neighbors, friends and family in transracial as opposed to inracial adoptions. Only 28 percent of parents in Simon and Alstein's (1981) study described aunts, uncles, and grandparents as initially approving and supporting the decision to adopt transracially. At seven or more years following adoption, many parents in the Simon and Alstein study characterized neighbors as nonsupportive. Friends, as contrasted with family and neighbors, were more supportive of the adoption. Zastrow (1977) reported that parents who had adopted transracially encountered less hostility than they had anticipated.

Ethnic Identity

While the majority of studies suggest similar social adjustment among inracial and transracial adoptees, transracial adoption may affect ethnic pride and identity. Andujo (1988) found that Mexican American adolescents who were adopted inracially were more likely than those adopted transracially to identify themselves as Mexican American. In contrast, the transracial adoptees were more likely to identify themselves as American. The inracial adoptees also demonstrated higher levels of pride in their Mexican American heritage. McRoy and colleagues (McRoy et al., 1982) content-analyzed open-ended responses pertaining to self-identity. Transracially adopted black adolescents, in contrast to those adopted by black families, were more likely to identify themselves as adopted. Also, the transracial adoptees were more likely to refer to issues pertaining to race in their self-descriptions.

Feigelman and Silverman (1983) studied three groups of transracially adopted children. Transracially adopted Colombian children evidenced little interest in their Hispanic heritage, presumably because their families had minimal social contact with Hispanic communities. Black and Korean adoptees showed stronger ethnic identifications than did the Colombian children. The Korean children often showed discomfort with their physical appearance. Adolescent transracially adopted Korean children in Kim's study (1978) had little sense of Korean identity and were often rejecting of the characteristically Asian aspects of their physical appearance.

Johnson, Shireman, and Watson (1987) found that inracially and transracially adopted black children had similar racial preferences and racial self-identifications at age 8. Similar preferences were also observed at age 13 (Shireman, 1988). Comparisons between the inracial and transracial adoptees at age 13 showed that the transracial adoptees were more comfortable in white culture and equally comfortable with respect to black culture (Shireman, 1988).

Several studies investigate the impact of living in an integrated community on the transracially adopted child. In Grow and Shapiro's (1974) study, transracial adoptive families often lived in predominately white areas. Those who lived in integrated areas reported more satisfaction with the adoption. Feigelman and Silverman (1983) found no link between integra-

tion of neighborhood and the social adjustment of black transracial adoptees. Yet integration did affect racial identification. Those who lived in
integrated neighborhoods and whose children attended integrated schools
reported that their children evidenced greater pride in and identification
with their black racial heritage. McRoy and colleagues (1982) emphasize
the importance of integrated community life: "If the parents had normal
and frequent contact with blacks and if the child, in turn, had similar
experiences, the child seemed to develop positive racial feelings" (p. 525).

Simon and Alstein (1977) administered projective tests to transracial
adoptees and their siblings. They concluded (Simon & Alstein, 1981):

As a group the children were more racially color blind and more indifferent to
race . . . than any other group reported in any previous study, including studies . . . in the United States . . . and other parts of the world. We found black
children who did not think that white children were smarter, cleaner or more
attractive than themselves. We found white children who did not think that black
children were dumber, meaner, less attractive, and so on (p. 1).

These "color blind" children, from Ladner's (1977) perspective, identified
with the human race rather than with their own racial group.

Concerns and Criticism

Many have questioned the utility and wisdom of a "color blind"
identification for minority children, who will be exposed to racism and
discrimination as a normal course of events (Jones & Else, 1979; Small,
1984). A strong racial identity is viewed as instrumental to the minority
adoptee (Ladner, 1977; Jones & Else; Small; Chestang, 1972). Chestang
emphasizes the pragmatic survival skills taught in black homes:

Can white parents equip a black child for the inevitable assaults on his personality
from a society that considers his color to be enough reason to reject him? . . . How
can the black child learn the necessary maneuvering, seduction, self-enhancement
through redefinition and many other tactics taught by black parents, by word and
deed, directly and indirectly? (p. 103).

Andujo (1988) expresses concerns for the transracially adopted Mexican
American children in her study. Without a sense of ethnic identity, she
questions whether they will develop a "sense of wholeness [and a] feeling
of belonging" (p. 534) in their adult years. She states further, "Once the
adoptees are beyond the confines of the immediate families, they will
experience the same interactive threats all minorities experience in society"
(p. 534).

Small (1984) identifies problems for children of mixed racial background. The adopting family, perhaps wanting a white child, may deemphasize or deny the child's minority or "colored" racial background. The larger society, in contrast, will note even the hint of minority ethnicity (i.e., slightly darker skin) and treat the child accordingly.

Transracial adoption has been criticized on political grounds. Small (1984) states that "the one-way traffic of black children into white families begs fundamental questions of power and ideology" (p. 129) and that the "black community is being used as a 'donor' group for white society" (p. 129). The National Association of Black Social Workers expressed "vehement opposition" to transracial adoption in 1972 (Feigelman & Silverman, 1983, p. 235), and this opposition appears to be continuing into the 1990s.

METHODS

Three major subgroups are formed for analysis. The *white, inracial* placement group is composed of families where all parents (two parents in the two-parent family, or one parent in the single-parent family) are white and the adopted child is also white. The *transracial* placement group is composed of families where all parents are white and the child is of minority status or biracial. In the *minority/mixed, inracial* (or simply *minority, inracial*) placement group at least one parent and the adopted child are of minority status or are biracial. Further, the child "matches" the ethnicity of at least one parent. Where either parent or child was biracial, they were considered to match if they shared any common racial background. For instance, a black parent and a biracial child, black and white, match as both share black ethnicity. The subgroups consisted of 467 placements in white, inracial families, 230 placements in minority/mixed, inracial families, and 63 transracial placements.

The above classification excludes some cases from any subgroup. For instance, three minority or biracial children were placed transracially with minority or biracial parents. Also, 18 families where at least one parent was of minority or biracial ethnicity adopted white children. These cases were excluded so as to more clearly distinguish the three major subgroups. Placements of biracial children who are part white in homes with white parents are included in the transracial group. This decision reflects what might be termed a social definition of race. It recognizes that the suggestion of minority status in physical appearance defines the child as a minority (Jones & Else, 1979; Small, 1984; Chimezie, 1975). The breakdown within the three subgroup classifications varied between the agencies in the study. Specifically, 60 percent (138 of 230) of minority, inracial placements, 51 percent (32 of 63) of transracial placements, but only 31 percent (146 of

467) of white, inracial placements were made by the Illinois DCFS, $p < .01$.

The possible choices for race were white, black, Asian, Native American, Hispanic, and other. The response "Other" usually conveyed a biracial parent or child. Undoubtedly, some children and parents who were biracial from a biological perspective were not categorized as such on this questionnaire.

FINDINGS

Sample and Service Characteristics

Table 8.1 presents the ethnicity of children in the minority, inracial, and transracial groups. A much higher percentage of children in the minority, inracial group are black. In contrast, the percentage of biracial children is higher in the transracial group. The pronounced difference in the ethnicity of the children in these two groups recommends caution in the interpretation of differences in outcome. (All of the children in the white, inracial group are white.)

Tables 8.2 and 8.3 compare the three subgroups on selected characteristics. Table 8.2 demonstrates that children in the white, inracial group were somewhat older at the time of entry into the home. The mean age of parents was oldest in the minority, inracial group, reflecting, in part, more frequent placements with grandparents. Incomes were markedly lower in this group. Table 8.3 highlights numerous differences. For instance, the percentage of children with handicaps is highest in the transracial group. The percentage of children with behavioral problems, defined by a score in the clinical

Table 8.1
Ethnicity of Children

Ethnicity	Minority/ mixed, inracial Freq.	%	Transracial Freq.	%
Black	167	73	6	10
Asian-American	0	0	5	8
Native American	25	11	11	17
Hispanic	15	7	19	30
Biracial (or multiracial)	23	10	22	35

Table 8.2
Selected Characteristics of Subgroups

Characteristic	Minority/ mixed, inracial			White, inracial			Transracial		
	M	SD	n	M	SD	n	M	SD	n
Age of children									
When entered home**	4.6	3.4	227	6.0	3.7	467	5.0	4.0	63
At survey*	11.4	3.5	230	10.6	3.9	467	10.5	4.1	63
Age of parents									
Respondent**	47.5	11.5	215	40.9	7.6	466	42.7	9.2	62
Mother**	47.1	11.5	208	40.6	7.5	455	42.4	8.9	60
Father**	48.1	11.3	139	42.4	7.7	427	44.4	8.9	50
# of children in home*	3.1	1.9	222	2.8	1.7	465	3.4	2.4	62
Family income ($)**	24,864	17,876	162	39,900	22,735	410	37,304	22,578	56

*$p<.05$, **$p<.01$

range on the CBC total problems scale, is highest in the white, inracial group. Adoptions by single parents and relatives were most common in minority, inracial placements. Children placed in minority, inracial homes were least likely to have experienced psychiatric or group home placement or sexual abuse prior to their adoption.

Patterns of contact with the adoption agency social worker varied according to subgroup, with families in the minority, inracial group reporting fewer postplacement visits with adoption agency social workers. Forty-eight percent (106 of 222) in this group reported no in-person contacts with their social worker after the adoptive placement, $p < .01$, compared with 21 percent (97 of 463) in the white, inracial group and 36 percent (22 of 61) in the transracial group. Some of the difference between the groups reflects the influence of other factors such as agency auspices, age of child at placement and at the time of the survey, urban residence, and the kinds of problems experienced by the child. It is noted that differences related to agency auspices reflect the effects of using different sampling methods in the different states. Even when the just-mentioned factors are controlled for in multivariate analysis, findings still suggest less contact for the minority, inracial families, $p = .02$.

Adoption Outcomes

Impact of adoption and parent-child relationship. Adoptive outcomes were most positive in the minority, inracial group. The percentages of

Table 8.3
Family, Child, and Service Characteristics by Type of Placement

Characteristic	Minority/ mixed, inracial %	n	White, inracial %	n	Transracial %	n
Adopted child is female	54	229	46	466	40	63
Adoption by relatives**	21	226	4	461	8	62
Subsidized adoption**	76	217	51	459	72	61
Adoption by foster parents**	53	225	37	465	53	62
Sibling placement	37	218	39	460	31	62
Single-parent adoption (status at placement)**	34	208	8	466	10	63
Adoptive mother graduated from college**	17	219	32	456	34	61
Child is handicapped**	14	230	21	467	38	63
Child has behavioral problems**	29	201	47	416	37	54
Child experienced disruption prior to adoption[a]	7	159	15	290	15	47
Group home or psychiatric placement prior to adopt[a]**	7	159	14	290	23	47
Sexual abuse prior to adopt (actual or suspected)[a]**	15	152	43	281	33	46

[a]Variable not included in Oklahoma DHS and Project Adopt questionnaires, hence, the smaller sample size.

*p<.05. **p<.01

parents reporting that the adoption's impact was very positive were: minority, inracial group, 58 percent (126 of 219); white, inracial group, 41 percent (190 of 465); and transracial group 53 percent (33 of 62), $p < .01$. Scores on the parent-child relationship scale also showed closer relationships in minority, inracial families. Mean scores were: minority, inracial group, 3.53 ($SD = 0.52$, $n = 226$); white, inracial group, 3.26 ($SD = 0.69$, $n = 451$); and transracial group, 3.26 ($SD = 0.71$, $n = 58$), $p < .01$.

The interpretation of why better outcomes are observed in the minority, inracial group is problematic. In large part, the better outcomes reflect the factors highlighted in Tables 8.1, 8.2, and 8.3, for example, the comparatively low incidence of sexual abuse in the minority, inracial group and the relatively higher frequency of behavioral problems or prior psychiatric placement for the adoptees in the white, inracial group. The analyses presented in Chapter 3 and those referred to in a separate article (Rosenthal,

Groze, & Curiel, 1990) suggest a modest trend towards better outcomes in minority families when other factors are statistically controlled for. An analysis comparing outcomes in minority, inracial families with those in transracial families does not offer definitive conclusions regarding outcome (Rosenthal, Groze, Curiel, & Westcott, in press). The reader should realize that a survey design such as is utilized in this study cannot control adequately for all of the possible confounding factors.

Table 8.4 focuses on the parents' assessment of the adoption's impact on the family and the age of the child at entry into the adoptive home. The excellent outcomes, as indicated by the percentage of "Very positive" responses, stand out for the minority, inracial group, particularly for children in the six- to -eight-year-old group.

While most of this chapter focuses on the three defined family subgroups, we also looked at outcomes according to the ethnicity of children irrespective of the family's makeup. The analysis points to very positive outcomes for minority children. For instance, the percentages of "Very positive" responses regarding family impact by ethnicity of the children were: white, 41 percent (198 of 485); black, 55 percent (92 of 166); Asian American, 67 percent (4 of 6); Native American, 61 percent (22 of 36); Hispanic, 65 percent (22 of 34); and biracial, 51 percent (25 of 49), $p < .01$.

School. Children in all three subgroups performed well in school. Among those aged 6 to 17, 100 percent (214 of 215) of children in the minority, inracial group, 99 percent (393 of 397) in the white, inracial group, and 94 percent (51 of 54) in the transracial group were attending school at the time of the survey, $p < .01$. School grades in the semester immediately preced-

Table 8.4
"Very Positive" Responses by Ethnicity of Family and Age at Entry into the Home

Age at entry	Minority/ mixed, inracial %	n	White, inracial %	n	Transracial %	n
Birth to 2 years	63	83	60	113	80	25
3 to 5 years	55	60	39	128	38	13
6 to 8 years	62	50	36	119	42	12
9 to 11 years	35	20	26	73	20	10
12 to 14 years	50	4	32	19	50	1
15 to 18 years	--	0	40	5	--	0

ing the survey were somewhat better in the transracial group, although differences did not achieve significance. The percentages of students earning a "B" average or better in the semester preceding the survey were: minority, inracial group, 52 percent (99 of 191); white, inracial group, 52 percent (167 of 319); and transracial group, 68 percent (28 of 41), $p > .05$. Among the three groups, parents in the white, inracial group were slightly less likely to report that their children enjoyed school: minority, inracial group, 72 percent (158 of 219); white, inracial group, 64 percent (267 of 419); and transracial group, 73 percent (40 of 55). This difference bordered on significance, $p = .06$.

Exploratory Analyses

Support from family and friends. Table 8.5 presents parents' perceptions of support from family and friends. On balance, differences between the groups are small. As expected, the trend is towards less approval and support in the transracial placement group. Given the strong associations of support and approval to outcome (see Chapter 3) and the excellent outcomes in minority, inracial families, the authors' expectation was that these families would report higher levels of support and approval than white, inracial families. Yet reports for these two subgroups were similar.

Family cohesion. While minority, inracial families reported the closest parent-child relationships, these families, paradoxically, scored lowest on a family functioning instrument measuring family cohesion, the overall closeness of family members to one another (FACES III, in Olson et al., 1985; see Chapter 6). The mean cohesion score for minority, inracial placements was 39.4 ($SD = 5.6$, $n = 195$). In contrast, higher levels of closeness were observed in the other two groups. Mean scores were 40.8 ($SD = 4.9$, $n = 455$) in white, inracial placements and 40.0 ($SD = 6.4$, $n = 58$) in transracial placements, $p < .01$. These differences in cohesion were in part due to the higher percentage of single parents in minority, inracial families. Among two-parent families, the same pattern was observed but differences were smaller and no longer significant.

The paradox of closer parent-child relationships and yet lower family cohesion in minority, inracial families intrigued us and suggested the need for more intensive analysis. Hence, we compared minority, inracial families and other families (the other two subgroups combined) on selected items from the cohesion scale. A clear pattern became evident. On those items focused squarely on the closeness of family members, the minority, inracial families actually scored higher on cohesion. For instance, 62 percent (131 of 210) of respondents in these families in contrast to 53 percent (276 of 519) in other families responded "Almost always" to the question "[How

Table 8.5
Support from Family and Friends

Question	Response to question		
	Yes, very much so %	Yes, somewhat %	No, not really %
Do your relatives approve of the adoption?			
Minority/mixed (n = 227)	81	17	2
White (n = 465)	76	22	1
Transracial (n = 62)	76	18	6
Do your spouse's relatives approve of the adoption?*			
Minority/mixed (n = 160)	72	23	5
White (n = 428)	70	26	4
Transracial (n = 52)	56	31	13
Have your friends been supportive of the adoption?			
Minority/mixed (n = 225)	83	14	4
White (n = 466)	81	17	2
Transracial (n = 63)	75	21	5

*p<.05 (T-test using three-point response scale.)

often do] family members feel very close to one another?", $p < .01$. Other items called for respondents to compare closeness, activities, or time with nuclear family members versus that with those outside the nuclear family. On these items, the response pattern was for greater closeness in the group composed of transracial and white, inracial families. For instance, 67 percent (347 of 521) in this group versus only 53 percent (110 of 207) in the minority, inracial group responded "Frequently" or "Almost always" to the question "[How often do] we like to do things with just our immediate family?", $p < .01$. This pattern of findings suggests that the lower score on cohesiveness in the minority, inracial group does not indicate less closeness within the nuclear family; instead, it suggests that family members experience greater closeness with those outside the nuclear family.

Resilience of minority, inracial placements. The findings presented in Table 8.6 convey the resilience of the minority, inracial placements. Factors that might be expected to cause major problems for the parent-child relationship appear not to do so in the minority, inracial adoptive families.

Six factors show different associations to the quality of parent-child relationship in the three subgroups. These factors (see Table 8.6) are

- Adoption by a "new" family (one that had not previously been a foster family to the adoptee)
- Older age of the child
- High family income
- Behavioral problems (measured by the Total Problems scale of the Child Behavior Checklist, Achenbach and Edelbrock, 1983)
- Learning disabilities
- The child's dislike of school

The presence of each factor is strongly associated with problematic parent-child relationship in the transracial placement group. In each case, the strength of association is weaker in the white, inracial group and weaker still in the minority, inracial group. Stated differently, these factors seem to generate serious problems in transracial placements, moderate problems in white, inracial placements, but only minor problems in minority, inracial placements.

Open-ended comments. The open-ended questions (see Chapter 4) encouraged written comments. The comments of the transracially adopting parents were searched for references to racial and ethnic issues. The almost total absence of such comments stood out. Only one negative comment was noted. This respondent commented on "the barrage of disrespect that seems inherent from his Latin background." It was unclear whether this comment referred to disrespect directed from others towards the child or from the child towards, presumably, the parents. One mother responded that it was difficult to learn how to groom the hair of a young black girl.

Several positive comments were noted. Regarding a multiracial boy, one mother commented on "the easy, comfortable way John accepts his different races." Another commented on the rewards of "seeing her grow to like her dark skin and curly hair and be proud of being 'black' rather than ashamed of being 'brown.' "

Response patterns. An unexpected finding was that minority, inracial families were less likely to respond to the first mailing of the questionnaire. Eighty-six percent of white, inracial families (400 of 467), 84 percent of transracial families (53 of 63), but only 70 percent of minority and mixed families (160 of 230) responded to the first mailing, $p < .01$. This finding perhaps resonates the experience of adoption agencies; additional outreach—in survey terms, a second mailing—may be necessary to recruit the involvement of minority families. Given that results suggest lower levels

Table 8.6
Parent-Child Relationship Scores for Factors Interacting with Type of Adoption

Factor	Minority/ mixed, inracial		White, inracial		Transracial	
	M	n	M	n	M	n
Foster family adoption**						
Yes	3.54	117	3.39	168	3.51	30
No	3.53	104	3.17	281	2.99	27
Age of child at survey***						
0 to 5 years	3.52	13	3.66	60	3.80	9
6 to 11 years	3.61	112	3.35	207	3.39	23
12 to 18 years	3.46	101	3.02	184	2.96	26
Family income*						
Less than $50,000	3.53	148	3.30	287	3.37	42
$50,000 or greater	3.65	11	3.09	110	2.80	9
CBC Total Problems score***						
29 or lower	3.69	119	3.65	184	3.68	29
30 or above	3.34	87	2.98	259	2.81	28
Learning disabilities*						
Yes	3.53	52	3.16	128	2.99	22
No	3.54	174	3.30	174	3.43	36
Enjoyment of school						
"Enjoys"	3.66	156	3.41	257	3.49	36
"Likes and dislikes about the same"	3.20	56	2.98	121	2.64	11
"Dislikes"	2.87	3	2.39	27	2.10	4

Note. Significance tests are tests of statistical interaction using either two-factor analysis of variance or multiple regression with the interaction term formed by multiplication of the factors. The interaction term for enjoyment of school, while not significant when all three groups are considered, is significant, $p<.01$, when only the minority/mixed, inracial and transracial groups are included in the analysis.

$^*p<.10$, $^{**}p<.05$, $^{***}p<.01$

of social work contact with minority families, more outreach may be needed.

DISCUSSION AND PRACTICE IMPLICATIONS

Differences between the three subgroups with respect to sample characteristics exceeded expectations. Most notably, children in the minority, inracial group stood out as least "damaged." These children were least likely to have experienced sexual abuse or group home or psychiatric placement prior to adoption. They were least likely to be handicapped and to evidence behavioral problems. The contrast with respect to ethnicity of the children in the minority, inracial and transracial groups stood out. Black children were placed transracially far less often than were other minority children. The transracial placement group is distinguished by an exceptionally high percentage of children with handicaps.

With respect to adoptive outcome, basically good outcomes were observed for all three groups. The exceptionally good outcomes in the minority, inracial group stand out. Differences in outcomes are explained to a considerable degree by differences in sample characteristics (see Tables 8.1 to 8.3).

Issues in Transracial Adoption

Clearly, transracial adoption has changed greatly since the late 1960s and early 1970s. The transracially adopting family then could perhaps be characterized as highly educated and politically liberal. While some families matching this characterization are included in the current study, they have been supplemented by the group of foster parent adopters, many of whom are moderately educated and traditional in terms of family and political values. In terms of adoptive outcomes, transracial adoptions by foster parents were much more successful than were those by "new" parents. The foster parent home provides an opportunity to develop a relationship with the child and make an informed choice prior to adoption. Such an opportunity, an advantage in any special-needs adoption, appears important for families considering transracial adoption.

While scholars have developed convincing theoretical and political arguments against transracial adoption and while some studies identify problematic outcomes, the preponderance of the data in this and other studies supports transracial adoption. In the current study, parents identified few problems and basically responded positively to questions concerning support from family and friends, thereby affirming that transracial adoption is viable for many children.

Changes in attitudes, life-styles, and demographics since the late 1960s and early 1970s mitigate some of the stigma of transracial adoption. As compared with the 1960s, more minority persons in the 1990s carry out working-class and middle-class roles. Also, interracial marriage increased substantially with respect to some minority groups (Ho, 1990). Further, society in the 1990s is increasingly characterized by a diversity of family types, including "blended" families and single-parent families. By 1990, transracial adoption had been a visible part of the national culture for 20 years. The 1960s were characterized by high hopes that the wars against poverty and racism would be won. By 1990, the idealistic hopes of many had been tempered, if not destroyed. Perhaps in this less idealistic but more pessimistic era, persons can make more realistic decisions regarding transracial adoption.

In the 1970s Simon and Alstein (1977) found that children in homes where parents had adopted transracially were "color-blind." The almost total absence of parent comments pertaining to issues of ethnicity and race suggests that the current study has identified a group of color-blind parents. While this blindness carries with it some advantages, parents should recognize that many children will need the opportunity to interact with same-race role models and friends.

In this study, it is not negative outcomes for transracial placements but instead positive ones for minority, inracial placements that argue convincingly for enhanced recruitment of minority families. This is perhaps most important for minority children with handicaps, as they are most likely to be placed transracially. The high percentage of transracial adoptions by foster parents generates the recommendation that minority parents be recruited for foster family placements that have the potential of becoming adoptive placements. The recruitment of more minority persons into the social work profession and the adoptions field is integral to the recruitment of minority parents. This will increase the comfort of minority applicants and the agency's understanding of minority families and communities.

Minority, Inracial Families

Many special-needs adoptees come from birth families where behavior was dysfunctional and often violent and where educational achievement was neither valued or rewarded. Consequently, these children often bring behavior problems and poor academic skills into the adoptive home. The adoptive family's ability to deal effectively with these issues is of central importance. Minority, inracial placements were distinguished from the other subgroups by the fact that problems with behavior and in school appear less damaging to the quality of parent-child relationship. Study findings suggest that many parents and children in minority, inracial families maintain close parent-child relationships even when the children experience serious problems in behavior or school. This resilience of parent-child relationship conveys a strong acceptance of the child as a valued family member and is a distinct asset in special-needs adoption.

Many minority communities (and working-class and lower-income communities as well) have greater tolerance for misbehavior and for modest academic achievement than do many middle- or upper-income, (often) white communities, which may place greater emphasis on academic achievement. Further, the values and norms of the minority or lower-income community may be more congruent with the experiences and expectations of the adopted child. This may facilitate transition into the home and increase the child's comfort with his environment.

In minority, inracial placements, parent-child relationships remain as close with teens as with younger children. This same pattern was not observed in the other subgroups. The close relationships between teens and adoptive parents in minority, inracial homes suggest that inracial placement may offer distinct advantages for older children. Particularly where problems arise due to discrimination or racism, minority parents possess experience-based problem-solving skills with which to help their children. The data suggest that relationships between minority teens and their parents are more often problematic in transracial placements. Issues or conflicts pertaining to racial identity undoubtedly strain parent-child relationships in many transracial adoptive homes.

MINORITY FAMILY SYSTEMS

Theory, research, and practice-based knowledge about family life often proceed on the undocumented assumption that the norms of the majority culture are best and most desirable for all, including ethnic minority groups (Mindel & Haberstein, 1976; Rodman, 1968). Such assumptions in adoption practice discriminate against and discourage minority and lower-income applicants.

Ho (1987) identifies six factors of minority family life: (1) racism, (2) for many, poverty, (3) stress stemming from value and procedural conflicts with external systems, (4) a common group history, often with immigrant status and distinctive physical traits, (5) a dual identity, functional in both minority and majority culture, and (6) varying degrees of English proficiency. While these factors define minority life as different and as unique, some factors may also define it as disadvantaged.

The social environment of the minority family is not unlike that of the adopted child. Kirk's seminal work in the early 1960s (Kirk, 1984) recognized the prejudice and disfavored social status of the adoptee and his or her family; Kirk's term was role handicap. Like the minority family, the adopted child experiences rejection and is "different." The authors posit that minority families identify with the adopted child's "minority" status. This identification enhances empathy and facilitates the child's transition into family and community.

Grier and Cobbs (1968) argue that Blacks are bound to the concept of equality; fairness and opportunity are core values. The provision of opportunity to the adopted child is congruent with this value. The adoptee's role handicap may kindle the strong sense of equality and opportunity in the black community.

The black family traditionally maintains an extensive kinship network of blood-related and nonrelated persons (Janzen & Harris, 1986). Nuclear family boundaries may be less rigid; strong linkages—across and within generations, with relatives and nonrelatives alike—are normative. These networks function as support systems to parent and child.

Black communities have a strong tradition of providing homes to children in need. As many persons grow up outside of the nuclear family, stigmatization is reduced. The adopted child is likely to encounter peers who are also being raised outside of the birth home. Seeing others in similar circumstances, the child is more likely to see himself as belonging and less likely to ask himself, "What did I do wrong that my situation is so different from those around me?"

Minority families scored slightly lower on the family cohesion measure. This may be an asset in the context of special-needs adoption. As discussed earlier, the lower cohesion score suggests that boundaries between the nuclear family and other systems are open and inclusive rather than exclusive. Many adoptees experienced rejection by previous parent figures. Close, intense relationships with new parents require social and emotional skills that they may not possess. If pushed too quickly into such relationships, acting-out behavior or even disruption may ensue. The flexible family boundaries of many minority families with increased opportunity for interaction with those outside the nuclear family may be preferable. This flexibility enables child and parent to develop a close relationship in a less pressured, less intense context.

Cognitive development studies have characterized Hispanic children as field dependent (Buriel, 1975; Ramirez & Price-Williams, 1974), that is, as having an external (environmental) rather than internal (self) orientation in decision making. As such, they are sensitive to environmental cues and may be less assertive, less individualistic, and less self-directing than their white-majority peers, many of whom are field independent. The field dependency concept may also be applied to Hispanic families in their interactions with external systems. Families direct less effort towards planning their future and more to adapting to what they perceive to be their fate. The saying *si Dios quiere*, "if it is God's will," expresses this orientation.

Such an orientation may be an asset in special-needs adoption. Adjustment to the adoptive family is a long-term process, often with prolonged behavioral management problems. While effective problem-solving skills are needed, equally important is patience, an ability to take one day at a time. In a paradoxical way, the day-to-day issues of economic survival faced by many minority and lower-income families may also be an asset. When one is focused on such issues, problems related to child behavior or modest school performance may seem less important and therefore less problematic.

The tolerance of many minority families was clearly demonstrated in this study; good parent-child relationships were often observed even when children exhibited behavior or school problems. Ho (1987) emphasizes that Hispanic and Native American families are influenced by a "being-in-becoming" orientation (p. 232). Achievement is deemphasized and the inherent self-worth and dignity of each person is recognized. Such a recognition of self-worth, even when personal relationship is strained or task performance is marginal, is at the heart of the excellent outcomes observed for minority families.

Chapter 9

Focus on Children with Handicaps

In special-needs adoption, children with handicaps represent a distinct and significant group. Because of their physical or mental impairments or medical problems, these children present unique challenges to child welfare services and to their adoptive parents. This chapter focuses on the 20 percent of study children (163 of 799) with vision, hearing, and other physical impairments, mental retardation, or serious medical conditions; the term *handicap* is used to apply generally to these conditions. Adoptive outcomes for children with handicaps are contrasted with those of children with other conditions, including learning disabilities, developmental delays, and behavior problems. Comments of parents are presented as exemplars of the particular rewards and problems often encountered.

LITERATURE REVIEW

The research on adopted children with handicaps shows some contradictory results, but on balance suggests that these adoptions are successful and provide parents with significant satisfaction. In general, the research has focused on the risk for disruption, factors associated with adoptive outcome, and characteristics of children with handicaps and the families who adopt them.

Several studies examine the association of handicap to risk for adoption disruption. Boneh (1979) found that both cognitive disability and physical disability predicted disruption. In Nelson's (1985) study, intellectual impairment was a modest predictor of adoption dissolution. In contrast, physical impairment was unassociated with dissolution. In a New Jersey–

, neurological handicap, retardation, and orthopedic handicap
ociated with risk for disruption (Boyne et al., 1984). The
presence of a nonorthopedic physical handicap was associated with reduced
risk. In a multistate study of special-needs adoption, children with physically and mentally disabling conditions were modestly underrepresented
among those whose adoptions disrupted (Urban Systems, 1985). In contrast, Partridge and colleagues (1986) found that the number of mental,
intellectual, physical, or medical problems of adoptees was moderately
associated with increased risk. Rosenthal, Schmidt, and Conner (1988)
assessed language, gross-motor, fine-motor, and academic skills. Higher
skill levels were modestly associated with intact outcome, but the association did not achieve significance. Coyne and Brown (1985) found a
disruption rate of 8.7 percent in a sample of 693 developmentally disabled
children, a rate that was lower than had been anticipated.

Other studies focus on intact families. Nelson (1985) found that 73
percent of families that adopted special-needs children were well satisfied
with the adoption. Given that intellectual and physical impairment were not
mentioned as significant predictors of parental satisfaction with the adoption, it can be deduced that the level of satisfaction of parents who adopted
children with these conditions is similar to that in the sample as a whole.
Franklin and Massarik (1969a, 1969b, 1969c) studied adoptions of children
with minor, moderate, and severe medical conditions. On balance, these
conditions caused less restriction of family activities than had been anticipated. Ratings of parental role satisfaction were good or excellent in 77
percent of adoptions. Particularly good outcomes were demonstrated for
lower-class families and upper-class families; results were less positive
among middle-income families, who were "perhaps too preoccupied
with . . . upward mobility to enlist [their] resources to cope with the
medically impaired child" (Franklin & Massarik, 1969c, p. 598). Glidden
and colleagues (Glidden, Valliere, & Herbert, 1988) observed highly
positive family impacts in a sample of British families that adopted mentally
retarded children or fostered them on a long-term basis. For instance, "62
percent of the mothers responded that they had become better people as a
result of the adoption, citing changes such as greater tolerance, less
selfishness, more sympathetic attitudes, and increased compassion"
(p.122). Gath (1983) observed highly positive family impacts in a follow-up
study of seven families who adopted or fostered children with Down's
syndrome.

Hockey (1980) examined adoptions of mentally retarded children. Outcomes in this study were more guarded than those previously described;
about one-quarter of the adoptions failed from the perspective of adoptee-
parent relationship. A key predictor of positive parent-child relationship

was the adoptive family's knowledge of the child's background and potential; more positive outcomes were observed when background information was provided. Upper-class families as contrasted with those with lower incomes experienced problems more often, particularly when they adopted children with mild retardation.

Several studies address the characteristics of and motivations of parents who adopt children with special needs and handicaps. Feigelman and Silverman (1983) found that families with lower incomes indicated a greater willingness to adopt children who were mildly retarded. They also found that single parents, fertile couples (as contrasted with infertile), and parents who shared child care tasks were more likely to adopt children with disabilities. Chambers (1970) found that families of lower social class and with shorter marriages and fathers with lower educational attainment were more willing to adopt children with intellectual handicaps. In Franklin and Massarik's study (1969a) "qualifications usually thought to influence eligibility adversely were significantly associated with placement of children with medical conditions" (p. 463). Factors associated with placement of these children included older age of the mother, fertility in the adopting couple, and the presence of at least two children in the home. This study showed that children with severe as opposed to moderate or minor conditions were most likely to be placed in families with lower social class position.

Deiner and colleagues (1988) found that most families adopting special-needs children were motivated by a prior attachment to the child formed either as foster parents or in some other capacity. The adopting parents had modest incomes and were often active in church. In contrast, in Glidden's study (Glidden et al., 1988) parents adopting retarded children were most often professional and highly educated.

To summarize, the balance of studies indicates that most parents who have adopted children with handicaps derive considerable satisfaction from these adoptions and that most such adoptions can be characterized as successful.

DEFINITION OF HANDICAP AND OTHER CONDITIONS

A wide range of conditions is encompassed by the study definition of handicap. Because the data reflect parents' perceptions reported in the mailed questionnaire rather than technical assessments or determinations, several refinements were necessary to clarify the data for effective analysis.

Handicap Conditions

Vision, hearing, and physical impairment. Only children who were enrolled in classes for the blind or visually impaired are included in the blind and vision impairment category. This restrictive definition excludes children with minor problems correctable by glasses. In contrast, all children whose parents indicated a hearing impairment are included in this category. The category of physical impairment includes a variety of conditions perceived by parents as handicaps. A partial list of responses includes crippled legs, partial paralysis, short arm and leg, brittle bone disease, limp, and poor coordination.

Serious medical conditions. Some of the chronic medical conditions mentioned by parents were judged by the researchers as potentially minor impairments. Hence, medical conditions were categorized as either minor or serious, and the minor conditions were excluded from the definition of handicap. A partial list of serious conditions includes epilepsy, heart problems, spina bifida, kidney and bladder problems, leukemia, and pulmonary hypertension. Some of the more common minor conditions were asthma, allergies, bronchitis, ear infections, obesity, and migraine headaches.

Within the category of serious medical conditions, a subgroup of children with life-threatening conditions was identified and analyzed separately. These conditions include osteosarcoma, muscular dystrophy, leukemia, and pulmonary hypertension.

Mental retardation. Based on parent reports, this category includes some children with mild intellectual deficits that might not meet the formal definition of retardation. Other children are severely or profoundly retarded.

Other handicaps. Two children with conditions that did not fit into any of the foregoing categories were included in the handicapped group: their impairments were "moderately severe burn scars" and "grade three brain bleed." In addition to the subgroup of children with life-threatening conditions, three other subgroups were identified: cerebral palsy, Down's syndrome, and seizure disorders.

Other Subgroups

Nonhandicap conditions. Results are presented for three conditions (developmental delays, learning disabilities, and behavior problems) that do not meet the study definition of handicap. The developmental-delay group is composed of children with mild or moderate delay in, for example, speech and language, fine- and gross-motor skills, or physical growth.

Delays in social and emotional functioning, for instance, conditions such as immaturity or short attention span, were not considered developmental delays. To distinguish developmental delays from mental retardation, mentally retarded children were specifically excluded. Thus, where both mental retardation and developmental delays were indicated by parents, the child was included in the mental retardation group but not in the developmental delay group. The learning disabilities group includes some children who are slow academically but who would not be considered learning disabled by formal criteria. The behavior problem group is defined by a score in the clinical range on the Total Problems Scale of the Child Behavior Checklist (Achenbach & Edelbrock, 1983), indicating a level of behavioral problems at approximately the 90th percentile or higher with respect to the sample of typical children that forms the checklist norms.

Multiple conditions. With the exception that a child cannot be in both the developmental-delay group and the mental retardation group, the aforementioned groups are not mutually exclusive. Thus, some children have more than one handicapping condition; others may have a handicapping condition and some other condition. For instance, a child could be hearing impaired, have a serious medical condition, and have learning disabilities.

Two additional subgroups were identified. The handicap and behavior problems group consists of children who meet the study definition for both behavior problems and handicap. The multiple handicaps group is composed of children with more than one handicapping condition. Vision, hearing, or other physical handicap, serious medical condition, and mental retardation are the specific conditions utilized in developing this group. The group ($n = 60$) consists of 39 children (65 percent) with two conditions, 19 (32 percent) with 3 conditions, and 2 (3 percent) with five conditions. While the reliance on parent reports made some misclassification unavoidable, the majority of children are classified appropriately.

FINDINGS

Characteristics of Families and Children

Tables 9.1 and 9.2 present selected characteristics for families of children with and without handicaps. The children with handicaps were younger at the time of adoption and were adopted by families with, on average, lower incomes. Children with handicaps were more often adopted by foster parents and single parents. The lower mean income in families who adopted handicapped children is only partially explained by the overrepresentation of single-parent and foster parent adopters among these families. Incomes of families who adopted children with handicaps were lower even when

Table 9.1
Selected Characteristics of Families by Handicap Status (Continuous Variables)

Characteristic	Children with handicaps			Children without handicaps		
	M	*SD*	*n*	*M*	*SD*	*n*
Age of child						
When entered home	4.2	3.7	162	5.9**	3.6	634
At survey	10.6	3.9	163	10.9	3.8	636
# of years child in home	6.3	3.8	162	5.0**	3.2	634
Age of parents						
Respondent	43.3	9.6	160	43.0	9.5	618
Mother	43.2	9.5	156	42.5	9.3	599
Father	44.3	10.0	124	43.8	8.8	520
Total # of children living in home	3.3	2.1	161	2.9*	1.8	626
Family income ($)	31,274	24,430	135	36,785**	21,527	522

*$p<.05$, **$p<.01$

statistical controls for these factors were introduced. These families more often received financial subsidies and tended to be larger. Children with handicaps were less likely to be placed with siblings or to have been sexually abused prior to adoption.

The racial background of children in the sample does not vary between children with handicaps and those without; however, the racial backgrounds of the adopting parents differ. A higher percentage of handicapped children were adopted by white parents. This difference in percentages is explained by transracial placement. Considering only minority and biracial children, 44 percent (26 of 59) of handicapped children but only 17 percent (40 of 237) of nonhandicapped children were placed transracially. This difference reached significance, $p < .01$.

Adoption Outcomes

Impact on the family. Responses are similar for families adopting children with and without handicaps. In both groups, 47 percent of

Table 9.2
Selected Characteristics of Families by Handicap Status (Dichotomous Variables)

Characteristic	Children with handicaps %	Children with handicaps n	Children without handicaps %	Children without handicaps n
Adopted child is female	44	162	49	635
Respondent is female	90	163	84	634
Either parent a biologi-cal relative of child	6	161	11	626
Child minority or biracial	38	160	38	633
At least one parent minority or biracial	23	161	34**	626
At least one parent same race as child	83	157	93**	626
Subsidized adoption	82	160	55**	613
Adoption by foster parents	55	161	40**	630
Sibling placement	23	158	41**	620
Single-parent adoption	22	157	14*	616
Adoptive mother graduated from college	26	155	28	613
Adoptive mother works at paid job[b]	53	118	63	498
Child experienced disrup-tion prior to adoption[a]	12	123	12	391
Group home or psychiatric placement prior to adopt[a]	15	123	13	391
Sexual abuse prior to adopt (actual or suspected)[a]	17	121	39**	373

[a]Variable not included in Oklahoma DHS and Project Adopt questionnaires, hence, the smaller sample size.

[b]Based on two-parent families only.

*$p<.05$, **$p<.01$

respondents report that the impact of the adoption on the family was very positive (see Table 9.3). Distinctly positive impacts are evident for the subgroup of children with Down's syndrome, with 78 percent of this group responding "Very positive." Highly positive impacts were also reported for children with serious medical conditions and for children with multiple handicaps.

Parent-child relationship. Table 9.4 presents four items probing parent-child interactions. On all questions, a substantial majority of parents report positive interactions. While the reports of parents of children with handi-

Table 9.3
Impact on Family, Parent-Child Relationship, and CBC Total Problems Score

Condition	N	Percent who responded "Very positive" regarding impact of adoption on family	Mean score on parent-child relationship scale	Mean score on CBC total problems scale
All handicapping conditions	163	47	3.39	41.1*
Vision, hearing, or physical	92	51	3.37	40.5
Blind or vision	8	57	3.68	26.5
Deaf or hearing	30	46	3.43	39.3
Physical handicap	64	52	3.33	43.0
Mental retardation	84	49	3.43	45.3**
Serious medical condition	62	60	3.43	37.5
Specific conditions				
Cerebral palsey	19	50	3.60*	32.2
Down's syndrome	9	78**	3.93**	26.1*
Seizure disorder	16	56	3.42	47.7
Life-threatening condition	16	60	3.26	38.2
Multiple handicaps	60	59	3.44	43.6
Children without handicaps	636	47	3.33	35.6*
Nonhandicap conditions				
Learning disabilities	227	39**	3.24**	47.4**
Developmental delays	105	37**	3.17*	48.3**
Minor medical	83	42	3.33	43.9**
Behavior problems	286	21**	2.96**	61.6*
Handicap and behavior problems	63	31**	3.07**	60.9**
Full Sample	799	47	3.34	36.7

Note. Because of missing values, sample size is approximate. All tests of significance compare cases that possess condition that defines that group to cases that do not possess condition.

*p<.05, **p<.01

Table 9.4
Selected Questions on Parent-Child Relationship by Handicap Status

Question	Children with handicaps		Children without handicaps	
	Freq.	%	Freq.	%
How do you and your child get along?				
Very well	110	68	411	65
Fairly well	44	27	197	31
Not so well	5	3	19	3
Very poorly	2	1	5	1
Do you feel close to your child?				
Yes, very much so	110	68	353	56
Yes, for the most part	37	23	223	35
Not sure	7	4	28	4
No	7	4	30	5
How often do you and your child spend time together which you both enjoy?				
Just about every day	120	74	418	67
About two or three times per week	25	15	142	23
About once a week	9	6	46	7
About once a month	5	3	13	2
Less than once a month	3	2	9	1
How would you rate the communication between you and your child?				
Excellent	78	48	243	38
Good	59	37	290	46
Fair	20	12	79	12
Poor	4	2	21	3

Note. No comparisons achieve significance.

caps are slightly more positive on each question, no differences achieved statistical significance. The question addressing closeness of relationship bordered on significance, $p = .051$.

Mean scores on the parent-child relationship scale do not reveal statistically significant differences between families adopting handicapped versus nonhandicapped children, $t = 0.89$ ($df = 771$), $p > .05$. The mean score for parents of children with handicaps was 3.39 ($n = 148$, $SD = 0.67$) while the mean for other parents was 3.33 ($n = 625$, $SD = 0.65$; see also Table 9.3). Outcomes for children with handicaps contrast markedly with those for children with conditions that do not define them as handicapped. For instance, behavior problems are strongly associated with negative outcomes. To a lesser degree, so also are learning disabilities and developmental delays. The data do not suggest that children who have both handicaps and behavior problems experience worse outcomes than do those who have behavior problems only. However, the higher mean score on the CBC Total Problems Scale for children with handicaps suggests the possibility that handicap may increase the possibility of behavioral problems (see Table 9.3).

The characteristics presented in Tables 9.1 and 9.2 were assessed for possible association to score on the parent-child relationship scale. This analysis was restricted to children with handicaps. For the most part, these associations were similar to those observed in the full sample. Younger age at entry into the adoptive home, younger age at the time of the survey, minority or biracial status of at least one adoptive parent, adoption by foster parents, lower family income, the adoptive mother not having graduated from college, and having the mother as respondent to the questionnaire predicted more positive parent-child relationship. These factors were significantly associated at the .05 level or below. The child's race bordered on significance; minority or biracial status predicted good relationship. Sexual abuse or group home or psychiatric placement prior to adoption predicted more problematic relationship, but these associations did not achieve significance, in part due to limited statistical power.

Factors interacting with handicap status. Three variables appear to interact with handicap status in the prediction of score on the parent-child relationship scale. These variables show different patterns of association for children with and without handicaps. The first interaction involves adoptions by foster parents. In these adoptions, parent-child relationship scores are slightly higher for children with handicaps than for children without handicaps. Yet in adoptions by "new" (nonfoster) families, the pattern is reversed, with slightly lower scores for children with handicaps than for children without. The second interaction involves family income. In families with moderate incomes (up to $50,000) handicapping condition is unassociated with parent-child relationship score. Yet in families with high incomes ($50,000 and above) handicapping condition predicts problematic parent-child relationship. Finally, gender of the respondent interacts with handicap status. Adoptive fathers report more problematic relationships when the child is handicapped. In contrast, when mothers respond, handicap status of the child is unassociated with parent-child relationship score. Table 9.5 presents these interactions.

The most pronounced interaction effect concerns family income. This interaction remains significant ($p < .05$) in factorial analysis of variance blocking for handicap status, foster parent adoption, gender of respondent, and high versus low income. The other interactions should be interpreted more tentatively. Even though the interactions reach statistical significance, they are of modest to moderate strength and convey general trends rather than compelling differences.

Family. The Family Adaptability and Cohesion Evaluation Scales (FACES III, in Olson et al., 1985) assess two dimensions of family functioning. The cohesion scale measures the emotional bonding between family members, while the adaptability scale measures flexibility in power structure, role relationships, and relationship rules (Olson et al., p. 3). Norms, based on a national sample of typical families, are available for both scales (see Chapter 6 for greater detail on FACES III).

Compared to the representative sample, families who adopted children with handicaps demonstrate greater adaptability. Their mean score on the adaptability scale was 25.7 ($SD = 5.2$, $n = 142$), while the mean in the

Table 9.5
Factors Interacting with Handicap in Prediction of Parent-Child Relationship

Factor	Children with handicaps		Children without handicaps	
	M	*n*	*M*	*n*
Type of adoption[**]				
Foster parent	3.59	81	3.41	250
Nonfoster parent	3.13	65	3.28	369
Family income[**]				
Less than $50,000	3.44	107	3.36	390
$50,000 or greater	2.61	16	3.19	122
Respondent[*]				
Adoptive mother	3.43	133	3.34	525
Adoptive father	3.00	15	3.32	98

Note. Significance tests pertain to the interaction effect.

[*]$p<.05$, [**]$p<.01$

normative sample was 24.1 ($SD = 4.7$, $n = 2453$). This difference reaches significance, $t = 3.59$ ($df = 2593$), $p < .01$. The mean score for these families was also higher than that for families who adopted children without handicaps (mean $= 24.7$, $n = 586$), t $= 2.11$ ($df = 726$), $p < .05$.

Similar levels of cohesion were observed among families that adopted children with handicaps (40.2, $SD = 6.1$, $n = 148$), those that adopted children without handicaps (40.3, $SD = 5.2$, $n = 594$) and those that form the normative sample for FACES III (39.8, $SD = 5.4$, $n = 2453$).

School. Almost all children ages 6 to 17 were attending school, including 97 percent (135 of 139) of children with handicaps and 99 percent (560 of 564) of other children. Of those attending school, 76 percent (102 of 135) of children with handicaps and 29 percent (164 of 560) of others were enrolled in special education curriculum either part-time or full time. Seventy-five percent (112 of 150) of parents of handicapped children in contrast to 65 percent (377 of 580) of other parents reported that their children enjoyed school (see Table 9.6); this difference bordered on significance.

Perceptions of Services and Support Systems

While social work services were, on balance, evaluated positively, parents of children with handicaps evaluated these services as somewhat less helpful than did other parents (see Table 9.6). The parents' perception of the accuracy of background information was, as expected, an important predictor of the parent's global rating of the impact of the adoption; for parents who adopted children with handicaps, this variable (measured on a three-point scale) correlated at .34 ($n = 143$, $p < .01$) with the adoption's impact on the family.

Families who adopted children with handicaps participated in various counseling and support services subsequent to the adoptive placement. Forty-two percent of children (67 of 158) received individual therapy (counseling), with 35 percent of parents (22 of 62) responding that these services were "Very helpful." Twenty-eight percent of families (45 of 158) participated in family therapy, with 39 percent (16 of 41) describing the services as "Very helpful"; 23 percent participated in parent support groups (37 of 159), with 50 percent (17 of 34) responding that they were "Very helpful"; and 43 percent (69 of 160) were in contact with other special-needs parents, with 49 percent (32 of 65) responding, "Very helpful."

Table 9.6 shows that parents of children with handicaps were somewhat more likely than other parents to be in contact with other parents of special-needs children. Findings may also be compared with the full sample (see Table 3.4). This comparison shows that parents of children with

Table 9.6
Enjoyment of School, Helpfulness of Services, and Contact with Special-Needs Parents

Condition	N	Responded that child "enjoys school"	Responded "Yes, very much so" regarding helpfulness of social work services	In contact with other special-needs parents since placement
			Percents	
All handicapping conditions	163	75	46**	43**
Vision, hearing, or physical	92	76	46*	36
Blind or vision	8	75	50	29
Deaf or hearing	30	77	54	41
Physical handicap	64	76	41**	33
Mental retardation	84	77*	46	52**
Serious medical condition	62	81	53	55**
Specific conditions				
Cerebral palsy	19	81	50	28
Down's syndrome	9	100	56	78**
Seizure disorder	16	75	53	27
Life-threatening condition	16	88	31	73**
Multiple handicaps	60	79	43*	55**
Children without handicaps	636	65	57**	28**
Nonhandicap conditions				
Learning disabilities	227	58**	49	35
Developmental delays	105	57*	42**	37
Minor medical	83	64	51	25
Behavior problems	286	52**	44**	39**
Handicap and behavior problems	63	65	38*	52**
Full Sample	799	67	55	31

Note. Because of missing values, sample size is approximate. All tests of significance compare cases that possess condition that defines that group to cases that do not possess condition.

*$p<.05$, **$p<.01$

handicaps were somewhat more likely to seek out all of the just-described services.

PARENT COMMENTS

In response to the survey's open-ended questions about the rewards and difficulties of the adoption, parents of children with handicaps sounded many of the same themes as other adopting parents. Other comments, however, clearly reflect the unique challenges facing children with handicaps and their families.

Services

While most reported that their social workers were helpful, supportive, and accessible, other parents identified areas of concern. Some parents responded that workers were insensitive to or uninterested in the needs of children with severe handicaps. One parent, for instance, noted that her social worker did not seem comfortable in the presence of her child, who was quadriplegic and also mentally retarded. Some parents commented on the heavy work demands on their workers and said that they had to "push" their workers to submit the necessary paperwork. In contrast, others noted that their social workers helped them with the legal and technical issues and thereby expedited the adoptive process. The social workers' knowledge of available services and help in linking families with these services was a key determinant of parent satisfaction.

Many parents described their financial subsidies as essential. One parent commented, "Our worker made sure we had a subsidy that covered everything needed by the child at the time of placement and in the future." In some instances, medical benefits did not adequately cover needed services leading to financial and emotional hardship for parent and child. One parent stated: "They provided me with some helpful information, but I need *services*. . . . They did not know my son would have hearing and speech problems, and be a slow learner." Even though some parents realized the extent of the child's handicap, they underestimated the extent of services that would be required. Other parents recognized that service needs would increase over time. Here are some selected parent comments.

Dane [boy, age 15, with brain damage and bent fingers from abuse] was older when placed, which presents a whole different set of problems. Some problems were not found until after placement or after finalization. Expenses for this type of adoption—medical, therapy, et cetera—were higher than expected.

As Emily [girl, age 6, with intellectual functioning at 6-month level] grows bigger, longer, and heavier, we grow older and less able to cope with the muscular tasks that are necessary in Emily's care. So far, all is fine, but we see difficulties in the future.

I would ask for more support to help Daniel [boy, age 14, severe scars and facial damage from abuse] adjust and deal with what happened to him. He will need corrective surgery in the next several years on his face and ear.

[Regarding Jimmie, boy, age 5, mild cerebral palsy, developmental delays, and asthma] If I had it to do over again, I would do it in a minute. I would make sure that dollar and hour amounts for therapy, speech, et cetera were clearly spelled out in the subsidy. I would make sure individual and family counseling were also included.

As in the full sample, the greatest dissatisfaction with services among those who adopted children with handicaps related to inaccurate or missing background information. One parent stated: "No information provided. Misrepresented handicap and history. No supportive services at all." Another commented on her 6-year-old daughter, who had cerebral palsy and was severely retarded:

More accurate information would have been medically helpful for us and child. We needed current medical records at time of placement, that is, we did not know that she had been on seizure meds so our doctor did not continue the meds. . . . When we finally realized that Sally had seizures, she had incurred more brain damage that could have been prevented.

Rewards

Parents responded candidly to the open-ended questions probing the rewards and difficulties of the adoptive experience. The comments pertaining to rewards centered on several themes. Mentioned perhaps most often was the joy in seeing children make developmental progress in a variety of areas—social, emotional, learning. Parents took joy in small bits of progress and in the tenacity of the children in spite of their impairments. Many children made progress that exceeded expectations. Also mentioned frequently was the simple joy in receiving love from the children. Some parents indicated that their adoption of a child with handicaps had helped other family members to develop into more caring persons. Here is a sample of parent comments.

Susan [girl, age 3, multiple handicaps] is a delight to work with. Although she is severely handicapped and physically ill a lot, she continues to fight. Her little gains have been giant steps, for she has improved in areas we were not sure she would.

Lucy [girl, age 6, cerebral palsy, mental retardation, and medical problems] has improved so much! From not being able to hold a baby bottle or turn over at 26 months, she is now crawling, sitting, standing, walking with help, feeding herself, saying three words, using sign language, and overall enjoying life. . . . Lucy has showed more love and hope than we ever thought she would.

Seeing Dave [boy, age 11, cerebral palsy and mild retardation] progress from a child labeled "severely retarded in need of long-term custodial care" to a child who is mainstreamed into a regular fourth grade class for academic subjects where he is on the honor roll.

When I think of all the accomplishments Ann [girl, age 14, cerebral palsy and seizures] has made, it makes us all very thrilled for her. She always smiles, regardless of how sick she is. Of course, she has her bad moments. Now that she is a teenager she gets moody.

Watching Jim [boy, age 3, moderate mental retardation] grow and learn—each new step is a cause for celebration.

Tommy [boy, age 5, cerebral palsy and severe retardation] has mellowed our children and they are much more aware of others with handicaps. They take the time to talk to them and to accept people the way they are. They have learned to reach out to others.

Difficulties

Just as parents experienced great joy in their children's developmental progress, their impairments were a source of distress and pain. One parent described the pain of "seeing him [boy, age 6] suffer from seizures and not being able to have them under control no matter how much medicine he is on." Another commented that "being 16 [with borderline retardation] is not easy for him; especially being teased about his lack of reading skills." Behavior problems, sometimes connected with the child's handicap, were mentioned often. One mother stated:

Because of Roger's [boy, age 15, mild retardation] mental disabilities, he lies a lot and does things you would expect from a much younger child. He is always in trouble at school and does not get his work done . . . very demanding when his pills wear off.

Other frequently mentioned problems included financial strain and difficulty in coordinating medical, social, and educational services.

DISCUSSION AND PRACTICE IMPLICATIONS

Families who adopted children with handicaps had lower mean incomes than other families even when controlling for confounding variables that might explain this difference. At least two interpretations are possible. The first is that less affluent families may be more willing to adopt children with handicaps. The second is that family income may influence the decisions of adoption workers; they may view higher-income families as more appropriate for the "healthiest" children, those with the fewest problems.

Closer examination of the data provides at least partial support for the first interpretation. The association between handicap condition and family income level is unique among the different special-needs characteristics. For instance, older age at placement, group home or psychiatric placement prior to adoption, and emotional/behavioral problems did not vary strongly according to income. The tentative interpretation that families with lower incomes may be more willing to adopt children with handicaps is supported by findings from two other studies (Feigelman & Silverman, 1983; Chambers, 1970). Some upper-income families may have experienced difficulty because their expectations were at odds with the child's capacities.

Given the lower mean income in families adopting children with handicaps, one would expect also to find lower educational levels. Yet the parents' educational level was unassociated with handicap status of the child. Given their higher-than-expected educational level, those families who adopted children with handicaps appear to have forgone some income as part of their decision to adopt. Clearly, higher educational level brings considerable advantages in the adoption of a child with handicaps. In particular, the family is better equipped to coordinate the sophisticated medical and educational services that the child may require and to advocate on behalf of the child's needs.

While handicapping condition predicted neither positive or negative outcome, developmental delay and learning disability predicted negative outcome. Some children in the handicapped group possess relatively minor handicaps. Nevertheless, the degree of impairment in development in this group is, on balance, much greater than that in the learning disabled and developmental-delay groups. Hence the major developmental impairments evident in the handicap group appear to be less problematic for the adoption than do the minor impairments that characterize the developmental-delay and learning disability groups. The trend towards better outcomes for children with major impairments is underscored by the particularly good outcomes for those with multiple handicaps and serious medical conditions.

Major impairments are readily apparent to the prospective adoptive parent. One parent responded, "I knew my daughter's problems were massive when I decided to adopt her and I chose to take the good with the bad." In contrast, minor impairments are more difficult to discern and may take the adoptive parent by surprise. Both major and minor impairments as described above affect the adoption's outcome much less than do behavioral problems, which strongly predict negative impact and problematic parent-child relationship (see also Chapter 10).

Children with handicaps experienced better outcomes in adoptions by foster parents. Foster parents have a clear, experience-based understanding of the child's needs and capacities. On the other hand, new (nonfoster) adoptive parents may overestimate the child's capacities or have unrealistic expectations that are untempered by experience.

Families adopting children with handicaps were characterized by high adaptability scores on the FACES III family assessment instrument (Olson et al., 1985). This suggests flexible assignment of tasks and roles and, perhaps, the active involvement of fathers and other children in caring for the handicapped child. Clearly, a flexible approach helps the family in successfully carrying out the multiple tasks and roles involved in raising a child with handicaps. The FACES cohesion results suggest that families with children that have handicaps experience a degree of emotional closeness that is similar to that in typical families. Results in this study for families adopting children with handicaps differed slightly from those of Deiner and colleagues (1988), who found that families who adopted special-needs children scored higher than typical families on both adaptability and cohesion.

Recent thinking regarding biological families with mentally retarded children emphasizes closeness, problem solving, and adaptation rather than pathology and dysfunction (Byrne & Cunningham, 1985). The positive family impacts and family interaction patterns reported in this study support this perspective. The majority of parents report close and rewarding relationships with their children and take considerable joy in the children's accomplishments.

Parents of children with handicaps participated often in parent support groups and also were frequently involved with other parents of special-needs children. Most evaluated these services positively, recommending their expansion. Several parents anticipated increased difficulties in lifting the child and performing necessary physical tasks as the child and parents grew older. Clearly, help in physical care as well as occasional respite care, perhaps for a vacation, are important service needs and underscore the need for a long-term commitment of agency support to the adopting families. Parents regarded their financial subsidies as essential. These subsidies should be comprehensive and long-term and should address individual and family counseling needs as well as medical and educational services.

Among minority and biracial children, those with handicaps were far more likely than others to be adopted transracially; 44 percent in this group but only 17 percent of others were adopted transracially. This finding generates a recommendation of enhanced recruitment of minority parents for minority children with handicaps.

In sum, study findings regarding the adoption of children with handicaps are highly positive. Particularly when the child's specific needs and capacities are well understood prior to the adoption, these adoptions are a rich and rewarding experience for both families and children.

Chapter 10

Focus on the Children's Behavior

A particularly complex aspect of adoption and social work practice revolves around behavioral issues. There are several behavioral dimensions to be considered with adopted children. First, there is the question of emotional adjustment to the adoption itself. Second, evidence of underlying biological or genetic influences on behavior makes it difficult to identify those childhood behaviors that result from environmental causes and those that are linked to the child's physiological makeup. Finally, for special-needs children, there may be a range of life experiences (i.e., abuse, neglect, and multiple prior placements) that shape behavior. These dimensions make behavior a difficult aspect of special-needs adoption to explore but underscore the importance of trying to understand the patterns of behavioral adjustment of special-needs adoptees.

Following a review of the literature that addresses behavioral issues in both infant and special-needs adoption, this chapter shifts the focus of inquiry to an analysis of behavioral issues in the current study of 799 children. We used a standardized behavioral checklist, the Child Behavior Checklist (CBC, Achenbach & Edelbrock, 1983), to compare the behavior of children in the current study with that in several other samples. The comparison groups include the clinical and nonclinical samples that comprise the checklist norms, a sample of children adopted at or near infancy (Brodzinsky, Schechter, Braff & Singer, 1984), and another sample of special-needs adoptees (Berry & Barth, 1989). The chapter also explores the associations of behavioral problems to gender, race, age at entry into the adoptive home, age at the time of the survey, and length of residence in the adoptive family home. Finally, implications for social work practice and for adoptive parents are presented.

PRIOR RESEARCH

Researchers have focused considerable attention on the behavioral adjustment of adopted children. While most investigations have explored behavioral issues related to those adopted as infants, the increase in the number of special-needs adoptions has precipitated several studies. Inquiry has centered on whether adoptees are (1) overrepresented in clinical populations, (2) more prone to behavioral problems, and (3) subject to different kinds of problems than nonadoptees.

Children Adopted At or Near Infancy

Clinical samples. In 1960, Marshall Schechter argued that adopted children were overrepresented among those in psychiatric treatment, beginning a period of significant debate on this subject. Brinich and Brinich (1982) cited 13 authors concurring and eight authors disagreeing with Schechter. McRoy, Grotevant, and Zurcher (1988), summarizing data from 15 studies, concluded that adopted children may be two to five times more likely to be referred for psychological treatment. Kadushin and Martin's (1988) summary suggests that nonrelative adoptees represent 1 percent of all children but almost 5 percent of those in child psychiatric and child guidance facilities.

Adoptees are overrepresented in several pediatric conditions including, most notably, hyperactivity (Dalby, Fox, & Haslam, 1982; Deutsch et al., 1982). Kenny, Baldwin, and Mackie (1967) found a disproportionate number of adoptees in a minimally brain-injured population with many exhibiting "the symptom cluster of hyperactivity, erratic attention span, emotional volatility, and defects in self-control" (p. 27). Reece and Levin (1968) also identified hyperactivity as a frequent problem for adopted children in clinical treatment. Silver (1970) found that the incidence of adoption in a sample of children with neurological learning disability was four times the expected rate.

Several studies demonstrate an association between adoptive status and the pattern of behavioral disturbance exhibited by children in mental health treatment. Specifically, adoptees in treatment appear more likely to experience problems related to aggression, antisocial behavior, or sexual acting out (Menlove, 1965; Offord, Hershey, Aponte, & Cross, 1969; Schechter, Carlson, Simmons, & Work, 1964; Work & Anderson, 1971; Borgatta & Fanshel, 1965, cited in Berry & Barth, 1989; Simon & Senturia, 1966;

Reece & Levin, 1968). Lifschitz, Baum, Balgur, and Cohen (1975, cited in Weiss, 1985) found higher rates of aggressive and delinquent behavior among 6- and 7-year-old adoptees who were referred to a child guidance center. These authors, however, observed lower rates of aggression among adoptees at ages 12 to 13. Weiss found that adopted adolescents in inpatient treatment were more likely to be diagnosed as having adjustment reaction and were more likely to have been arrested prior to admission. This review is selective and does not attempt to cover all studies. Weiss (1985), for instance, cites several studies showing no difference in symptoms or diagnosis between adoptees and nonadoptees.

McRoy, Grotevant, and Zurcher (1988) compared two groups of adolescents in residential treatment. One group was composed of adoptees, while the other was not. For girls only, the adoptees demonstrated higher levels of externalized (acting-out, aggressive, etc.) behavioral problems.

While the balance of findings supports the overrepresentation of children in clinical treatment, this finding by itself is not sufficient to support a conclusion that adopted children are more vulnerable to emotional problems. Adoptive families, in part due to their generally high socioeconomic status, may be more likely to seek treatment (Kirk, Jonassohn, & Fish, 1966). Also, the stresses and uncertainties of adoptive parenthood may lead parents to seek treatment at the earliest sign of difficulty. Notably, the studies reviewed have focused on the childhood and adolescent years, and we are unaware of any significant body of research that suggests an overrepresentation of adult adoptees in clinical or psychiatric treatment. Brinich and Brinich (1982), for instance, found that adoptees represented 5 percent of child patients but only 1.6 percent of adult patients at a psychiatric institute; the representation of adult adoptees was actually below the authors' estimate of their representation in the general adult population.

Nonclinical samples. Brodzinsky and colleagues (1984) administered the Child Behavior Checklist (CBC, Achenbach & Edelbrock, 1983) to parents of adopted and nonadopted children, ages 6 to 11. The adoptees ($n = 130$) were adopted shortly after infancy (mean = 3.2 months, range 3 days to 3 years, 6 months). The nonadoptees ($n = 130$) were matched in terms of age and gender. Adopted girls evidenced greater behavioral problems than did nonadopted girls on both the internalizing (inhibited, withdrawn behavior, etc.) and externalizing (acting-out, aggressive behavior, etc.) scales. Differences were greater in the externalizing area. Comparisons of adopted and nonadopted boys showed adopted boys to have greater problems on the externalizing dimension. Adopted boys scored higher also on internalizing problems, but this difference did not reach statistical significance. In addition to the major internalizing and externalizing scales, the CBC also has numerous subscales. For both boys and girls, the difference between adoptees and nonadoptees was most pronounced on the hyperactivity subscale, with adoptees more often evidencing problems.

Brodzinsky and colleagues (1984) also administered the Hahnemann Elementary School Behavior Ratings to the children. Adopted children scored more poorly on each of the five Hahnemann scales: originality, school involvement, irrelevant talk, negative feelings, and school achievement. Hoopes (1986) found that teachers rated adopted children higher on restless, nervous habits and hostility than a control group of nonadoptees.

Others have also found increased problems in nonclinical samples. Bohman and Sigvardsson's longitudinal study of adopted and nonadopted children showed a greater incidence of emotional problems among 10- and 11-year-old adopted boys but not among girls (Bohman, 1970, cited by Brodzinsky et al., 1984). The boys often evidenced problems of "hyperactivity, poor concentration, poor peer relations, defiance and aggressiveness" (Bohman, 1972, quoted by Hoopes, 1986, p. 3). By age 15, differences between groups were quite small (Bohman and Sigvardsson, 1980) and by ages 18 and 22, no important differences were evident (Bohman & Sigvardsson, 1982, cited in Brodzinsky et al.; Bohman & Sigvardsson). Lindholm and Touliatos (1980) found increased levels of conduct problems, personality problems, and socialized delinquency in a nonclinical sample of adopted children. In contrast to the just-described findings, Brodzinsky and colleagues cited five studies that did not find differences between nonclinical samples of adoptees and nonadoptees. At least two studies showed that adoptees do not experience greater problems than nonadoptees with respect to self-concept, social adjustment, or identity formation (Stein & Hoopes, 1985; Norvell & Guy, 1977); a third study suggests that adoptees may experience more problems in these areas (Simmons, 1980, cited in Stein and Hoopes, 1985).

In sum, a limited body of research on nonclinical populations suggests that adopted children may be at higher risk for behavioral problems. Brodzinsky (1987) contends that this risk is largely limited to the latency and adolescent years. Those younger than about age 6 (Brodzinsky) as well as those who have reached adulthood do not appear to be at greatly increased risk for emotional or behavioral problems. Further, Brodzinsky emphasizes that the great majority of adopted children are functioning within normal levels and may be regarded as free from serious emotional difficulties.

Adopted Children with Special Needs

Research on special-needs adoption primarily has focused on the link between behavioral issues and the risk for adoption disruption. Most investigators have concluded that the presence of behavioral problems greatly increases this risk (Partridge et al., 1986; Urban Systems Research, 1985; Boneh, 1979; Berry & Barth, 1989; Boyne et al., 1984; Reid et al., 1987; Sack & Dale, 1982). Acting-out, aggressive, or externalized behavior as contrasted to withdrawn, inhibited, or internalized behavior is most strongly associated with risk for disruption. Self-abusive behavior and punishment-seeking behavior also appear to predict disruption. For instance, Partridge and colleagues (1986) list six significant ($p < .01$) behavioral predictors: sexual promiscuity, physically injuring others, stealing, vandalizing, threatening or attempting suicide, and wetting or soiling bed or clothes. Sack and Dale describe punishment-seeking behavior, soiling, urinating and smearing feces to express hostility, and stealing and hoarding in a group of children whose adoptions had disrupted. Reid and colleagues (1987) noted two themes in a group of children who had previously been in residential treatment and were adopted when older: (1) "child reacted with extreme verbal abuse or with physical aggression to a typical parent request" (p. 146) and (2) "provocative deviant behavior such as stealing, fire setting, destroying parents' possessions, and running away [resulting in] parents [using] excessive physical force, corporal punishment, name calling [and] threats" (p. 146–147).

Berry and Barth (1989) administered the CBC to 85 families who had adopted children age 3 and older. In about one-third of these families, the adoption had disrupted, while in the rest it remained intact. On both the internalizing (withdrawn, inhibited behavior, etc.) and externalizing (acting-out, aggressive behavior, etc.) scales, the sample in both the disrupted and intact groups evidenced far greater levels of behavioral problems than did the nonclinical sample on which the CBC was normed. Scores of the disrupted and intact groups were similar on the internalizing scale, but the disrupted group demonstrated greater problems among externalizing behaviors. With respect to subscales, scores of both groups were particularly higher than the CBC norms on hyperactivity; this scale did not, however, discriminate between the two groups. Strong distinctions between the intact and disrupted groups were evident on the specific behaviors of threatening people, cruelty and meanness to others, involvement in many fights, and arguing a lot.

Tizard (1979) studied children adopted at 2 years of age or older following institutional placement. At age 8 "between a half and two-thirds of the children were described [by their teachers] as very restless, quarrelsome, disobedient, and attention-seeking at school" (p. 537). Nevertheless, the majority of parents were well satisfied with the adoptions; further, these children demonstrated many fewer problems than children who remained in institutions or were reunited with their families of origin.

THE CHILD BEHAVIOR CHECKLIST

The primary behavioral measure used is the 118-item behavior problems section of the Child Behavior Checklist (Achenbach & Edelbrock, 1983). Two distinct samples provide norms. The clinical sample was composed of children who were at the intake stage of treatment at 42 mental health centers. The children in the nonclinical sample were selected at random from a metropolitan area. Norms were calculated separately for three age groups (4- and 5-year-olds, 6- to 11-year-olds, 12- to 16-year-olds) for each gender. Each CBC item has a three-point response continuum: 0 = Not True, 1 = Somewhat or Sometimes True, and 2 = Very True or Often True. Scale scores are calculated by summing responses to individual items.

The three major scales of the CBC are Total Behavioral Problems, Internalizing, and Externalizing. Internalized behavior is often "fearful, inhibited, [and] overcontrolled" (Achenbach & Edelbrock, 1983, p. 31) while externalized behavior is often "aggressive, anti-social, [and] undercontrolled" (Achenbach & Edelbrock, p. 31). The total problems scale, based on all 118 items, cuts across all age/gender groups. Internalizing and externalizing scales are also available for each group, but within each group different items comprise the scales. As mentioned earlier, these scales represent the major dimensions of behavior. Within each group there are also numerous shorter scales, most of which measure subdimensions of internalizing and externalizing behavior. Specific subscales differ from group to group, although there is considerable overlap.

The chapter reports normalized T scores for internalizing and externalizing. These scores are scaled so that the mean score of the nonclinical group is approximately 50 points, with a standard deviation of about 10 points. Further, the shape of distribution of these scores is more in accordance with the normal curve than is that of the raw scores. Higher T scores indicate higher problem levels.

The CBC definition of the clinical range is helpful in interpreting findings. For the Total Problems, Internalizing, and Externalizing scales, the clinical range is defined approximately as a score in the upper 10 percent of the nonclinical normative group; the exact percentage differs by group and scale. In other words, a score in the clinical range conveys that a child has more pronounced behavioral problems than about 90 percent of his or her peers. In the six CBC age/gender groups, the percentage of children in the clinical sample scoring in the clinical range on the total problems scale ranged from 71 to 77 (see Tables 10.3 and 10.4). These consistently high percentages support the validity of the clinical range in discriminating clinically significant behavior. For the subscales, the clinical range represents approximately the upper 2 percent of the nonclinical sample.

To compare across age and gender groups, we developed two scales based on but distinct from the CBC's own internalizing and externalizing scales. Our crosscutting scales are composed of the 20 items common to each of the six CBC age/gender externalizing scales (alpha = .91) and the 18 items common to each internalizing scale (alpha = .82). For both scales, responses to individual items are summed and the resulting total is divided by the number of items. Hence, scale scores represent mean responses.

The CBC was not designed for administration to parents whose children are mentally retarded. In the current study, some parents who indicated retardation for their children did nevertheless complete the CBC. The findings presented include these children. Special analyses of the three major scales, while not presented here, suggest that the decision to include these children did not substantively affect the results. When children with retardation were specifically excluded, findings differed only slightly from those presented in this book. Of the 799 families in the total study sample, 757 completed the behavior problems section of the Child Behavior Checklist; these families comprise the sample for the current chapter.

FINDINGS

CBC Scale Scores

Tables 10.1 and 10.2 present raw scores on the Total Problems, Internalizing, and Externalizing scales for the adoption sample and the clinical and nonclinical CBC samples. For 4- and 5-year-olds, mean scores for the adoptive and nonclinical samples are similar on all three scales. Neither male nor female adoptees in this age range demonstrate significant behavioral problems. In comparison to nonclinical samples, scores of 6- to 11-year-old adoptees are elevated substantially on both the Total Problems and Externalizing scales. Internalizing scores are elevated somewhat for girls in this age group but hardly at all for boys.

Scores for 12- to 16-year-old adoptees are elevated on all three scales for both boys and girls. Scores in externalizing differ more from the nonclinical group than do scores in internalizing. In general, scores for adoptees in this age group are elevated more than are the scores of 6- to 11-year-old adoptees. While mean scores for both 6- to 11-year-olds and 12- to 16-year-olds are significantly elevated on many scales, these scores do not exceed those observed in the CBC clinical sample.

In sum, the major CBC scales suggest significant behavioral problems for latency-age and adolescent adoptees but not for those age 4 and 5. On balance, scores are elevated by about the same amount for boys and girls, conveying essentially the same severity of behavioral problems for children

Table 10.1
Behavior Problem Scores of Boys in Adoption and CBC Samples

| Age group and scale | Adoption sample | | | CBC samples[a] | | | | |
| | | | | Clinical | | Non-clinical | | |
	M	SD	n	M	SD	M	SD
4- to 5-year-olds							
Total problems	27.0	19.6	26	59.8	30.1	24.1	14.2
Internalizing	9.7	6.8	26	25.1	15.6	9.7	6.8
Externalizing	12.9	12.5	26	29.7	15.6	11.3	7.8
6- to 11-year-olds							
Total problems	36.0	22.2	177	58.9	24.0	21.7	15.0
Internalizing	11.7	8.8	177	23.1	12.2	8.4	6.7
Externalizing	20.0	12.4	177	30.5	13.1	10.8	8.2
12- to 16-year-olds							
Total problems	40.4	29.1	159	53.1	24.7	17.5	15.6
Internalizing	15.8	11.5	159	21.4	12.3	7.4	7.4
Externalizing	20.1	15.4	159	26.5	13.0	8.4	8.4

[a]See Table 10.3 for sample sizes.

Table 10.2
Behavior Problem Scores of Girls in Adoption and CBC Samples

| Age group and scale | Adoption sample | | | CBC samples[a] | | | | |
| | | | | Clinical | | Non-clinical | | |
	M	SD	n	M	SD	M	SD
4- to 5-year-olds							
Total problems	27.0	17.8	26	58.8	29.1	25.2	17.1
Internalizing	11.4	8.3	26	28.7	14.9	10.8	9.3
Externalizing	11.5	9.6	26	21.2	13.6	8.4	6.6
6- to 11-year-olds							
Total problems	36.7	24.6	185	58.4	26.2	19.9	14.2
Internalizing	11.3	9.2	185	23.7	12.6	7.7	6.3
Externalizing	22.1	15.5	185	32.5	15.7	10.7	8.6
12- to 16-year-olds							
Total problems	39.0	27.9	121	55.8	26.3	16.6	14.1
Internalizing	14.7	12.0	121	24.4	12.7	7.0	6.5
Externalizing	18.3	14.7	121	26.9	14.2	7.3	7.6

[a]See Table 10.4 for sample sizes.

irrespective of sex. The degree of elevation tends to be greater for externalized than for internalized behavior.

The study also examined the percentages of children scoring in the clinical range. Percentages for the major scales are presented in Chapter 3 (see Table 3.6) while those for the subscales are in Tables 10.3 (boys) and 10.4 (girls). Among children age 6 and above, the percentage of adopted children in the clinical range exceeds that in the nonclinical sample on most major scales and on numerous subscales. Among the different subscales, the high percentage of adoptees scoring in the clinical range on hyperactivity stands out. In several of the age/gender groups, this percentage is similar to that in the clinical CBC sample. Thus, hyperactivity appears to be an important behavioral problem for many families that adopt special-needs children.

Comparisons to Other Studies

Table 10.5 compares T scores in internalizing and externalizing to Brodzinsky's sample of children adopted at or near infancy (Brodzinsky et al., 1984). Also included is Brodzinsky's matched control group of children not adopted and the two CBC normative samples. All samples in Table 10.5 are composed of children age 6 to 11.

The internalizing scores of the special-needs adoptees are quite similar to those of the children adopted in infancy. On the externalizing dimension, however, the special-needs adoptees show higher T scores, indicative of more serious problems. Hence, the current sample is distinguished from typical adoptees primarily by externalized behavior problems.

Findings can also be compared with those of Berry and Barth (1989). This comparison concerns T scores aggregated across the age/gender groups; in other words, T scores for the full samples are compared. The children in Berry and Barth's intact (nondisrupted) group, all adopted at age 3 or older, scored higher in both internalizing and externalizing behaviors than did the children in this study. Mean T scores were: children in this study, internalizing, 56.2 ($SD = 10.6$, $n = 694$) and externalizing, 59.4 ($SD = 11.3$, $n = 694$); Berry and Barth intact group, internalizing, 66.1 ($n = 57$) and externalizing, 64.0 ($n = 57$). On balance, then, the current sample demonstrates fewer behavioral problems. The fairly low response rate (29 percent) in the Berry and Barth study may have affected their findings; perhaps the mean level of behavioral problems among special-needs adoptees is not as high as that in Berry and Barth's sample.

Given that the distribution of the T scores has been normalized, approximate percentiles can be estimated for children in the current sample. The mean score for internalizing in the current sample is at approximately the 73rd percentile with reference to the nonclinical CBC sample. In other

Table 10.3
Scores in Clinical Range for Boys in CBC and Adoption Samples (Percentages)

	Ages 4-5			Ages 6-11			Ages 12-16		
	CBC samples			CBC samples			CBC samples		
Scale	Clin-ical (n=100)	Non-clin. (n=100)	Adop-tion (n=26)	Clin-ical (n=300)	Non-clin. (n=300)	Adop-tion (n=177)	Clin-ical (n=250)	Non-clin. (n=250)	Adop-tion (n=159)
Aggressive	61	6	12	43	2	14	26	4	16
Delinquent	29	2	4	40	4	25	35	3	27
Depressed	37	4	0	31	2	3	--	--	--
Hostile withdrawal	--	--	--	--	--	--	33	2	25
Hyperactive	--	--	--	34	3	31	46	4	33
Immature	42	3	12	--	--	--	23	3	38
Obsessive-compulsive	--	--	--	30	2	13	22	2	18
Schizoid (or anxious)	14	2	4	31	3	10	16	2	6
Sex problems	14	0	0	--	--	--	--	--	--
Social withdrawal	37	3	4	28	2	10	--	--	--
Somatic complaints	25	3	0	14	2	2	20	2	9
Uncommunicative	--	--	--	44	6	13	20	2	13

Table 10.4
Scores in Clinical Range for Girls in CBC and Adoption Samples (Percentages)

Scale	Ages 4-5			Ages 6-11			Ages 12-16		
	CBC samples		Adoption	CBC samples		Adoption	CBC samples		Adoption
	Clinical (n=100)	Non-clin. (n=100)	tion (n=26)	Clinical (n=300)	Non-clin. (n=300)	tion (n=185)	Clinical (n=250)	Non-clin. (n=250)	tion (n=121)
Aggressive	32	2	8	46	3	21	27	2	12
Anxious obsessive	--	--	--	--	--	--	35	2	12
Cruel	--	--	--	21	2	12	35	1	23
Delinquent	--	--	--	23	2	14	41	2	21
Depressed	23	2	0	50	3	11	--	--	--
Depressed withdrawal	--	--	--	--	--	--	43	2	13
Hyperactive	27	2	15	44	2	34	--	--	--
Immature hyperactive	--	--	--	--	--	--	37	2	36
Obese	18	2	0	--	--	--	--	--	--
Schizoid (or anxious)	31	3	0	--	--	--	21	2	18
Schizoid obsessive	--	--	--	19	1	12	--	--	--
Sex problems	13	3	8	21	2	15	--	--	--
Social withdrawal	29	2	23	45	3	12	--	--	--
Somatic complaints	25	2	0	19	2	4	36	3	14

Table 10.5
***T* Scores on Child Behavior Checklist for Five Samples of Children, Ages 6–11**

| Gender and study | Current study | | Brodzinsky study[a] | | CBC samples[b] | |
	M	*n*	Adopted *M*	Control group *M*	Clinical *M*	Non-clinical *M*
Girls						
Internalizing	55.2	185	56.8	52.5	67.0	51.3
Externalizing	60.5	185	57.7	49.8	68.1	51.0
Boys						
Internalizing	55.0	177	54.9	53.0	65.6	51.2
Externalizing	59.8	177	55.9	49.3	68.1	51.0

[a]Combined sample size for boys and girls was 130.

[b]See Tables 9.3 and 9.4 for sample size.

words, the mean score indicates a greater level of problems than those demonstrated by about 73 percent of typical children. The mean score for externalizing is at about the 83rd percentile.

Age and Time in the Home

Table 10.6 presents the association between the three behavioral scales and the child's age both at entry to the adoptive home and at the time of the survey. For both of these variables, behavioral problems increase with age. The increase in problems in relationship to age at the time of the study reflects, in part, the influence of age at placement; those who were older at the time of the study were more likely to have been placed when older. Findings for those age 0 to 2 at the time of the study should be viewed cautiously, as these children were younger than the age range for which the CBC was designed.

Table 10.6 also presents the level of behavioral problems in relationship to the length of time that the child had lived in the adoptive home when the survey was conducted. Behavioral problems do not vary in any discernible pattern that is associated with time in the home. This finding was contrary to our expectation, which had been for a decrease in behavioral problems as time in the home increased. Time in the home was investigated further using multiple regression. Yet this analysis was problematic. One would like to

Table 10.6
Behavior Problem Scores by Age and Time in Home

Age or time in home	n	CBC total problems M	CBC total problems SD	Common internal items[a] M	Common internal items[a] SD	Common external items[a] M	Common external items[a] SD
Age at entry into home							
0 to 2 years	214	29.2	24.8	0.18	0.24	0.35	0.36
3 to 5 years	207	37.4	25.5	0.25	0.23	0.47	0.37
6 to 8 years	188	38.5	25.9	0.30	0.26	0.47	0.37
9 to 11 years	113	44.6	25.8	0.35	0.28	0.56	0.39
12 to 14 years	28	40.3	30.0	0.33	0.28	0.48	0.39
15 to 18 years	4	51.0	36.3	0.51	0.61	0.59	0.35
Age at time of study							
0 to 2 years	11	17.4	14.9	0.04	0.07	0.20	0.22
3 to 5 years	70	25.7	18.1	0.11	0.14	0.36	0.33
6 to 8 years	152	34.0	21.1	0.21	0.19	0.43	0.32
9 to 11 years	210	38.1	24.9	0.27	0.24	0.44	0.36
12 to 14 years	203	38.4	28.1	0.30	0.28	0.48	0.42
15 to 18 years	105	42.8	32.2	0.34	0.33	0.52	0.43
Months resided in home at time of survey							
0 to 11 months	24	34.0	18.9	0.23	0.20	0.43	0.28
12 to 23 months	77	36.1	22.7	0.25	0.24	0.41	0.32
24 to 35 months	109	37.4	24.6	0.27	0.27	0.46	0.36
36 to 47 months	117	36.6	24.4	0.23	0.23	0.47	0.38
48 to 59 months	108	38.2	26.1	0.28	0.26	0.47	0.37
60 to 71 months	76	44.9	27.6	0.32	0.28	0.56	0.39
72 to 95 months	98	31.1	23.0	0.22	0.21	0.40	0.36
96 to 119 months	69	28.7	26.5	0.22	0.26	0.34	0.37
120 months and up	76	40.6	34.4	0.30	0.34	0.47	0.46

[a]Due to missing values, sample sizes are approximate; in all cases, sample size is accurate to within three cases.

control statistically for two confounding variables, age at entry into the home and age at the time of the survey and, having done so, assess the effect of time in the home. Yet time in home, age at entry, and age at survey can not be entered in a single regression as these three variables represent only two independent pieces of information. When controlling for age at the time of the survey, total behavioral problems decrease as time in the home increases (beta $= -.12$, $p < .01$, $n = 745$). Yet when controlling for age at entry into the home, the opposite pattern is observed; total behavioral problems increase as time in the home increases (beta $= .10$, $p < .01$, $n = 754$). While findings in this area are equivocal, they clearly do not indicate a marked drop in problematic behavior as time in the home increases.

Given that both age at entry into the home and time in the home are of interest, Table 10.7 controls for both of these factors. Following the same pattern as demonstrated in Table 10.6, behavioral problems for most age groups increase modestly over about the first 6 years in the home. In comparison to other groups, the behavioral problem scores for those children who had been in their homes for 6 to 9 years were quite low. These low scores are in part due to the fact that a high proportion of these children entered their adoptive homes when they were quite young (see Table 10.7). Also, a high proportion of these children were of minority status or biracial, a factor associated with lower behavioral problem scores. (The mean score for minority and biracial adoptees was 32.2, $n = 278$, while that for white children was 39.4, $n = 519$, p < .01.) Even taking these factors into account, the CBC scores in this group were quite low and may in part reflect sampling error as well as the effects of using different sampling methods in different states. We are unable to offer a convincing explanation as to why behavior problems decreased for adoptees in their homes for 6 to 9 years.

Behavior Problems and Adoptive Outcome

The association of behavioral scores to parent perceptions of adoptive outcome was examined. As discussed in Chapter 3, externalizing problems correlate more strongly with perceptions of outcome than do internalizing

Table 10.7
Total Behavior Problems Score by Age at Entry and Number of Years in Home

	Years in Home								
	Less than 1 year		1 year to less than 3 years		3 years to less than 6 years		6 years to less than 10 years		10 years or more	
Age at entry into home	M	n	M	n	M	n	M	n	M	n
0 to 2 years	10	2	24	34	28	57	22	65	43	56
3 to 5 years	34	9	35	44	40	87	36	29	32	18
6 to 8 years	40	8	40	58	40	78	33	42	38	2
9 to 11 years	39	3	43	37	47	63	40	10	--	0
12 to 14 years	--	0	41	12	42	15	4	1	--	0
15 to 18 years	28	2	103	1	45	1	--	0	--	0
Total	34	24	37	186	39	301	30	167	41	76

problems (see Table 3.15). Indeed, among all variables in the study, externalized behavioral problems correlate most strongly with outcome.

The impact of the adoption on the family showed a somewhat different association to time in the home than did the CBC total problems score. As just discussed, behavioral problems worsened slightly over the first six years in the adoptive home. In contrast, perceptions of the adoption's impact improved modestly across this time frame. These perceptions improved still more for children who had been in the home for more than six years, reflecting in part the influence of younger age at placement (see Table 10.7) as well as a higher percentage of minority and biracial adoptees. The percentage of families responding "Very positive" for the five time periods designated by the columns in Table 10.7 were, respectively, 38 percent ($n = 24$), 45 percent ($n = 185$), 45 percent ($n = 301$), 52 percent ($n = 164$), and 52 percent ($n = 75$). Hence, while behavioral problems may increase modestly or stay about the same, the parent's perception of the adoption's impact seems to improve modestly as time increases (see Figure 3.2 and related discussion).

As the CBC scores of the sample children were elevated most on the hyperactivity subscales, the association of hyperactivity to parent-child relationship was examined. This association was studied separately for each of the four age/gender groups for which a hyperactivity subscale exists (see Tables 10.3 and 10.4). Correlations ranged from $-.45$ to $-.58$, suggesting that high levels of hyperactivity predict problematic relationship.

DISCUSSION AND PRACTICE IMPLICATIONS

Externalized Behavioral Problems

Significant behavioral problems were indicated for special-needs adoptees during latency and adolescence. In contrast, the 4- and 5-year-old adoptees evidenced no major difficulties. These findings support Brodzinsky's (1987) conclusion that adopted children evidence greater behavioral problems primarily in middle childhood and adolescence. Contrary to findings from some studies (Devaney, 1982; Bohman, 1970, cited in Brodzinsky et al., 1984; Shireman, 1988; Seglow, Pringle, & Wedge, 1972, cited in Brodzinsky et al.), adopted boys did not demonstrate greater behavioral difficulties than did adopted girls.

Externalized behavioral problems (aggressive behavior, acting-out, etc.) more so than internalized problems (withdrawn, inhibited behavior, etc.) seem to distinguish the behavior of several groups of adopted children. To underscore this conclusion, we reiterate findings from this and related studies.

Several studies demonstrate that adoptees in clinical treatment are often seen for problems related to acting-out and aggressive behavior (Menlove, 1965; Offord et al., 1969; Schecter et al., 1964; Work & Anderson, 1971; Borgatta & Fanshel, 1965, cited in Berry & Barth, 1989; Simon & Senturia, 1966; Reece & Levin, 1968). Brodzinsky and colleagues (1984) found that latency-age children adopted as infants tended to be distinguished from nonadoptees somewhat more by external problems than by internal problems. In Berry and Barth's (1989) study of children adopted at age 3 or older, externalized but not internalized problems discriminated between disrupted and intact adoptions. The current group of special-needs adoptees were distinguished from those adopted as infants by externalized behavior but were similar regarding internalized behavior. Similarly, externalized behavior more than internalized behavior discriminated the current sample from the CBC nonclinical sample. Finally, external behavior was associated more strongly with parental perceptions of parent-child relationships and with the adoption's impact on the family.

It is noted that the stronger associations for external behavior may be partially due to the fact that such behavior is easier to measure than is internal behavior. Stated differently, the generally higher reliability of measurements for external behavior may in part explain the stronger associations.

Hyperactivity

The current study demonstrates an exceptionally high percentage of adoptees scoring in the clinical range for hyperactivity. This is in accord with findings from other studies (Dalby et al., 1982; Deutsch et al., 1982; Brodzinsky et al., 1984; Berry & Barth, 1989; Hoopes, 1986; Bohman, 1972, cited in Hoopes, 1986). Hyperactivity showed a moderate to strong relationship to quality of parent-child relationship, suggesting that it causes significant hardship. Yet responses to the open-ended question, "What was most difficult [about this child's adoption]?" seldom mentioned hyperactive behaviors. The most common responses invariably called attention to "traditional" acting-out and aggressive behaviors—lying, cheating, stealing, conflict with authorities, poor control of temper. Thus, while hyperactivity is both common and difficult, it may not by itself generate problems that are serious enough to result in disruption. This interpretation corresponds with Berry and Barth's (1989) finding that level of hyperactivity did not discriminate between intact and disrupted adoptive placements.

Even if hyperactive behavior by itself may not lead to disruption, it clearly presents major problems for many parents who adopt special-needs children. In response to the question probing what was most difficult, many commented on the high level of attention demanded by their children (see Chapter 4). These demands may reflect the high level of hyperactive behavior in the sample.

The third edition of *Diagnostic and Statistical Manual* of the American Psychiatric Association (American Psychiatric Association, 1987), defines Attention Deficit Hyperactivity Disorder (ADHD). To be diagnosed as ADHD, a child must display at least 8 of 14 behaviors prior to the age of 7 for a period of at least 6 months. Representative behaviors include fidgeting, easy distraction, restlessness, and excessive talking. Several researchers have studied the etiology of ADHD, in particular contrasting the roles of genetic, biological, perinatal, and environmental factors (Anastopoulos & Barkley, 1988; Rapoport & Ferguson, 1981; Graham & Stevenson, 1987; Lambert & Hartsough, 1984). While emphasizing the methodological limitations of many studies, Anastopoulus and Barkley (1988) conclude:

A large number and variety of biological circumstances have been implicated in the etiology of ADHD. Many of these, including neurological damage and the ingestion of food additives and sugar, have not held up well under close scientific scrutiny. Others, such as those pertaining to genetic transmission, biological variation of inborn temperamental differences, mesial frontal and frontal-limbic dysfunction, elevated lead levels, and prenatal exposure to nicotine and alcohol, have received sufficient theoretical and empirical support to warrant further serious consideration as etiological mechanisms (p. 90).

This review clearly suggests an important role for biological factors in the etiology of the single behavioral problem that is most pronounced among special-needs adoptees. The impacts of environmental factors, for instance abuse, neglect, and multiple placements, can often be discerned in observing the behavior and adjustment of special-needs adoptees. It is important, however, to recognize also that biological factors, including genetic factors, influence behavior. Indeed, behavior thought to be due to environmental factors or dysfunctional dynamics may reflect biological or genetic causation. Clearly, a "bad seed" hypothesis (i.e, when adoptive parents attribute problems to genetic factors beyond their control) provides a ready excuse that parents use to distance themselves from their child's problems as well as possible solutions. Yet the opposite perspective, the view by many social workers and others that social factors are always paramount can be equally counterproductive. A balanced approach that recognizes the importance of biological as well as environmental factors is crucial for effective assessment and practice.

In addition to raising the potential for stressful interactions with parents, ADHD places the child at higher risk for both learning and behavior problems in school. The combination of ADHD and strained interactions at home and school, in turn, may direct the adopted child towards serious externalized behavior problems (aggressive behavior, delinquency, etc.) that may result in disruption. Effective treatment for the child with ADHD may require medication or a combination of medication and behavioral management techniques. While symptoms of hyperactivity or impulsiveness may decline with medication or behavior management, effective help for the child with ADHD requires ongoing, long-term management efforts by the adoptive parents.

Behavior Problems: A Longer-Term Perspective

The failure of problem behaviors to decline markedly as length of time in the home increased was contrary to expectations. Some parents commented that the process of integrating the child into the home had taken longer than they had anticipated. Study findings suggest that the special-needs adoptive parent should anticipate the possibility of an extended period of difficult behavior, perhaps declining in intensity slowly over time. This interpretation is presented tentatively. A longitudinal design with frequent measurements in the year following adoption is needed to adequately study behavioral trends across time. Further, a longitudinal design could assess whether those children age 4 and 5 in the current study, relatively free of problem behavior at the time of the survey, will develop serious problems in their latency and adolescent years.

The lower levels of problem behavior among minority youth are due in large part to less damaging experiences prior to adoption. In particular, minority youths were less likely to have experienced sexual abuse and group home or psychiatric placement. Chapter 8 presents discussion of the particular strengths of minority families in dealing with behavior problems.

Responses to open-ended questions in the current study clearly highlighted external behavioral problems as the single most difficult area for adoptive parents (see Chapter 4). Parents referred often to lying, stealing, and destruction of property on the part of adoptees. The punishment-seeking behaviors described by Reid and colleagues (1987) and Sack and Dale (1982) were also mentioned, although comments rarely carried the intensity conveyed by the authors of these studies. The relative absence of parent comments regarding the most severe behavior problems—brutal physical assaults, suicide attempts, and ongoing sexual assault—suggests that such behaviors were quite infrequent. Since such events often lead to disruption, their low frequency in this sample of intact families is not surprising. (See Chapter 4 for parent comments regarding behavioral problems.)

Concluding Comments

Notwithstanding the high levels of behavioral problems and the negative association of these problems to parental satisfaction, most special-needs parents were well satisfied with their decision to adopt. Normative behavior is not a requisite condition for successful special-needs adoption. The overall picture emerging from this study is one of nonnormative behavior on the part of many children but generally good satisfaction on the part of most parents. The high level of behavioral problems underscores the need many special-needs families have for specialized professional services. Berry and Barth (1989) suggest that both behavior management training and intensive family preservation services should be utilized more often with adoptive families. Other authors demonstrate the effectiveness of parent-preparation and parent-support groups (Feigelman & Silverman, 1983; Elbow & Knight, 1987; Gill, 1978; Tremitiere, 1979).

While it is beyond the scope of this book to offer a full explication of what constitutes adoption-sensitive social work or mental health practice, several clear-cut needs emerge. Both Berry and Barth's (1989) social and cognitive model of adoptive family adjustment emphasizing stressors, tasks, and coping resources and McRoy and colleagues' (1988) multiple-cause model of emotional disturbance in adopted adolescents provide valuable frameworks for structuring helping interventions. From the perspective of the parent, this study points out certain themes and corresponding parental needs:

The child's progress may not match the parents' expectations, thus the need for realistic expectations.

Behavioral problems will likely persist over time, thus the need for effective behavioral management.

Parents may encounter sheer physical exhaustion, thus the need for rest or respite.

Parents may face emotional exhaustion, thus the need for support and understanding.

Schools may be unable to deal with the child's learning barriers or behavioral problems, thus the need for ongoing involvement and advocacy in the school setting.

The addition of a new family member affects the family system and family subsystems, thus the need to anticipate potential changes.

From the child's perspective, other issues are raised. The process of bonding with new parents may rekindle memories of rejection by the birth parents. When the child has experienced multiple moves prior to adoption, he or she may anticipate that the adoptive placement will disrupt. When the child is adopted into a new family, he or she will deal with "family shock" in adjusting to a new set of spoken and unspoken family rules and habits. When the socioeconomic status of the adopting family differs from the status the child is accustomed to, additional adjustments will be necessary. The child will need to unlearn destructive behaviors and learn behaviors that are functional in the new setting. Somehow, the child must acquire a sense that he or she truly belongs in his or her new family and community.

Even with the best parenting and mental health services, many special-needs adopted children exhibit behavioral problems over extended periods of time. There are no pat strategies to cope with behavior issues, but adoption professionals might start the search for ideas with those who are most intimately experienced in special-needs adoption. Many special-needs parents have parented children—biological, foster, and adoptive—from diverse backgrounds and as such may be regarded as experts in parenting. The social work or mental health professional will do well to draw on this expertise in helping these special families deal with the very difficult behavioral problems that they often encounter.

Chapter 11

Focus on Selected Topics

The variables involved in special-needs adoption are diverse and many, and the large data set involved in this study allowed the opportunity to look at several selected topics, though not in the depth afforded issues discussed in earlier chapters. This chapter briefly explores four such issues: (1) contact between adoptees and their biological families following placement, (2) the special difficulties encountered when placing siblings as a group, (3) the agencies' patterns (and perhaps biases) of selecting families for specific adoptees, and (4) the self-esteem of special-needs children. Each of these issues has import for practitioners in the field and may point to issues for future investigation.

CONTACTS WITH BIOLOGICAL FAMILY

Contact with the biological family may be a source of stress and challenge for both the adopted child and his or her new family. At the same time, contact may be an essential component of the processes of healing, growing, coping, and moving on that each special-needs child must undergo. This section examines the experiences of the children in visiting siblings, biological parents, and extended family, discusses what can be expected as a result of such visitation, and suggests how adopting parents and social service workers can best manage these contacts or prepare children for the experience.

Method

The questionnaire probed whether the children in the study had been in contact with any member of their biological families (nuclear or extended) since the adoptive placement. Contact was defined as in-person, telephone, mail, or any other kind of contact. Respondents were asked to exclude contacts between the child and any biological relatives (usually siblings) who also lived in the adoptive home. Where contact had been made, respondents described the nature of the contact and assessed its effects on both the child and the adoptive family. Both close-ended and open-ended questions were used. Data presented in this section were drawn from the overall three-state sample except in a few instances where the Oklahoma Department of Human Services and the Kansas samples were scrutinized in closer detail.

Nature of Contacts

Respondents described many different kinds of contacts. An analysis of 143 contacts from the Oklahoma DHS and Kansas samples showed that 71 percent of children had visited in person and 20 percent communicated by phone or mail. In 9 percent of cases the nature of the contact could not be determined. Some children had active ongoing contacts, for example, monthly meetings with their birth parents or siblings; others had very sporadic contacts, for example, the exchange of Christmas or birthday cards. Several of the contacts were accidental, such as chance meetings in the park. Others occurred as a result of everyday life circumstances. One birth mother, for instance, worked in the supermarket where the adoptive parents shopped. Several parents described meetings of siblings that had taken place without their prior knowledge. In the Oklahoma DHS and Kansas samples, 115 families responded to a probe asking whether contacts would continue; 78 percent responded affirmatively, 12 percent responded "No," and 10 percent were unsure.

Table 11.1 presents the percentage of contacts for the full sample and selected subsamples. In the full sample, about one-third of the families reported contacts. When adoptions by relatives and foster parents are excluded from consideration, about one-quarter of families report contacts between the child and biological family.

Contact was most common with birth family siblings. Table 11.1 identifies which biological family members had contact with the adopted child. The "Parents" category may be considered a "nuclear family" category; it includes contacts with parents only as well as contacts with both parents and biological family siblings. In contrast, the "Siblings only"

Table 11.1
Contacts with Child's Biological Family Since Adoptive Placement
(Percentages)

Contact	Full sample	Adoptions by foster parents	Adoptions by relatives	Foster and relative adoptions excluded
Family member contacted	(n=790)	(n=343)	(n=78)	(n=396)
Parents[a]	11	17	36	3
Siblings only[a]	16	16	8	16
Grandparents	5	10	8	5
Aunts, uncles, or cousins	5	5	1	2
Any of above or unspecified	34	41	60	26
Effect of contact				
For the child	(n=267)	(n=137)	(n=43)	(n=101)
Mostly good	28	30	28	26
Both good and bad points	33	28	23	45
Not much effect	25	25	33	21
More harm than good	13	18	16	9
For the adoptive family	(n=263)	(n=134)	(n=43)	(n=100)
Mostly good	27	25	23	29
Both good and bad points	28	28	23	32
Not much effect	32	33	39	29
More harm than good	12	14	14	10

[a]The parents category includes some situations where both parents and siblings were contacted. The siblings only category includes only those situations where siblings were contacted but the parents were not.

category includes only situations where siblings but not parents were contacted. In the full sample, about one-tenth of the families reported contacts between the child and one or more of the birth family parents. Yet when adoptions by relatives and foster parents are excluded, contacts with the biological parents were quite rare (3 percent). In the full sample, about one family in every six reported contact with a biological family sibling.

Assessments of Contacts

Table 11.1 also presents adoptive parent assessments of the effect of contact for both the child and the adoptive family. On balance, assessments are similar with respect to the child and the adoptive family. The major difference is that the response choice "Not much effect" is used more often in reference to the adoptive family. Also, the assessments are quite similar for the various samples and subsamples presented.

These assessments could be characterized as moderately positive. For instance, in the full sample only 13 percent assess the visits as having caused the child "more harm than good." The assessment of "more harm than good" varied, however, depending upon whom the child visited. Table 11.2 shows that visits with birth parents are assessed more negatively than are those with other family members.

Contacts with the biological family were also analyzed in relation to the adoptive parents' assessment of the impact of the adoption. In other words,

Table 11.2
Effect of Contact for the Child by Family Member Contacted (Percentages)

Effect	Parents[a] (n=85)	Siblings only[a] (n=124)	Grand-parents (n=60)	Aunts, uncles, cousins (n=42)
Mostly good	21	31	32	31
Both good and bad	29	40	28	33
Not much effect	29	19	30	26
More harm than good	21	10	10	10

[a]The parents category includes some situations where both parents and siblings were contacted. The siblings only category includes only those situations where siblings were contacted but parents were not.

was contact associated either negatively or positively with overall satisfaction with the adoption? For this analysis, the adoption's impact was divided into two categories, "Very positive," and any other response. Overall, those whose children visited biological family members were somewhat less likely to choose "Very positive"; 42 percent (112 of 265) of those whose children visited chose this response versus 49 percent (250 of 508) of those whose children did not visit, $p = .07$. This same pattern was also evident when the analysis focused on the specific family member visited. Forty-three percent (36 of 83) of the parents whose children visited birth parents, 38 percent (47 of 123) of the parents of those who visited siblings, 40 percent (23 of 58) of the parents of those who visited grandparents, and 42 percent (18 of 43) of the parents of those who visited aunts or uncles responded "Very positive." The analysis with respect to siblings reached significance, $p < .05$.

Comments from Parents

Narrative responses from parents underscore both the negative and positive experiences encountered when their adopted children were in touch with their biological families.

Negative comments. Negative comments typically emphasized the emotional stress and changed behavior triggered by the contacts. Parents described lapses in personal hygiene, depression and withdrawal, hyperactive behavior, sexual acting out, reduced effort in school, acting-out behavior in home and school, and other behavioral reactions. Several parents interpreted the behavior as regressive, often repetitive of problem behaviors that the child had shown when he or she first moved into the home.

Often the contacts rekindled the child's wish to return to the birth home. On the other hand, contacts sometimes left the child feeling guilty about his or her improved living situation. This was particularly the case where siblings remained in the biological family home or had been adopted by a family of lower socioeconomic status. Following are some of the more serious problems as described by parents:

She was upset and remembered the [sexual] abuse, [resulting in] nightmares.

Our son was torn between two families. His siblings pressured him to remain part of their "family" (although a family structure no longer existed). He felt guilty for being part of a new (and much better) situation, knowing life was quite difficult for the siblings.

Contacts [with siblings] were very disruptive to child. He went back to bed-wetting, nightmares, baby behavior—he could not handle it.

Jessie becomes upset about his brother's failures. His brother brings up things about their past that Jessie would just as soon forget.

[Court-ordered visits with biological mother were] emotionally bad for child—caused confusion when she was little—now anger as she gets older.

One day after visit [with sister], Joan showed high anxiety, hyperactivity, and sexual acting out.

Really don't think this is good for him. Reopens wound. He is very happy now, has come a long way.

[Visit with sisters made the child] more nervous, old habits returned—wet pants, brother sucked thumb, couldn't sleep, bad dreams, constipation.

Positives and negatives. Often parents noted positive effects along with the negative. For instance, the parent in the preceding comment added that the child gained a sense of "security that sisters did exist and were OK." Often parents stated that visits had negative effects in the short run, usually in terms of disturbed behavior, but more positive effects in the long run. As one parent stated, "Stress!! In the long run, visits are constructive; in the short run, they stress our kids and us."

Positive comments. The positive comments reflected one of two major themes. First, some comments reflected simply that the children enjoyed seeing members of their birth families. Second, the visits affirmed to the children the reality that they could not return to their homes. Sometimes the visits reaffirmed that while their birth parents cared for them, they could not take care of them. Just as the visits sometimes triggered feelings of guilt, they also sensitized the children to the expanded opportunities available in their adoptive homes. Many adoptive parents made positive comments about visits with grandparents and aunts and uncles. Frequently, these extended family members had been a source of support to the child prior to the adoption. Similarly, many of the children were quite close to their siblings, and these visits were often rewarding.

Following are some representative comments. The first comment points out advantages to the adoptive family as well as to the children:

The reality of who their mother is needs to be faced. It was not the girls' fault that they were given up ('rejected') by her. . . . They need to hear and see this over and over again. Also, each time we see her, my husband and I get more bits of information that help us understand our children better.

[It is] good for my son to continue contact with his brothers and to be able to put unpleasant and pleasant memories in proper perspective.

[Regarding an aunt and uncle] We were afraid of meeting them at first. . . . When we realized they wouldn't interfere or take him back and they found out he was well taken care of, loved, and thriving, we could both relax and as a result are a very close "family" and friends.

Amy was his care-giver when Daniel was a baby even though she was only four. There is a bond between the two of them. . . . Even though both are happy with their families, they love each other and need to be close once in a while.

Good because the child loves her mother very much. And to let them know she loves them. That helps them a lot.

[Regarding siblings] They feel a need to have some contact. They are very satisfied. They are always tickled to see how much they resemble each other. . . . Their contact with the bio-father has on its own shown them results of mistakes and things they do not want to do with their life. (E.g., they both read paper and saw he was arrested.) They see he is very poor also and not neat—doesn't hold a job—they see importance we place on working, responsibility, neatness, et cetera, and have on their own chosen this way as best for them.

Discussion

For most children, contacts with relatives were at least moderately positive. These contacts helped children to view the birth family—its strengths and its weaknesses—more realistically. Findings in this study very closely mirror those of Nelson (1985). In Nelson's study one-half of the respondents were "glad" (p. 108) that their adoptive child was in contact with a biological relative, while only 9 percent expressed dissatisfaction. Yet the negative comments expressed by adoptive parents clearly show that visits, particularly visits with biological parents, may trigger highly problematic behavior. Hence, where an adoption is particularly stressful or where a visit may induce added stress, the adoptive family may be advised to restrain or monitor visitation. This advice is consistent with that of Barth & Berry (1988), who concluded that contact with family or prior caretakers "seems to be a desirable addition for an adoption that is progressing smoothly, but is a threat to risky placements (p. 152)."

ADOPTIONS OF SIBLING GROUPS

The placement of siblings as a group represents a special challenge because of the obvious difficulties of managing the impact of not just one special-needs child but several in a single family unit. On balance, this study found very little difference between the characteristics of children placed individually and those adopted as a sibling group. Nor was there any significant difference in the assessment of satisfaction about the adoption's outcome between the full sample and parents of sibling groups. In the open-ended questions, however, the parents of siblings tended to express more negative experiences, reflecting the greater difficulties of these adoptions.

Findings

Overall, the sibling placements were similar in most aspects to those of other special-needs children in the sample.

Characteristics of placements. Those adopted in sibling groups and others were of similar age at the time of the survey (mean = 10.8 years for each group) and at the time of entry into the home (mean = 5.8 years and 5.3 years). Neither gender or ethnicity were associated with placement as part of a sibling group. Thirty-nine percent (157 of 404) of boys and 35 percent (132 of 372) of girls were placed in sibling groups, $p > .05$, as were 35 percent (101 of 290) of minority or biracial children and 39 percent (187 of 482) of white children, $p > .05$. As might be expected, sibling group placements were less common in single-parent families; 23 percent (26 of 115) of these placements versus 40 percent (254 of 640) of placements in two-parent families were sibling group placements, $p < .01$. Sibling group placements were also less common in adoptions by foster parents; 31 percent (104 of 335) of these adoptions in contrast to 42 percent (186 of 438) of adoptions by new parents were sibling group adoptions, $p < .01$. Finally, those placed in sibling groups (11 percent, 20 of 186) and others (15 percent, 47 of 317) were equally likely to have experienced group home or psychiatric placement prior to adoption, $p > .05$.

Outcomes. In the full sample, parents adopting single children rather than siblings were slightly more likely to evaluate the adoption's impact on the family as very positive, (48 percent, 227 of 477, versus 45 percent, 128 of 283, p .05.) This same analysis was rerun including only those children with siblings in their birth family, that is, those children for whom sibling group placement was a possibility. Again, differences were not significant; in this analysis the percentage of "Very positive" responses was slightly higher in sibling placements (45 percent versus 44 percent, 144 of 329). A third analysis compared those who had birth family siblings (whether placed as a sibling group or separately) to those who did not. Outcomes were much more positive for children without birth siblings; 56 percent (83 of 148) of adoptive parents for this group versus 44 percent (271 of 610) for children with birth siblings responded "Very positive," $p = .01$. Yet the more positive outcome for those without birth siblings was attributable to the younger age of this group and did not hold in multiple regression analysis controlling for age at entry into the home and at the time of the survey.

Outcomes varied modestly with respect to the child's birth order within his or her sibling group (i.e., with respect to the siblings from his/her birth family who were also placed in the adoptive home). Where the study child was the oldest in the group, 51 percent (61 of 120) of parents responded "Very positive" regarding family impact. This compares with 45 percent (15 of 33) for parents of middle siblings and 37 percent (43 of 116) for parents of youngest siblings, $p = .10$. This finding should be viewed tentatively.

As findings from two studies suggest lower disruption rates for sibling placements when there are no other children in the home at the time of placement (Barth & Berry, 1988; Boneh, 1979), we attempted to investigate this question, using several different statistical techniques. There was, however, no indication that the presence of other children presented more problems in sibling group placements than in other placements.

Child behavior. Mindful that Reid and colleagues (1987) observed good outcomes in sibling group placements of older, emotionally disturbed children, we explored the association of sibling group placement to the child's behavioral problems. The mean score on the total behavioral problems scale of the Child Behavior Checklist (Achenbach & Edelbrock, 1983) was slightly lower for children placed in sibling groups, 34.3 ($SD = 25.4$, $n = 283$), versus 38.3 ($SD = 26.6$, $n = 459$) for other children, $p < .05$.

Parent comments. While the questionnaire did not prompt specifically for comments regarding sibling group placement, a good number were made, with the majority expressing negative experiences.

Parent comments identified several common themes. Several stated that siblings were kept together more by agency policy than because this was in their interests. Others felt that the presence of siblings in the home kept alive memories of the biological family, thereby blocking the process of emotional separation from the birth family and preventing bonding with the adoptive family. Also, pairs of siblings often reinforced each other's misbehavior, sometimes setting up a dynamic of "us" (siblings) versus "them" (adoptive parents). Several parents simply stated that adopting two or more children at the same time was difficult. Selected parent comments on sibling group adoptions follow:

If I had it to do over, I would not adopt two children at the same time. They reinforce each other's bad habits.

We adopted two special-needs children, and this was just too much for our family. One child's needs were more severe than the other's, and he is no longer in our home.

Although it is nice having adopted two siblings and keeping them together, I am convinced that more progress could have been made with both children socially and academically if they had been placed in separate families and encouraged to communicate positively with each other. They have tended to reinforce each other's [bad] attitudes. [They've] got each other and don't have to fit in.

We spent three days with our sibling group before adopting. The oldest, who is now hospitalized, acted as he is—severely emotionally disturbed. But because the social worker said he was normal, we thought it was normal "testing behavior!" We should have listened to our gut when we saw him eating feces, et cetera.

Adopt one at a time.

The boys were first together in their first adoptive home. Our home was the third adoptive home. Someone put these boys together even though they had never been together, and together they were a disaster. Each set of adoptive parents asked that they be separated. We finally succeeded after the older one requested to leave.

A minority of comments spoke to the benefits of sibling group placement. One family related a year-long ordeal to reunite two siblings; they were reunited and both adoptions have worked well: "They are now just like any other normal brother and sister." One parent stated, "I really have enjoyed getting two children because they at least knew they had each other and very often that helped."

Discussion

The data do not argue convincingly for or against the practice of sibling group placement. This decision, then, will often be a difficult one and one where individual circumstances will predominate. Hegar (1988) stresses the importance of bonds between siblings—these bonds are perhaps stronger than we as adults commonly acknowledge. Bonds between siblings may be particularly strong when parenting has been inadequate. Hegar's review of research suggests that the presence of siblings may reduce the trauma that children experience when they are placed in foster care or otherwise separated from their parents.

Sibling placement would appear to be contraindicated where previous sibling placements have failed and where relationships between siblings are destructive. While some parents expressed reservations regarding visits between siblings who had been separated, these visits should probably be encouraged when they are perceived as important to the child. For instance, one parent described how such sibling contact had been important in helping her daughter come to grips with her situation and change her attitudes and behavior for the better. The lower behavior problems score of those adopted as siblings speaks well for sibling group adoption but may only reflect that siblings with behavior problems are less likely to be placed in sibling groups.

While the quantitative data show no differences between sibling and nonsibling placements, the parents' narrative comments suggest the need for special efforts to prepare parents for the difficulties of adopting siblings.

PATTERNS OF ADOPTIVE PLACEMENT

Are children with particular characteristics adopted more often by particular types of families? While other chapters have explored factors of race and handicap, this section focuses primarily on the association of adoptive family income and adoption by foster parents to selected characteristics of children and cases.

Findings

Table 11.3 presents case characteristics according to family income, and certain patterns emerge. Children with handicaps were more often adopted by lower-income as contrasted to higher-income families. Sexually abused children, on the other hand, were frequently adopted by middle- and upper-income families. Children with serious behavioral problems as indicated by a score in the clinical range on the CBC were found more often in middle-income and higher-income families. The study design does not allow one to conclude whether this association is causal, that is, whether the expectations of higher-income families somehow lead to behavior problems. Adoptions by relatives were much more common in the lowest income group. The percentage of sibling group adoptions increased with family income. The percentage of adoptions by foster parents was considerably lower among parents in the highest-income groups. As expected, adoptions by single parents were overrepresented among lower-income adopters.

The characteristics presented in Table 11.3 were also examined in association to foster parent adoption. Families where the parents were previously foster parents to the adopted child were more likely to adopt children who were younger than age 6 when they entered the home (69 percent versus 47 percent), children with handicaps, and minority or biracial children (48 percent versus 31 percent). These adopters were more often single parents at the time of adoption (20 percent versus 12 percent) and at least one parent was more often of minority status (38 percent versus 27 percent). Foster parent adopters were less likely to adopt children who had experienced adoption disruptions (9 percent versus 15 percent), sus-

Table 11.3
Selected Characteristics by Income Level

Case characteristic	Lowest to $24,999 %	n	$25,000 to $39,999 %	n	$40,000 to highest %	n
Child age 6 or older when entered home	62	210	54	200	52*	246
Child is female	51	209	56	200	56	247
Respondent is female	93	208	82	200	78**	247
Either parent a biologi-cal relative of child	17	206	7	199	2**	244
Subsidized adoption	78	203	57	197	43**	243
Adoption by foster parents	52	208	46	198	29**	247
Sibling placement	32	204	41	200	44*	243
Single-parent adoption	29	199	14	200	5**	246
Child minority or biracial	55	207	29	200	24**	246
At least one parent minority or biracial	49	209	21	199	21**	244
At least one parent same race as child	92	205	90	199	90**	242
At least one biological child of adoptive parents in home	33	203	38	199	38	245
Adoptive mother graduated from college	16	202	26	191	48**	241
Child is handicapped	42	210	36	200	32	247
Child scores in clinical range on CBC total problems scale	36	176	45	176	46*	227
Child experienced disrup-tion prior to adoption[a]	11	142	16	120	8	145
Group home or psychiatric placement prior to adoption[a]	11	142	13	120	16	145
Sexual abuse prior to adopt (actual or suspected)[a]	18	139	45	115	43**	143

[a]Variable not included in Oklahoma DHS and Project Adopt questionnaires, hence, the smaller sample size.

*$p<.05$, **$p<.01$

pected or actual sexual abuse prior to adoption (27 percent versus 42 percent), group home or psychiatric placement prior to adoption (11 percent versus 17 percent), and children with behavioral problems (36 percent versus 45 percent). Also, adoptions of sibling groups were less common (31 percent versus 43 percent). Finally, foster parent adoptions were also subsidized more often (77 percent versus 48 percent). The other factors presented in Table 11.3 did not discriminate significantly between foster parent and other adopters.

The overrepresentation of minority parents and minority children in foster parent adoptions occurs largely because Illinois DCFS, the state with the largest percentage of minority adoptive placements, utilized foster parents more often than did the other participating agencies. When analyses are conducted within the different agencies, this overrepresentation is no longer present; in fact, trends in the opposite direction were sometimes evident.

Discussion

One motivation for this analysis of placement patterns was to see whether children with selected special-needs conditions or problems, for instance, older age at adoption, handicaps, prior group home or psychiatric placement, and behavioral problems, were more likely to be placed in families with lower socioeconomic status. Such a pattern could suggest that these families were viewed as highly acceptable for children with serious problems but less so for children with less serious problems.

Children with handicaps (vision, hearing, or other physical handicaps, retardation, or serious medical conditions) were more likely to be placed in lower- and moderate-income families, a finding consistent with other studies (Chambers, 1970; Nelson, 1985, with respect to intellectually impaired children). Yet the data do not suggest that lower socioeconomic status was associated with other special-needs characteristics. In fact, the opposite pattern was evident for many factors, including behavioral problems, sexual abuse, and group home or psychiatric placement prior to adoption. Moderate- and upper-income families were also more likely to adopt sibling groups.

We speculate that the patterns shown in Table 11.3 may reflect the preferences of adopting families rather than those of the agencies. That is, higher-income families may be more willing to deal with behavioral problems and sibling groups but less open to the adoption of children with serious handicaps. Higher-income families may believe that behavioral problems but not severe physical or mental handicaps can be conquered or erased. Therefore, they may feel more comfortable adopting the child with behavior problems who has the potential to model their high achievement orientation. Similarly, moderate- and lower-income families may adopt children with handicaps more often because they are willing to do so. Clearly, adoption has the best prognosis for successful outcome when the family's expectations and the child's characteristics are similar.

The overrepresentation of single parents among those who had previously been foster parents to their adopted child was not expected. The data suggest that this is a fairly common route to adoption for singles.

THE SELF-CONCEPT OF SPECIAL-NEEDS ADOPTEES

Subsequent to the surveys conducted in Illinois, Kansas, and Oklahoma, special-needs adoptive families in Iowa completed the same questionnaire. Generating the sample randomly from a list of subsidized adoptions, 199 families from the sample of 280 responded (71 percent). Again, results were excellent, with 49 percent of the families responding "Very positive" and 24 percent of the families responding "Mostly positive" regarding the adoption's impact on the family.

In addition to completing the survey, responding parents were asked if they were willing to have their children complete the Piers-Harris Children's Self-Concept Scale, a standardized measure of self-esteem. Children in 29 percent of families (57) agreed to complete the self-concept instrument. Fifty percent (24 of 48; 9 cases missing) of these children were interviewed with family members present, 13 percent (6) were interviewed alone, and 38 percent (18) completed the instrument with assistance from their parents.

The instrument was administered in some instances by research assistants from the University of Iowa School of Social Work. Each item was read aloud and the child responded verbally. Where parents administered the instrument, they followed this same protocol.

The Piers-Harris Children's Self-Concept Scale

The Piers-Harris Scale is an 80-item, self-report questionnaire focusing on a child's conscious self-perceptions. Piers (1984) describes self-concept as "a relatively stable set of self-attitudes reflecting both a description and an evaluation of one's own behavior and attributes" (p. 1).

In addition to the overall self-concept scale, the Piers-Harris also contains six subscales.

- The *behavior* subscale measures "the extent to which the child admits or denies problematic behaviors" (p. 38).

- The *intellectual and school status* subscale reflects "the child's self-assessment of his or her abilities with respect to intellectual and academic tasks, including general satisfaction with school and future expectations" (p. 38).

- The *physical appearance and attributes* subscale indicates "the child's attitudes concerning his or her physical characteristics, as well as attributes such as leadership and the ability to express ideas" (p. 39).

- The *anxiety* subscale measures "general emotional disturbance and dysphoric mood" (p. 39).

- The *popularity* subscale reflects "the child's evaluation of his or her popularity with classmates, being chosen for games, and [the] ability to make friends" (p. 39).

- The *happiness and satisfaction* subscale "taps a general feeling of being a happy person and easy to get along with, and feeling generally satisfied with life" (p. 39).

Norms have been developed for the total scale and the subscales. For the total self-concept score, the normative sample consisted of 1,183 schoolchildren ages 8 to 18 from a public school system in a small town in Pennsylvania. Since no consistent sex or grade differences were found, only one normative score was developed. The norms for the subscales were based on a sample of 485 public school children. The authors suggest caution in comparing children to the norms. For the reader interested in reliability and validity of the scale, the *Piers-Harris Children's Self-Concept Scale Revised Manual 1984* is recommended (Piers, 1984).

The presented results include percentile scores, the child's percentile relative to the normative samples. For example, a percentile score of 63 indicates a higher score than 63 percent of the children in the normative sample.

Findings

Total scale and subscale scores for all respondents and for children ages 8 to 18 are presented in Table 11.4. The total self-concept score for all special-needs adoptees ranged from a percentile score of 4 to a percentile score of 97. The mean self-concept score was at the 74th percentile. In other words, on average, the self-concept of the average respondent exceeds that of 74 percent of the normative sample. Hence, as a group, the special-needs adoptees evidenced excellent self-esteem. Mean scores for all subscales were above the 50th percentile, with some exceeding the 70th percentile.

Discussion

The administration of the Piers-Harris instrument revealed that the level of self-concept of special-needs adoptees may, on balance, be similar to that

Table 11.4
Self-Concept of Special-Needs Adoptees

Scale	M	SD	Range	Percentile score M	Range
All children (n = 57)					
Total self-concept	61.0	13.9	25-77	74	4-97
Behavior	13.0	3.3	3-16	51	1-95
Intellectual and school status	13.8	2.9	7-17	70	12-98
Physical appearance and attributes	10.1	2.9	2-13	74	2-97
Anxiety	10.0	3.7	1-14	58	1-97
Popularity	8.7	2.7	2-12	52	4-97
Happiness and satisfaction	8.7	1.8	3-10	72	2-90
Children aged 8 to 18 (n = 44)					
Total self-concept	60.5	14.1	25-77	71	4-97
Behavior	12.6	3.5	3-16	51	1-95
Intellectual and school status	13.6	3.1	7-17	70	12-98
Physical appearance and attributes	9.7	3.0	2-13	73	2-97
Anxiety	9.8	4.0	1-14	58	1-97
Popularity	8.6	2.8	2-12	52	4-97
Happiness and satisfaction	8.6	1.9	3-10	72	2-90

of children in the United States as a whole. Results should be interpreted with caution due to moderate response rate and sample size and due to the presence of children's parents at some interviews. These cautions notwithstanding, results are encouraging and suggest that many adoptees develop good self-images in spite of problem-filled backgrounds. The generally high levels of self-esteem support Kadushin's (1967) view that the effects of early trauma can often be reversed and, to some degree, overcome.

Chapter 12

Practice Recommendations:
Special-Needs Adoption in the 1990s

While previous chapters focus largely on empirical findings, the current chapter shifts attention to the implications of the study's findings for adoption practice in the 1990s and beyond. Briefly summarized, the mailed survey of almost 800 families who adopted children with special needs revealed the following findings:

- Seventy-five percent of respondents evaluate the adoption's impact on the family as "mostly" or "very positive."

- A high percentage of the children, about 41 percent, demonstrate clinically significant behavioral problems.

- Among all variables examined, acting-out, aggressive behavioral problems most influence the parent's perception of adoptive outcome.

- Hyperactivity is the single behavioral problem that most distinguishes special-needs adoptees from typical children (nonadoptees).

- Most of the special-needs adoptees do well in school; in this study 99 percent of children ages 6 to 17 were attending school and 52 percent earned grades of B average or higher in their most recent semester.

- While the most positive outcomes were for those adopted when very young (younger than about age 5), many children adopted when older, particularly those adopted in adolescence, experienced excellent outcomes.

- Adoptions by minority parents show outcomes that are even more positive than those of the sample as a whole; these better outcomes reflect in part the fact that minority children, on average, had less-damaging experiences prior to adoptive placement.

- Families with lower incomes and educational levels, those who adopted as single parents, and those who adopted their foster children experienced distinctly positive outcomes.
- Special-needs adoptive families are characterized by close emotional relationships and by flexibility with respect to roles, tasks, and rules.
- The provision of thorough and accurate background information is strongly associated with positive adoptive outcome.

Several cautions are recommended in the interpretation of findings. First, the results may be biased due to nonresponse; in other words, those who did not respond (40 percent of the potential sample) may have experienced less positive outcomes than those who did (60 percent). Second, some respondents may have given socially desirable rather than honest responses. These two phenomena influence findings to an unknown degree. Given that a survey design rather than an experimental design was used, many observed relationships may not be causal in nature, but instead may reflect the effects of extraneous factors. Finally, the great majority of children in the current study had been in their homes for longer than a year at the time of the survey. Thus, this study does not address adequately the challenges and problems encountered in the year directly following placement. A design specifically focused on this time period could do so.

RECOMMENDATIONS FOR RECRUITMENT

Visible, ongoing recruitment activities are essential (Coyne, 1986). Often, however, these activities may be limited in scope or secondary in importance to the myriad of other tasks that must be carried out in the adoption agency. In the long term such a failure to prioritize recruitment creates hardship for both workers and children awaiting placement. Recruitment tools such as brochures, videos, radio and television announcements (such as "Wednesday's Child"), newspaper columns, and personal networking can be used successfully in recruiting campaigns. Also, prospective parents and children awaiting adoption may be invited to a get-together, a time to visit and talk with one another. Sometimes, an unexpected person in a child's life, perhaps a teacher, neighbor, or caseworker, may step forward to adopt. Similarly, a potential adoptive parent may emerge from within the child's extended family system. Adoption workers need to be flexible, ready to take advantage of such opportunities. In 1990, National Adoption Week was expanded into National Adoption Month (November), providing an excellent time to focus public attention on adoption.

The successful special-needs adoptive program is flexible and creative in its recruiting of families. Coyne (1986) recommends that agencies identify specific types of families needed and use market-based strategies to reach them. Similarly, we recommend that agencies consider recruitment of several specific target groups.

First, older persons are an underutilized resource in special-needs adoption. Increased life expectancy, improved health habits and medical care, and incentives for early retirement enhance opportunities for adoption by this group. Numerous periodicals target the older adult and can be used in disseminating information about special-needs adoption.

Second, there is the gay and lesbian community. This controversial recommendation is based on several observations. The gay community was the first to respond to the AIDS crisis, developing social and other services prior to state and federal governments (Shilts, 1987). Also, this community possesses well-developed resources and organization capability. Many states do not discourage gay and lesbian people from adopting special-needs children and have employed them as foster and adoptive parents without incident. However, the recruitment strategy is typically passive; that is, while not denied the opportunity to adopt, gay and lesbian people are not actively pursued as adoptive parents. With almost half of available children still waiting adoptive placement and with the increase in adoptable children from the crack, cocaine, and AIDS epidemics, active recruitment strategies should be developed.

Third, given the good adoption outcomes for low-income families, recruitment should target these families, including those on public assistance. Already, some states are experimenting with recruiting and training families on public assistance to foster special-needs children. The opportunity to foster or to adopt provides the welfare participant with an opportunity to contribute to society and provides the child with a permanent home.

We do not recommend indiscriminate recruitment among these groups but instead suggest that workers evaluate potential adoptive placements according to each child's needs. For instance, some older parents may not have the physical stamina to parent children with some disabilities. Similarly, having a gay or lesbian adoptive parent might be uncomfortable for some children or quite difficult in some communities. Yet whatever disadvantages exist must be balanced against the usually much more serious consequences that result from growing up in long-term foster or group home care.

Given that nearly half (47 percent in 1985; Tatara, 1988) of the children in out-of-home placement are of minority status, enhanced recruitment of minority parents is strongly recommended. In particular, agencies should recruit minority foster parents who have the potential and motivation to adopt. This effort is enhanced by involvement of minority persons at all levels of adoption practice, including casework, administration, and foster parenting. While our strong preference is for inracial placement, this goal is not realistic for all minority children, particularly those with serious handicaps and disabilities. Findings from this and other studies recommend that transracial adoptions provide good permanent homes for many children and are an important resource.

RECOMMENDATIONS FOR PREPLACEMENT SERVICES

Background Information

Many parents responded that background information on the adopted child was insufficient. The need for accurate and complete information about the child is emphasized. Those who work in child welfare realize how easy it is to lose track of a child's past in the course of the multiple moves, caretakers, and placements that may be encountered. Information from a biopsychosocial perspective across the child's history including photographs, letters, schoolwork, testing and evaluation information, medical and psychiatric records, and social history should be gathered and made available to adoptive parents. It is particularly important that information about prior physical or sexual abuse be shared with the adoptive parents. Withholding such information due to fears that prospective parents will be deterred from the adoption is unfair to parent and child and makes dealing with future problems all the more difficult. The gathering of background information can be tedious, requiring the worker to become a "detective" on the child's behalf; nevertheless, this knowledge is essential for both the parent and the child.

The desire of many special-needs parents in this study for more depth in background information seems to us to parallel the search that many adopted at infancy undertake to learn about or make contact with their birth families. Neither adoptive parent or child desires that the child exist without a past. Instead, knowledge of the past strengthens the adoptive family system.

Preparation for Adoption

Several writers discuss the importance of preparing the child and family for adoption. We review selected writings below and offer our own recommendations.

Chestang and Heyman (1976) suggest that good preparation should clarify the adoption process, explain the difference between adoption and foster care, and deal with a child's fear and resistance to change. These authors emphasize the importance of direct, honest responses to parental inquiries and advise that parents need to be educated about the "honeymoon period" that may be encountered.

Even foster parents need assistance in preparing for the role change from foster to adoptive parent. Many foster parents, accustomed to consulting social workers on a myriad of matters, have difficulty accepting the increased autonomy that is inherent in the role of adoptive parent. In Meezan & Shireman's study (1985), 79 percent of foster families who adopted reported that the adoption had had a positive effect on their family.

Katz (1986) submits that successful adoptions of emotionally disturbed children depend less on issues of child psychopathology and more on parental characteristics that help a family incorporate a child without encountering intolerable family distress. Successful adopting families often demonstrate:

1. tolerance of one's own ambivalence and/or strong negative feelings . . . 2. refusal to be rejected by the child and the ability to successfully delay gratification of parental needs . . . 3. the ability to find happiness in small increments of improvement . . . 4. parental role flexibility . . . 5. [a] systems view of their family . . . 6. firm entitlement . . . 7. intrusive and controlling qualities . . . in a caring way . . . 8. humor and self-care and . . . 9. [an] open versus a closed family system (pp. 574–577).

Agencies can look for these qualities as they screen applicants. Perhaps even more important, adoption preparation services can enhance these qualities. For instance, agencies can foster the families' sense of entitlement and "ownership" of the child by "providing full background information as a right of adoptive families and by empowering them to truly act as parents with maximum authority and decision-making power in the child's life from the beginning of the placement" (Katz, 1986, p. 574). Similarly, the provision of respite services encourages self-care, while parent support groups encourage "humor and the venting of feelings as vital strategies in coping with stress" (Katz, 1986, p. 577).

These aforementioned writers focused primarily on preparation of children in family foster care settings. Many children who are free for adoption, however, reside in group care or residential treatment centers. Group care has its roots in the orphanage—long-term substitute care and a custodial orientation—while adoption is rooted in the benefits of family life. Now, new perspectives are needed. Donley and Haimes (1988) emphasize that residential group care providers and adoption workers need to collaborate in adoption preparation.

When moving children from group care into adoptive families, adoption workers need to carefully examine certain assumptions. First, workers should not assume that children can cope socially or emotionally with a family setting. Second, adoption workers should not assume that staff in residential programs are committed to the goal of adoption. Residential or group care staff may see adoption workers as naive, as playing the role of the rescuer, or as interfering in the child's treatment.

In preparing children from group care for adoption, residential and adoption workers need to work closely with one another. Preparation should draw on the child's attachment to key residential staff, as this may facilitate the development of attachment to the adoptive parents. The workers should clarify the child's gains in treatment and utilize these gains in developing the service plan. In addition, group care staff can teach parents behavior management skills and help the child to disengage from the group program. Wheeler (1978) and Aust (1981) recommend the use of a life book, a scrapbook of photos, drawings, mementoes, and memories from the child's life experiences, to help children integrate their past, assess the present, and plan for the future.

Thus, preparation for both family and child is needed. Whenever possible, prior caretakers should be actively involved both to support the child and to provide valuable information for the family. Contacts with other parents who have adopted help the parent to develop realistic expectations. One respondent stated:

The preparation for adoption was extremely helpful. We had a chance to hear from other adoptive parents of older [special-needs] children and to discuss hypothetical situations. Visits in the homes of two families with similar adoptions were also very valuable.

Preparation for Adoption at Four Oaks in Iowa

Four Oaks, Incorporated, a private, nonprofit family service agency in Cedar Rapids, Iowa, has developed several group-based services to prepare children in group and foster homes for adoption. These services include:

Sexual Abuse Survivors Group. This group facilitates the healing process for victims of sexual abuse by eliciting feelings that have been denied or suppressed. In the process, the child gains control over these feelings, improves coping skills, and increases self-esteem. Techniques used to assist children in identifying and communicating feelings include creative visual expression, role playing, and physical touch where appropriate and therapeutic.

Separation and Loss Group. This group facilitates the grieving process by identifying and processing feelings related to separation and loss. The group informs children about child welfare, foster care, and adoption services, helps them to understand good and bad qualities of their birth parents, and explores reasons why they cannot live with their birth families. Children gain a perspective on past, present, and future families. An ending ritual helps them to deal with termination of the group.

Adoption Preparation Group. This group prepares children for the logistics and pragmatics of adoption including recruitment, preplacement visits, placement, and finalization. Differences between adoption and foster care are emphasized and any questions about adoption are answered.

Four Oaks also prepares foster and adoptive families, sometimes using foster care as a training ground for potential adoptive families. The training covers the characteristics and problems of special-needs children, including attachment difficulties, hyperactivity, sexual and physical abuse of children, relationships with birth parents, and the grieving process. The logistics of adoption are explained, including the court process, placement phases, and adoption disruption. Lastly, the training focuses on changes that special-needs adoption brings to the family system. Participants discuss issues such as integrating the child into the family and coping with day-to-day living, building trust, "claiming" the child as part of the family, and developing behavior management skills.

RECOMMENDATIONS FOR POSTPLACEMENT SERVICES

Adoption-Sensitive and Family-Based Services

Families face enormous challenges and strains in adopting a special-needs child, and these strains may be compounded by major gaps in postplacement services. For example, families may experience difficulty in finding mental health specialists who are also experienced in the dynamics of special-needs adoption. Some families indicate that practitioners do not understand their motivation for adopting a special-needs child. When the therapist does not support the family in its objective of providing a permanent home, therapy can be a catalyst towards disruption rather than permanency.

Family therapy should help parents gain a sense of entitlement to the child. The therapist should be alert to parents' sometimes unrealistic expectations for change or progress. Where parents are infertile, therapy may need to focus on their sense of loss in not being able to conceive a biological child and how infertility influences their interactions with the adopted child. Some parents will need ongoing help in coming to grips with the reality that they may desire more closeness than the child can give.

A family systems perspective is especially important in therapy with special-needs adoptive families (Groze & Gruenwald, 1991). Crisis in adoptive families often results from the stress of adding a new family member rather than from chronic dysfunctional patterns; stated differently, the problem is not a dysfunctional family system but instead the family system's reaction to the stress of rapid change. Some mental health practitioners, inexperienced with the realities of child welfare, may be too quick to portray children as severely disturbed. Others may not understand or support the parents' desires to adopt a child with behavioral problems, thereby undermining the family's confidence and increasing the risk for disruption. A family-oriented approach reduces the "victim blaming" that often results when child rather than family becomes the primary target of intervention.

Adoption-related issues surface throughout the stages of family life (Bourguignon and Watson, 1987; Duhl, 1986; Winkler, Brown, van Keppel, & Blanchard, 1988). Therapy should not be viewed as time limited, but instead as a normative part of an adoptive family's experience (Winkler et al., 1988). Many families, in particular less-educated or lower-income families, may need help in locating and initiating these services.

Behavior Management

In addition to services that are adoption-sensitive and family-based, families need behavior management skills. As one parent wrote, the family needed "resources for creative discipline—there were very few that fit the category of an older child. Most that were given to us were for young children."

Straightforward behavior management skills appropriate to the emotional maturity of the children are required. As many special-needs children do not have age-appropriate skills for controlling their behavior, parents may need to implement rules and discipline that "feel" appropriate for younger children. Rules and consequences should be explicit and clearly followed. Behavioral contracts may be useful. Parents should be attuned to small increments of improvement so that these can be reinforced. Given the skills that many children possess for provoking arguments, parents must learn to administer discipline without losing control. Relaxation techniques, support groups, therapy, and respite can all help in this regard. (Specific suggestions for the hyperactive child are in Chapter 10.)

Some families will benefit from training in programs like PET (Parent Effectiveness Training) and STEP (Systematic Training for Effective Parenting), although the curriculum may need to be modified to emphasize adoption issues.

Respite Care

Respite care services, providing rest and temporary relief from parenting, are highly valued by special-needs adoptive parents. Respite care may be delivered outside of the family's residence, either in a specialized respite facility or a family home; or the respite provider may come to the adoptive family home. Respite services may be used during emergencies, during times of peak stress, or simply to provide a break from day-to-day routines.

Respite care services have been used successfully to maintain family stability (Halpern, 1985). In one study, services were associated with an immediate significant reduction in maternal stress (Rimmerman, 1989).

Specialized respite services are particularly important to families with medically frail or handicapped children, as many of these families have difficulty in arranging babysitting through traditional means. The availability of good respite services may help encourage families to foster or adopt children with AIDS (Tourse & Gundersen, 1988). In a recent study, foster families for children with AIDS received approximately 32 hours of respite care weekly (Gurdin & Anderson, 1987). This experience suggests that agencies need to commit significant resources in order to develop effective respite services.

Support Groups

In this study, adoptive parents evaluated support groups as well as informal contacts with other special-needs parents as more helpful than individual and family therapy. Single adoptive parents were particularly positive in their assessments regarding the helpfulness of support groups. Supportive services have several advantages when compared with traditional counseling services. First, participation does not carry the negative stigma that is attached to therapy. Second, as Whittaker and Tracy (1987) indicate, support by informal helpers can link families with other formal and informal services. Third, therapy services are not readily available in some areas. Whenever possible, support groups should be integrated into a community's network of professional and paraprofessional services (Winkler et al., 1988). While some support groups are self-sustaining, other groups may require the active involvement of adoption staff.

Adoptive parent support groups in Oklahoma participate in a variety of activities for parents, children, and families. Some activities fit the traditional view of how a support group operates: parents meet together to discuss the stresses and joys of adoptive parenthood, to brainstorm solutions to problems, and, of course, to support one another. Jane Conner, longtime coordinator of adoption programs for the Oklahoma Department of Human

Services, commented on the depth of sharing and involvement that characterized the interactions of one group (personal communication, December 1, 1990). Yet group members also participate in nontraditional activities such as camping trips, helping with child care, and simply enjoying each other's company.

In 1990, 19 special-needs adoptive parent groups, many sponsored by the Prairie Fire grant coordinated by Lutheran Social Services in Oklahoma City, met in urban and rural areas of Oklahoma. This grant provided for a statewide conference that brought together parents and children from across the state. Such activities build a much-needed sense of community among adoptive parents. As one parent commented, other special-needs adoptive families can become the "lifeline" that helps sustain a placement when friends, neighbors, or relatives disapprove.

Educational Programming

Despite the encouraging findings related to school attendance and performance, parent responses to open-ended questions point out recurring problems. School administrators and teachers may misinterpret the reasons why some special-needs adoptees lag behind in school. Deficits due to a lack of educational opportunity in the birth family setting may be falsely attributed to intellectual deficits or retardation. On the other hand, many adoptees do indeed have serious learning disabilities or handicaps that require specialized educational services. Even while Section 504 of the Rehabilitation Act of 1973 mandates that school systems provide specialized services to meet individual learning needs, obtaining such services can be difficult and can generate conflict between adoptive parents and school staff. Social workers and parents need to advocate on the child's behalf in order to obtain the best possible educational services.

Many children in the study, even those with average or above-average intelligence, lagged far behind their peers in school and often lacked needed motivation. Hence, parents must have realistic expectations, individualized according to the child's needs and capacities.

The enterprising adoption worker can help sensitize teachers to adoption issues. Melina (1990) recommends that teachers (1) be alert to the difficulties posed by assignments related to family issues (e.g., creating a family tree), (2) examine their own values about adoption and the role of heredity and environment, (3) be receptive to learning more about adoption and its effects, and (4) work closely with adoptive parents and professionals in understanding the special needs of the child.

Needless to say, the hyperactivity demonstrated by many special-needs children has adverse implications in the school setting. Perhaps empathetic understanding on the parent's part—derived from firsthand experience—can help teachers and others in the school system to develop the extra patience needed to work effectively with the child. While work with school administrators can be frustrating, successful negotiation of school tasks is essential if the adoption is to remain intact.

Financial Subsidies

Financial subsidies provide tremendous benefits to families and children. In most states, subsidies cannot exceed the amounts received by foster families (Barth and Berry, 1988; Shaffer, 1981) and are paid on a monthly basis until the child reaches majority age (Waldinger, 1982).

Several problems may be encountered in the delivery of subsidies. Bureacratic red tape may slow the process. As is clear in parent comments, both parents and workers need to advocate to ensure the child's subsidy. Where workers did so, families expressed appreciation. Sometimes a sense of secrecy surrounds the subsidy. No one is quite sure how to obtain one or what the specific criteria are. In some states, parents must request subsidies, while in others, subsidies are discussed only after a decision regarding adoption has been made. Means tests based on family income may also be required.

Subsidies should be readily available to all children with special needs, and policies requiring means tests should be discarded. Further, workers need to inform all potential families about subsidies prior to their decision regarding adoption. Adoption subsidies are often lower than foster care payments and may not increase as the child gets older (Barth and Berry, 1988). Clearly, a lower payment scale creates financial hardship for many adoptive families and functions as a barrier to timely adoptive placement.

Medicaid benefits may be provided to the child as part of the subsidy agreement. Medicaid provides only limited access to the health care services needed by children (Schor et al., 1988). In addition, many providers do not accept Medicaid. Financial subsidies may be critical in obtaining needed medical benefits, for example, braces or a pair of glasses for school sports, that fall outside of Medicaid's funding criteria.

For better and sometimes for worse, American society is highly materialistic. For status-conscious adolescents in particular, clothes play an important role in facilitating acceptance by a peer group. Subsidies may provide adoptive families with the means to meet some material needs and to enable the child to take part in enriching activities such as trips, concerts, baseball games, and horseback riding—precisely those experiences not available in the birth family. In this study, lower-income families experienced excellent outcomes. Clearly, these families hold expectations that are congruent with the needs and expectations of children. The provision of adequate subsidies is essential in recruiting these families and in enabling these families to effectively meet the children's needs.

TOWARDS THE YEAR 2000: ADOPTION DURING THE ERA OF AIDS AND EXTENSIVE DRUG USE

Child welfare practitioners face a new challenge: how to serve the influx of medically fragile children into foster and adoptive care. Three groups of children, those with AIDS, those with the AIDS virus but without symptoms of AIDS, and children with prenatal exposure to drugs present perhaps the greatest challenges.

AIDS and HIV-Infected Children

At present no cure has been discovered for acquired immune deficiency syndrome (AIDS). Moreover, AIDS attacks the victim's immune system, rendering them susceptible to a host of serious infections that may lead to death. Children represent about 2 percent of diagnosed cases of AIDS, a number that quadrupled during the two-year period from 1987, when there were about 500 cases, to 1989, when cases numbered about 2000 (Koop, 1987; CDC, 1987; CDC, 1988; CDC, 1990). The majority of known cases of pediatric AIDS (88 percent) involve children younger than the age of 5 (Select Committee, 1987; Hutchings, 1988). More than three-fourths of these cases result from transmission of the virus from infected mother to child. About 25 percent to 50 percent of babies born to infected mothers eventually contract AIDS (Johnson et al., 1989). While 75 percent to 80 percent of children die within about one year of being diagnosed with AIDS (Select Committee), the survival period is highly variable; some children with congenital infections have reached the age of 9 with relatively few physical symptoms (Koop, Select Committee; Hutchings). With improvements in treatments and medications, the projected life span of persons with AIDS will very likely continue to increase.

Minorities of color are represented disproportionately among victims. Black children, for instance, represent 15 percent of the U.S. child population but 53 percent of juvenile AIDS cases. Similarly, Hispanic children comprise 10 percent of the child population but 24 percent of juvenile AIDS cases (Quinn, 1987; Hutchings, 1988; Select Committee, 1987; CDC, 1988).

For every child with AIDS, 3 to 5 children are infected with the HIV virus; that is, they are seropositive or HIV positive. In 1991, an estimated 10,000 to 20,000 children were HIV infected (Oleske, 1987). Although infected with the virus, these children do not have the life-threatening diseases associated with AIDS or meet the diagnostic criteria for AIDS that have been established by the Center for Disease Control.

Although children with HIV infection may be free of AIDS symptoms, the infection may lead to retardation in growth (Plotkin, 1987) or dysfunction of various organ systems. Some children have a lesser manifestation of the disease known as AIDS-Related Complex, or ARC. They may have severe medical problems, including developmental disabilities, that will require a comprehensive and multidisciplinary approach (Olson, 1989). In one study, only 5 percent of HIV-infected children performed at age levels in all areas on comprehensive developmental evaluations (Boland, 1987).

Caring for a child with AIDS requires extensive involvement with medical services and special attention to hygienic conditions in the home. Also, the family must deal with negative reactions of neighbors, relatives, school officials, and service providers and cope with the terminal nature of the child's illness (Anderson, 1986). These social, economic, and psychological difficulties may lead to contact with the public child welfare system (Anderson, 1986).

Experts estimate that 25 percent to 33 percent of infants born with AIDS or HIV will not be cared for by their biological parents (Tourse and Gundersen, 1988; Melina, 1987; Boland, Evans, Connor, & Oleske, 1988). Adoption will be the best plan for permanency for those who cannot be reared in their birth homes. Adoption agencies need to aggressively recruit families for children with AIDS and HIV infection. The provision of adequate subsidies, respite care, and pre- and postplacement services will expedite these adoptive placements. Given the excellent outcomes for children with serious medical conditions observed in this study, we anticipate that many parents could derive considerable satisfaction in adoptions of these children.

Drug-Exposed Infants

An increasing number of child welfare cases are drug related. For instance, drug-related child abuse cases increased by 72 percent from 1985 to 1988 (FOCUS, 1990). As many as 375,000 babies are born with exposure to illegal drugs each year (FOCUS, 1990). Anonymous testing of newborn infants in one major East Coast city indicated that between 11 percent and 20 percent of newborn infants had been exposed to illicit drugs (FOCUS, 1990). Drug-exposed infants and children are vulnerable to abuse, neglect, and abandonment by their often drug-addicted parents. As many as 30 to 50 percent of drug-exposed children may enter foster care (FOCUS, 1990).

Drug-exposed children often suffer significant medical and behavioral problems, including difficulties in psychomotor development (Little, Anderson, Ervin, & Worthington-Roberts, 1989), temperament, sleep, attachment behavior (Lesser-Katz, 1982; Wachsman, Schuetz, Chan, & Wingert, 1989), and physical development (Kaye, Elkind, Goldberg, & Tytun, 1989). They require regular medical and neurobehavioral evaluations.

Drug-exposed children will often be candidates for adoption. Many will be adopted when they are quite young and will appear to be relatively healthy, masking potential problems that may develop later. Agencies need to provide complete background information and inform families regarding what is and is not yet known about the consequences of drug exposure.

SPECIAL-NEEDS ADOPTION WORKS

Special-needs adoption works. Adoption workers know this from their own practice. This study and others empirically confirm the practitioners' experience. During the 1970s and 1980s, adoption reached outward to new families and to new children. Perhaps the guiding philosophy of the new adoptive movement was expressed in the phrase "No child is unadoptable." The parallel phrase that best describes the findings of this study is "No family is unadoptable." The outreach to different types of families from many walks of life—minority families, relatives, foster parents, single parents, low-income and less-educated families—was central to the positive adoptive outcomes that we found.

The field of adoption needs to continue to reach out to new parents and new children and to recognize the dignity of persons from all segments of society. More liberal financial subsidies are needed, as is greater access to both pre- and postplacement services. Study findings recommend an increased emphasis on special-needs adoption and show significant benefits for children and parents.

From a pragmatic perspective, every child should not be adopted. Some children with severely abusive behavior cannot be managed in a family setting. Some children do not want to be adopted. For instance, some adolescents in long-term substitute care may feel that adoption undermines their connection to the biological family. The best decision in such an instance depends on the specifics of the individual situation.

Yet for almost all children who cannot return to their biological families, adoption is the best plan. Blame for problems experienced by children in foster care is too easily attributed to "the system." Foster care is not ruinous for all children and all do not experience multiple moves. Most children experience their foster parents as caring people. Many evidence significant social and cognitive gains in foster care. If blame is to be assigned, societal conditions—poverty, unemployment, racism, drugs, crime, and limited health, educational, and social programs—contribute most to the crisis in foster care. These problems, in combination with inadequate funding, ultimately lead to ineffective administrators, burned-out social workers, and cruel, uncaring parents.

Yet the core problem is that foster care, by its very nature, does not offer the permanency of adoption, either during childhood or, as Barth and Berry (1988) assert, after the child reaches adulthood. When a foster family moves out of state, the child, no matter how closely attached, most likely stays behind. Similarly, a death, family emergency, or any other change in circumstances may require the family to cease its fostering. Granted that disruptions occur, the adopted child is in the family to stay and has the opportunity to become a full and permanent family member. The high level of self-esteem among the special-needs adoptees in the Iowa sample attests to the ameliorative and rich benefits of adoption. So, too, does the child who exclaimed with joy several times at the finalization of his adoption: "Mom, we did it."

References

Achenbach, T. M. & Edelbrock, C. (1983). *Manual for the child behavior checklist and revised child behavior profile*. Burlington, VT: Department of Psychiatry, University of Vermont.

Alstein, H. (1984). Transracial and intercountry adoptions: A comparison. In Paul Sachdev (Ed.), *Adoption: Current issues and trends* (pp. 195–203). Toronto: Butterworth.

American Psychiatric Association. (1987). *Diagnostic and statistical manual of mental disorders* (3rd ed., revised). Washington, DC: Author.

Anastopoulos, A. D., & Barkley, R. A. (1988). Biological factors in attention deficit–hyperactivity disorder. *Behavior Therapist, 11*, 47–53.

Anderson, G. R. (1986). *Children and AIDS: The challenge for child welfare*. Washington, DC: Child Welfare League of America.

Andujo, E. (1988). Ethnic identity of transethnically adopted Hispanic adolescents. *Social Work, 33*, 531–535.

Aust, P. H. (1981). Using the life story book in treatment of children in placement. *Child Welfare, 60*, 535–560.

Bagley, C., & Young, L. (1979). The identity, adjustment and achievement of transracially adopted children; a review and empirical report. In G. K. Verma & C. Bagley (Eds.), *Race, education and identity* (pp. 192–219). New York: St. Martin's.

Barth, R. P., & Berry, M. (1988). *Adoption and disruption: Rates, risks, and responses*. New York: Aldine De Gruyter.

Barth, R. P., Berry, M., Yoshikami, R., Goodfield, R. K., & Carson, M. L. (1988). Predicting adoption disruption. *Social Work, 33*, 227–233.

Beavers, W. R. (1976). A theoretical basis for family evaluation. In J. M. Lewis, W. R. Beavers, J. T. Gossett, & V. A. Phillips (Eds.), *No single thread: Psychological health in family systems* (pp. 46–82). New York: Brunner/Mazel.

Beavers, W. R. (1982). Healthy, midrange, and severely dysfunctional families. In F. Walsh (Ed.), *Normal family processes* (pp. 45–60). New York: Guilford Press.

Beavers, W. R., Hulgus, Y. F., & Hampson, R. B. (1988). *Family competence and family style evaluation manual*. Dallas, TX: Southwest Family Institute.

Berman, L. C., & Bufferd, R. K. (1986). Family treatment to address loss in adoptive families. *Social Casework, 67*, 3–11.

Berry, M., & Barth, R. (1989). Behavior problems of children adopted when older. *Children and Youth Services Review, 11*, 221–238.

Bohman, M., & Sigvardsson, S. (1980). A prospective, longitudinal study of children registered for adoptions: A 15-year follow-up. *Acta Psychiatrica Scandinavica, 61*, 339–355.

Boland, M. G. (1987). Management of the child with HIV infection: Implications for service delivery. In B. K. Silverman & A. Waddell (Eds.), *Report of the surgeon general's workshop on children with HIV infection and their families* (pp. 41–43). Washington, DC: U.S. Government Printing Office.

Boland, M. G., Evans, P., Connor, E. M., & Oleske, J. M. (1988). Foster care needs of children with HIV infection. *Aids and Public Policy Journal, 3*, 8–9.

Boneh, C. (1979). *Disruptions in adoptive placements: A research study*. Boston: Massachusetts Department of Public Welfare.

Bourguignon, F. P., & Watson, K. W. (1987). *After adoption: Manual for professionals working with adoptive families*. Springfield, IL: Illinois Department of Children and Family Services.

Bourguignon, J. P. (1989a). Single-parent adoptions. Workshop presented at Sustaining Adoption National Conference, Charleston, SC, May 10–12.

Bourguignon, J. P. (1989b). *Toward successful adoption: A study of predictors in special needs placements*. Springfield, IL: Illinois Department of Children and Family Services.

Boyne, D., Denby, L., Kettenring, J. R., & Wheeler, W. (1984). *The shadow of success: A statistical analysis of outcomes of adoptions of hard-to-place children*. Westfield, NJ: Spaulding for Children.

Branham, E. (1970). One-parent adoptions. *Children, 17*, 103–107.

Brinich, P. M., & Brinich, E. B. (1982). Adoption and adaptation. *Journal of Nervous and Mental Disease, 170*, 489–493.

Brodzinsky, D. M. (1987). Adjustment to adoption: A psychosocial perspective. *Clinical Psychology Review, 7*, 25–47.

Brodzinsky, D. M., Schechter, D. E., Braff, A. M., & Singer, L. (1984). Psychological and academic adjustment in adopted children. *Journal of Consulting and Clinical Psychology, 52*, 582–590.

Buriel, R. (1975). Cognitive styles among three generations of Mexican-American children. *Journal of Cross-Cultural Psychology, 6*, 417–429.

Byrne, E. A., & Cunningham, C. C. (1985). The effects of mentally handicapped children on families—a conceptual review. *Journal of Child Psychology and Psychiatry and Allied Disciplines, 26*, 847–864.

Camarata, C. (1989). *Profile of Hispanic adoptive families in Texas*. Austin, TX: Texas Department of Human Services.

CDC. See Center for Disease Control.

Center for Disease Control (CDC). (1987, December). *AIDS Weekly Surveillance Report—United States*. Atlanta, GA: AIDS Program, Center for Infectious Diseases.

Center for Disease Control. (1988, December). *AIDS Weekly Surveillance Report—United States*. Atlanta, GA: AIDS Program, Center for Infectious Diseases.

Center for Disease Control. (1990). *HIV/AIDS Surveillance, Year-End Edition*. Atlanta, GA: AIDS Program, Center for Infectious Disease.

Chambers, D. E. (1970). Willingness to adopt atypical children. *Child Welfare, 49*, 275–279.

Chestang, L. (1972). The dilemma of biracial adoption. *Social Work, 17*, 3, 100–105.

Chestang, L. W., & Heymann, I. (1976). Preparing older children for adoption. *Public Welfare, 34*, 35–40.

Child Welfare League of America (CWLA). (1988). *Standards for adoption service (rev. ed.)*. Washington, DC: Child Welfare League of America.

Chimezie, A. (1975). Transracial adoption of black children. *Social Work, 20*, 296–301.

Classified Index of Industries and Occupations. (1982). Washington, DC: U.S. Department of Commerce, Bureau of the Census.

Cohen, J. S. (1984). Adoption breakdown with older children. In P. Sachdev (Ed.), *Adoption: Current issues and trends* (pp. 129–138). Toronto: Butterworth.

Coyne, A. (1986). Recruiting foster and adoptive families: A marketing strategy. *Children Today, 15*, 30–33.

Coyne, A., & Brown, M. E. (1985). Developmentally disabled children can be adopted. *Child Welfare, 64*, 607–615.

Dalby, J. T., Fox, S. L., & Haslam, R. A. (1982). Adoption and foster care rates in pediatric disorders. *Developmental and Behavioral Pediatrics, 3*, 61–64.

Davis, R. M., & Bouck, P. (1955). Crucial importance of adoption home study. *Child Welfare, 34*, 20–21.

Day, D. (1979). *The adoption of black children*. Lexington, MA: D. C. Heath.

Deiner, P. L., Wilson, N. J., & Unger, D. G. (1988). Motivation and characteristics of families who adopt children with special needs: An empirical study. *Topics in Early Childhood Special Education, 8*, 15–29.

Deutsch, C. K., Swanson, J. M., Bruell, J. H., Cantwell, D. P., Weinberg, F., & Baren, M. (1982). Overrepresentation of adoptees in children with the attention deficit disorder. *Behavior Genetics, 12,* 231–238.

Devaney, N. (1982). Adjustment of the older adoptive child: Process and relationship. Unpublished doctoral dissertation, Birmingham, AL: University of Alabama.

DiGiulio, J. F. (1987). Assuming the adoptive parent role. *Social Casework: The Journal of Contemporary Social Work, 68,* 561–566.

Donley, K. S. (1990). Understanding survival behaviors: System children in adoption. Presentation sponsored by Four Oaks, Inc., Cedar Rapids, Iowa, September 6–7.

Donley, K. S., & Haimes, R. S. (1988). New dimensions in child placement: Residential group care-adoption collaboration. In R. Small & G. Carmen (Eds.), *Permanence and family support: Changing practice in group child care* (pp. 229–244). Washington, DC: Child Welfare League of America.

Dougherty, S. A. (1978). Single adoptive mothers and their children. *Social Work, 23,* 311–314.

Duhl, F. J. (1986). *Issues in special needs adoptions for mental health practitioners.* Boston: Boston Family Institute.

Elbow, M. (1986). From caregiving to parenting: Family formation with adopted older children. *Social Work, 31,* 366–370.

Elbow, M., & Knight, M. (1987). Adoption disruption: Losses, transitions, and tasks. *Social Casework: The Journal of Contemporary Social Work, 68,* 546–552.

Falicov, C. J. (1988). Family sociology and family therapy contributions to the family development framework: A comparative analysis and thoughts on future trends. In C. J. Falicov (Ed.), *Family transitions: Continuity and change over the life cycle* (pp. 3–51). New York: The Guilford Press.

Falk, L. L. (1970). A comparative study of transracial and inracial adoptions, *Child Welfare, 49,* 82–88.

Fanshel, D. (1962). Approaches to measuring adjustment in adoptive parents. In *Quantitative approaches to parent selection* (pp. 18–35). New York: Child Welfare League of America.

Fanshel, D. (1972). *Far from the reservation.* Metuchen, NJ: Scarecrow Press.

Feigelman, W., & Silverman, A. R. (1977). Single-parent adoptions. *Social Casework, 58,* 418–425.

Feigelman, W., & Silverman, A. R. (1983). *Chosen children: New patterns of adoptive relationships.* New York: Praeger.

Festinger, T. (1986). *Necessary risk.* Washington, DC: Child Welfare League of America.

Fliegenspan, J. (1979). Getting through the system. In Dawn Day (Ed.), *The adoption of black children* (pp. 43–62). Lexington, MA: D. C. Heath.

FOCUS. (1990, Spring). Newsletter from the National Council on Disability.

Franklin, D. S., & Massarik, F. (1969a). The adoption of children with medical conditions: Part I—Process and outcome. *Child Welfare, 48,* 459–467.

Franklin, D. S., & Massarik, F. (1969b). The adoption of children with medical conditions: Part II—The families today. *Child Welfare, 48,* 533–539.

Franklin, D. S., & Massarik, F. (1969c). The adoption of children with medical conditions: Part III—Discussions and conclusions. *Child Welfare, 48,* 595–601.

Gath, A. (1983). Mentally retarded children in substitute and natural families. *Adoption and Fostering, 7,* 35–40.

Gershenson, C. P. (1984a). Community response to children free for adoption. *Child Welfare Research Notes #3.* (Available from Children's Bureau, Administration for Children, Youth, and Families, Box 1182, Washington, DC 20013.)

Gershenson, C. P. (1984b). The twenty-year trend of federally assisted foster care. *Child Welfare Research Notes # 8.* Administration for Children, Youth, and Families, Office of Human Development Services. See address in Gershenson, 1984a.

Gill, M. M. (1978). Adoption of older children: The problems faced. *Social Casework, 59,* 272–278.

Gill, O., & Jackson, B. (1983). *Adoption and race.* London: Batsford Educational; New York: St. Martin's.

Glidden, L. M., Valliere, V. N., & Herbert, S. L. (1988). Adopted children with mental retardation: Positive family impact. *Mental Retardation, 26,* 119–125.

Goetting, A. (1986). Parental satisfaction: A review of research. *Journal of Family Issues, 7,* 83–109.

Graham, P., & Stevenson, J. (1987). Temperament and psychiatric disorder: The genetic contribution to behaviour in childhood. *Australian and New Zealand Journal of Psychiatry, 21,* 267–274.

Grow, L. J., & Shapiro, D. (1974). *Black children—white parents.* New York: Child Welfare League of America.

Groze, V. (1986). Special-needs adoption. *Children and Youth Services Review, 8,* 363–373.

Groze, V., & Gruenewald, A. (1991). PARTNERS: A model program for special needs adoptive families in stress. *Child Welfare, 70,* 581–589.

Gurdin, P., & Anderson, G. R. (1987). Quality care for ill children: AIDS-specialized foster family homes. *Child Welfare, 66,* 291–302.

Halpern, P. L. (1985). Respite care and family functioning in families with retarded children. *Health and Social Work, 10,* 138–150.

Hartman, A. (1979). *Finding families: An ecological approach to family assessment in adoption.* Beverly Hills, CA: Sage.

Hartman, A. (1984). *Working with adoptive families beyond placement.* New York: Child Welfare League of America.

Hayes, M., & Jennings, G. (1989, October). Adoptive children and adoptive families. Paper presented at the American Association for Marriage and Family Therapy Annual Conference, San Francisco, CA.

Hegar, R. (1988). Sibling relationships and separations: Implications for child placement. *Social Service Review, 62*, 446–467.

Ho, M. K. (1987). *Family therapy with ethnic minorities*. Newbury Park, CA: Sage.

Ho, M. K. (1990). *Intermarried couples in therapy*. Springfield, IL: Charles C. Thomas.

Hockey, A. (1980). Evaluation of adoption of the intellectually handicapped: A retrospective analysis of 137 cases. *Journal of Mental Deficiency Research, 24*, 187–202.

Hoopes, J. L. (1986, March). The adopted child in school: High risk for learning disabilities (ERIC document). Paper presented at the Annual Conference of the Association for Children and Adults with Learning Disabilities, New York City.

Hutchings, J. J. (1988). Pediatric aids: An overview. *Children Today, 3*, 4–7.

Imber-Black, E. (1988). *Families and larger systems: A family therapist's guide through the labyrinth*. New York: Guilford.

Jackson, B. (1976). *Family experiences of inter-racial adoption*. London: Association of British Adoption and Fostering Agencies.

Jaffee, B., & Fanshel, D. (1970). *How they fared in adoption*. New York: Columbia University Press.

Janzen, C., & Harris, O. (1986). *Family treatment in social work practice*. Itasca, IL: F. E. Peacock.

Johnson, J. P., Nair, P., Hines, S. E., Seiden, S. W., Alger, L., Revie, D. R., O'Neil, K. M., & Hebel, R. (1989). Natural history and serologic diagnosis of infants born to human immunodeficiency virus-infected women. *American Journal of Diseases of Children, 143*, 1147–1153.

Johnson, P. R., Shireman, J. F., & Watson, K. W. (1987). Transracial adoption and the development of black identity at age eight. *Child Welfare, 66*, 45–55.

Jones, C. E., & Else, J. F. (1979). Racial and cultural issues in adoption. *Child Welfare, 58*, 373–382.

Jordan, V. L., & Little, W. F. (1966). Early comments on single-parent adoptive homes. *Child Welfare, 45*, 536–538.

Kadushin, A. (1967). Reversibility of trauma: A follow-up study of children adopted when older. *Social Work, 12*, 22–33.

Kadushin, A. (1970). *Adopting older children*. New York: Columbia University Press.

Kadushin, A., & Martin, J. (1988). *Child Welfare Services* (4th ed). New York: Macmillan.

Kadushin, A., & Seidl, F. W. (1971). Adoption failure: A social work postmortem. *Social Work, 16*, 32–38.

Kagan, R. M., & Reid, W. J. (1986). Critical factors in the adoption of emotionally disturbed youths. *Child Welfare League of America, 65,* 63–73.

Katz, L. (1986). Parental stress and factors for success in older-child adoption, *Child Welfare, 65,* 569–578.

Kaye, K., Elkind, L., Goldberg, D., & Tytun, A. (1989). Birth outcomes for infants of drug-abusing mothers. *New York State Journal of Medicine, 89,* 256–261.

Kenny, T., Baldwin, R., & Mackie, J. B. (1967). Incidence of minimal brain injury in adopted children. *Child Welfare, 46,* 24–29.

Kim, D. S. (1978). Issues in transracial and transcultural adoption. *Social Casework, 59,* 477–485.

Kirk, H. D. (1984). *Shared fate: A theory and method of adoptive relationships* (2nd ed). Port Angeles, WA: Ben-Simon.

Kirk, H. D., Jonassohn, K., & Fish, A. D. (1966). Are adopted children especially vulnerable to stress? *Archives of General Psychiatry, 14,* 291–298.

Koop, C. E. (1987). Excerpt from keynote address. In B. K. Silverman & A. Waddell (Eds.), *Report of the surgeon general's workshop on children with HIV infection and their families* (pp. 3–5). Washington, DC: U.S. Government Printing Office.

Ladner, J. (1977). *Mixed families: Adopting across racial boundaries.* Garden City, NY: Doubleday.

Lahti, J. (1982). A follow-up study of foster children in permanent placements. *Social Service Review, 56,* 556–571.

Lambert, N. M., & Hartsough, C. S. (1984). Contribution of predispositional factors to the diagnosis of hyperactivity. *American Journal of Orthopsychiatry, 54,* 97–109.

Lesser-Katz, M. (1982). Some effects of maternal drug addiction on the neonate. *International Journal of Addictions, 17,* 887–896.

Lindholm, B. W., & Touliatos, J. (1980). Psychological adjustment of adopted and nonadopted children. *Psychological Reports, 46,* 307–310.

Little, R. E., Anderson, K. W., Ervin, C. H., & Worthington-Roberts, B. (1989). Maternal alcohol use during breast-feeding and infant mental and motor development at one year. *New England Journal of Medicine, 321,* 425–430.

Maris, R. W. (1988). *Social problems.* Chicago: Dorsey.

McRoy, R. G., Grotevant, H., & S. Zurcher. (1988). *Emotional disturbance in adopted adolescents.* New York: Praeger.

McRoy, R. G., & Zurcher, L. A., Jr. (1983). *Transracial and inracial adoptees.* Springfield, IL: Charles C. Thomas.

McRoy, R. G., Zurcher, L. A., Lauderdale, M. L., & Anderson, R. N. (1982). Self-esteem and racial identity in transracial and inracial adoptees. *Social Work, 27,* 522–526.

McWhinnie, A. M. (1967). Adopted children: How they grow up. London: Routledge and Kegan Paul.

Meezan, W. & Shireman, J. F. (1985). Antecedents to foster parent adoption decisions. *Children and Youth Services Review, 7,* 207–224.

Melina, L. R. (1986). *Raising adopted children.* New York: Harper and Row.

Melina, L. R. (1987). Agencies face issue of placing babies with AIDS. *Adopted Child, 6,* 1–4.

Melina, L. R. (1990). Teachers need to be more sensitive to adoption issue. *Adopted Child, 9,* 1–4.

Mendes, H. A., & Roberts, R. W. (1979, Fall). Helping adoptive single-parent families [Special issue]. *Social Work Papers of the School of Social Work,* University of Southern California, *15,* 31–35.

Menlove, F. L. (1965). Aggressive symptoms in emotionally disturbed adopted children. *Child Development, 36,* 519–532.

Mindel, D. H., & Haberstein, R. W. (Eds.). (1976). *Ethnic families in America: Patterns and variations.* New York: Elsevier.

Minuchin, S., & Fishman, H. C. (1981). *Family therapy techniques.* Cambridge, MA: Harvard University Press.

Nelson, K. A. (1985). *On the frontier of adoption: A study of special-needs adoptive families.* Washington, DC: Child Welfare League of America.

Norvell, M., & Guy, R. F. (1977). A comparison of self-concept in adopted and non-adopted adolescents. *Adolescence, 12,* 443–448.

Offord, D. R., Hershey, M. D., Aponte, J. F., & Cross, L. A. (1969). Presenting symptomatology of adopted children. *Archives of General Psychiatry, 20,* 110–116.

Oleske, J. (1987). Natural history of HIV infection II. In B. K. Silverman & A. Waddell (Eds.), *Report of the surgeon general's workshop on children with HIV infection and their families* (pp. 24–25). Washington, DC: U.S. Government Printing Office.

Olson, D. H. (1989). Circumplex model of family systems VIII: Family assessment and intervention. In D. H. Olson, C. S. Russell, and D. H. Sprenkle (Eds.), *Circumplex model: Systemic assessment and treatment of families.* New York: Haworth.

Olson, D. H., McCubbin, H. I., Barnes, H., Larsen, A., Muxen, M., & Wilson, M. (1985). *Family inventories.* St. Paul, MN: Family Social Science, University of Minnesota.

Olson, D. H., Russell, C. S., & Sprenkle, D. H. (1979). Circumplex model of marital and family systems II: Empirical studies and clinical intervention. In John Vincent (Ed.), *Advances in family intervention, assessment and theory.* Greenwich, CT: JAI Press, 128–176.

Olson, D. H., Russell, C. S., & Sprenkle, D. H. (1983). Circumplex model of marital and family systems VI: Theoretical update. *Family Process, 22,* 69–83.

Olson, S. (1988). Pediatric HIV: More than a health problem. *Children Today, 3,* 8–9.

Partridge, S., Hornby, H., & McDonald, T. (1986). *Legacies of loss: Visions of gain, an inside look at adoption disruption.* Portland, ME: University of Southern Maine, Human Services Development Institute.

Piers, E. V. (1984). *Piers-Harris children's self-concept scale. Revised Manual 1984.* Los Angeles: WPS.

Plotkin, S. A. (1987). Introduction. In B. K. Silverman & A. Waddell (Eds.), *Report of the surgeon general's workshop on children with HIV infection and their families* (pp. 1–2). Washington, DC: U.S. Government Printing Office.

Proch, K. (1981). Foster parents as preferred adoptive parents: Practice implications. *Child Welfare, 60,* 617–625.

Quinn, T. C. (1987). The global epidemiology of the acquired immunodeficiency syndrome. In B. K. Silverman & A. Waddell (Eds.), *Report of the surgeon general's workshop on children with HIV infection and their families* (pp. 7–10). Washington, DC: U.S. Government Printing Office.

Ramirez, M. III, & Price-Williams, D. R. (1974). Cognitive styles of children of three ethnic groups in the United States. *Journal of Cross-Cultural Psychology, 5,* 212–219.

Rapoport, J. L., & Ferguson, H. B. (1981). *Developmental Medicine and Child Neurology, 23,* 667–682.

Reece, S. A., & Levin, B. (1968). Psychiatric disturbances in adopted children: A descriptive study. *Social Work, 13,* 101–111.

Reid, W. J., Kagan, R. M., Kaminsky, A., & Helmer, K. (1987). Adoptions of older institutionalized youth. *Social Casework: The Journal of Contemporary Social Work, 68,* 140–149.

Rimmerman, A. (1989). Provision of respite care for children with developmental disabilities: Changes in maternal coping and stress over time. *Mental Retardation, 27,* 99–103.

Ripple, L. (1968). A follow-up study of adopted children. *Social Service Review, 42,* 479–497.

Rodman, H. (1968). Family and social pathology in the ghetto. *Science, 161,* 756–762.

Rosen, M. (1977). *A look at a small group of disrupted adoptions.* Chicago: Chicago Child Care Society.

Rosenthal, J. A. (1985). Adoption disruption in Colorado: A correlational study. In Delores M. Schmidt (Ed.), *Special needs adoption: A positive perspective* (pp. 38–41). Denver: Colorado Department of Social Services.

Rosenthal, J. A., & Groze, V. (1990). Special needs adoption: A study of intact families. *Social Service Review, 64,* (3), 475–505.

Rosenthal, J. A., Groze, V., & Curiel, H. (1990). Race, social class and special needs adoption. *Social Work, 35* (6), 532–539.

Rosenthal, J. A., Groze, V., Curiel, H., & Westcott, P. A. (1991). Transracial and inracial adoption of special needs children. *Journal of Multicultural Social Work, 1* (3), 331–332.

Rosenthal, J. A., Schmidt, D., & Conner, J. (1988). Predictors of special needs adoption disruption: An exploratory study. *Children and Youth Services Review, 10,* 101–117.

Roundtable. (1990). Newsletter of the National Resource Center for Special Needs Adoption, vol. 4, p. 18.

Sack, W. H., & Dale, D. D. (1982). Abuse and deprivation in failing adoptions. *Child Abuse and Neglect, 6,* 443–451.

Schechter, M. D. (1960). Observations on adopted children. *Archives of General Psychiatry, 10,* 109–118.

Schechter, M., Carlson, P. V., Simmons, J. Q. III, & Work, H. H. (1964). Emotional problems in the adoptee. *Archives of General Psychiatry, 10,* 37–46.

Schmidt, D. M., Rosenthal, J. A., & Bombeck, B. (1988). Parents' views of adoption disruption. *Children and Youth Services Review, 10,* 119–130.

Schor, E. L., Aptekar, R. R., & Scannell, T. (1988). The health care of children in out-of-home care: A white paper. In *Summary of a Colloquium on the Health Care of Children in Foster Family Care, January 8–9, 1987— Washington, DC* (pp. 1–31). Washington, DC: Child Welfare League of America.

Seglow, J., Pringle, M. K., & Wedge, P. (1972). *Growing up adopted.* Windsor, England: National Foundation for Educational Research in England and Wales.

Select Committee on Children, Youth and Families. (1987). *A generation in jeopardy: Children and AIDS.* (House of Representatives, 100th Cong., 1st sess.). Washington, DC: U.S. Government Printing Office.

Shaffer, G. L. (1981). Subsidized adoption in Illinois. *Children and Youth Services Review, 3,* 55–68.

Shilts, R. (1987). *And the band played on: Politics, people, and the AIDS epidemic.* New York: St. Martin's.

Shireman, J. F. (1988). *Growing up adopted: An examination of major issues.* Chicago: Chicago Child Care Society.

Shireman, J. F., & Johnson, P. R. (1976). Single persons as adoptive parents. *Social Service Review, 50,* 103–116.

Shireman, J. F., & Johnson, P. R. (1985). Single-parent adoptions: A longitudinal study. *Children and Youth Services Review, 7,* 321–334.

Shireman, J. F., & Johnson, P. R. (1986). A longitudinal study of black adoptions: Single parent, transracial, and traditional. *Social Work, 31,* 172–176.

Silver, L. B. (1970). Frequency of adoption in children with the neurological learning disability syndrome. *Journal of Learning Disabilities, 3,* 306–310.

Silverman, A. R., & Feigelman, W. (1981). The adjustment of black children adopted by white families. *Social Casework: The Journal of Contemporary Social Work, 62,* 529–536.

Simon, N. M., & Senturia, A. G. (1966). Adoption and psychiatric illness. *American Journal of Psychiatry, 122,* 858–868.

Simon, R. J., & Alstein, H. (1977). *Transracial adoption.* New York: Wiley.

Simon, R. J., & Alstein, H. (1981). *Transracial adoption: A follow-up.* Lexington, MA: Lexington Books.

Simon, R. J., & Alstein, H. (1987). *Transracial adoptees and their families: A study of identity and commitment.* New York: Praeger.

Small, J. W. (1984). The crisis in adoption. *International Journal of Social Psychiatry, 30,* 129–142.

Small, J. W. (1987). Working with adoptive families. *Public Welfare, 45,* 33–41.

Smith, D. W., & Sherwen, L. N. (1983). *Mothers and their adopted children: The bonding process.* New York: Tiresias.

Stein, L. M., & Hoopes, J. L. (1985). *Identity formation in the adopted adolescent.* New York: Child Welfare League.

Talen, M. R., & Lehr, M. L. (1984). A structural and developmental analysis of symptomatic adopted children and their families. *Journal of Marital and Family Therapy, 10,* 381–391.

Tatara, T. (1988). *Characteristics of children in substitute and adoptive care based on FY 85 data.* Washington, DC: American Public Welfare Association.

Tizard, B. (1979). Adopting older children from institutions. *Child Abuse & Neglect, 3,* 535–538.

Tourse, P., & Gundersen, L. (1988). Adopting and fostering children with AIDS: Policies in progress. *Children Today, 3,* 15–19.

Tremitiere, B. T. (1979). Adoption of children with special needs—the client-centered approach. *Child Welfare, 58,* 681–685.

Triseliotis, J., & Russell, J. (1984). *The outcome of adoption and residential care.* London: Heineman Educational Books.

Unger, C., Dwarshuis, G., & Johnson, E. (1981). Coping with disruption. In *Adoption disruptions* (pp. 15–51). Washington, DC: U.S. Department of Health and Human Services.

Urban Systems Research and Engineering. (1985). *Evaluation of state activities with regard to adoption disruption.* Washington, DC: Urban Systems Research and Engineering.

Valentine, D., Conway, P., & Randolph, J. (1988). Placement disruptions: Perspectives of adoptive parents. *Journal of Social Work and Human Sexuality, 6,* 133–153.

Wachsman, L., Schuetz, S., Chan, L. S., & Wingert, W. A. (1989). What happens to babies exposed to phencyclidine (PCP) in utero. *American Journal of Drug and Alcohol Abuse, 15,* 31–39.

Waldinger, G. (1982). Subsidized adoption: How paid parents view it. *Social Work, 27,* 516–521.

Walsh, F. (1982). *Normal family processes.* New York: Guilford.

Ward, M. (1981). Parental bonding in older-child adoptions. *Child Welfare, 60,* 24–34.

Weiss, A. (1985). Symptomatology of adopted and nonadopted adolescents in a psychiatric hospital. *Adolescence, 20,* 763–774.

Westhues, A., & Cohen, J. S. (1990). Preventing disruption of special-needs adoptions. *Child Welfare, 69,* 141–155.

Wheeler, C. (1978). *Where am I going? Making a life story book.* Juneau, AK: Winking Owl Press. Cited in Aust, P. H. (1981), Using the life story book in treatment of children in placement. *Child Welfare, 60,* 535–560.

Whittaker, J. K., & Tracy, E. M. (1987, Winter). Supporting families: Linking formal and informal helping in family preservation services. *Permanency Report, 5* (1), 5.

Winkler, R. C., Brown, D. W., van Keppel, M., & Blanchard, A. (1988). *Clinical practice in adoption.* Elmsford, NY: Pergamon.

Woods, F. J., & Lancaster, A. C. (1963). Cultural factors in Negro adoptive parenthood. *Social Work, 7,* 14–21.

Work, H. H., & Anderson, H. (1971). Studies in adoption: Requests for psychiatric treatment. *American Journal of Psychiatry, 127,* 948–950.

Zastrow, C. (1977). *Outcome of black children/white parent adoptions.* San Francisco: R & E Research Associates.

Zwimpfer, D. M. (1983). Indicators of adoption breakdown. *Social Casework: The Journal of Contemporary Social Work, 64,* 169–177.

Index

Academic achievement: and handicapped adoptions, 160, 165; impact of adoption on, 30–31; and minority adoptions, 138–39, 144–45; parental expectations and, 53–54; parental responses to, 68; recommendations for dealing with problems regarding, 214–15; and single-parent adoptions, 117; and transracial adoptions, 31

Achenbach, T. M., 115

Adaptability: in adoptive families, 100–101, 107, 109–10; definition of, 97–98; underlying dimensions of, 102, 105

Adolescent children: adaptability in families with, 101, 109; behavioral problems in, 183; cohesion in families with, 100, 109; outcome for, 38; parent satisfaction and, 54; transracial adoption and, 132. *See also* Age of children

Adopted children: background information on, 10, 55–56; contact with biological family by, 189–95; former ties of, 68; interviews with young adults who were, 75–92; relationship between adoptive parents and, 34–36, 48, 49; self-concept in, 202–4; stress resulting from special needs of, 95–96; in study, 21–23; trends regarding, 2–4. *See also* Age of children

Adoption: difficulties from parental perspective, 62–69; historical perspective of, 1–4; impact of AIDS on, 216–17; impact of drug use on, 217–18; legislative impact on, 1; placement patterns in, 199–202; preparation for, 208–10; recruitment of families for special-needs, 206–8; rewards from parental perspective, 58–62; success of special-needs, 218–19; two-tiered system for, 4. *See also* Adoption outcome; Disruption

Adoption Assistance and Child Welfare Act of 1980 (P.L. 96–272), 1–2

About the Authors

JAMES A. ROSENTHAL is Associate Professor of Social Work at the University of Oklahoma, Norman. Dr. Rosenthal worked for eight years in public child welfare, both in direct practice and in research and evaluation. He has conducted research and published in several child welfare areas, including child abuse and neglect, home-based treatment, juvenile justice, and special-needs adoption. He is an adoptive father.

VICTOR K. GROZE is Assistant Professor at the University of Iowa School of Social Work in Iowa City. Dr. Groze has over ten years of clinical and supervisory experience working with families in adoption, adolescent services, and substance abuse treatment. His research has focused on institutional abuse and neglect and special-needs adoption.